Praise for *Jour*

I am grateful that books provide a way for minds to meet outside the constraints of distance and time. I found the books of John Pontius after he had passed away. But thanks to his writings, I know certain particulars about John's life and what he believed.

In his books, John did a brave thing—he documented his journey of discipleship. He got specific about the principles that helped him know the Savior. He shared stories about the gospel actually working in his life.

We are told to hunger and thirst after righteousness. We are taught to ask and seek and knock. We are instructed to seek wisdom out of the best books. That implies real work and effort. It includes thinking hard, listening to others with real intent, and on occasion, stretching beyond what is known and comfortable. At times we might stumble into error, but we stay humble and keep reorienting on the real goal—coming to Christ.

John Pontius wrote openly about some of the spiritual lessons he learned. I see beautiful value in this. I see an earnest attempt to demonstrate that a relationship with Christ is real and attainable, that it is within reach for anyone who wants it.

I admire John Pontius and anyone with the guts to express their true beliefs in an environment that can be incredibly harsh, accusatory, and critical of anything spiritual. It is my hope that many of us will find the courage to share what we have learned while seeking Christ. I believe the citizens of this world need more of these examples, not less of them.

—Brandon Mull, #1 *New York Times* Best-Selling Author

For the true seeker and truth seeker within the restored gospel of Jesus Christ, there are very few literary works on this earth that could possibly compare to those brought forth by Brother John Pontius, no doubt through much sacrifice, pleadings, and tears. This book is no exception.

When I first opened the manuscript for *Journey to the Veil II: Path of Discipleship* at Terri's kind invitation, and before even reading the printed word, the Lord's Spirit enveloped me with an unanticipated assurance of the spiritual feast to be had within its pages. *Journey to the Veil II* includes John's very personal, sacred writings that will prove to be a literal, unspeakable, and timeless spiritual treasure for every soul who drinks deep from its well. John's words, which no doubt were given him of the Spirit, once again arise, seemingly from the dust, to lift a world desperately needing such an instantaneous infusion of God's word, hope, love, and light.

Although John is no longer with us in the flesh, his words come to life once again by uplifting the soul and pointing us all to the absolute reality of the Living Christ, and of our own personal invitation to seek His face, rend the veil by eradicating all unbelief, and know Him as we, too, are known. There is no greater vision in mortality than the vision Brother Pontius puts forth in this work. May we all travel the journey of belief in Christ through our longingness and unquenchable desire and need to know Him, even unto a bestowed, living faith in Him, and subsequently to an actual perfect knowledge of Him, even while in mortality as the Lord wills.

Thank you, John, for paying us a friendly and loving visit from the other side of the veil through your Spirit-filled words contained in this much-needed and timely work.

—Steven Anthony Bishop, Amazon #1
National Best-Selling Author
*Putting On Christ—A Road Map for Our Heroic
Journey to Spiritual Rebirth and Beyond*

I highly recommend this great and final work of the late John Pontius, *Journey to the Veil II: Path of Discipleship*. John's words, I believe, are some of the most poignant of our day. John is a man who dedicated almost every day, hour, and minute of his life to the sacred pursuit of learning to identify the voice of the Holy Spirit, and then flawlessly obeying it. John was not seeking the notoriety or praise of the world; in fact the converse is true. In the final days of his mortal probation, when the Spirit whispered to him to unveil some of his deepest thoughts and feelings via a blog, John was reluctant to do so. In his words: "Since I am not generally attracted to the whole concept of blogging, which appeared to me as a way of promoting one's self, the term, 'unblogging' seemed to fit me better—thus the genesis of 'UnBlog My Soul.'" Both *Journey to the Veil I* and *II* are compilations of these now-well-known "UnBlogs."

There is a very real "born again" transformation that must take place within each of us on our path to exaltation. This book will inspire you to submit to such a transformation, and to more personally know your Lord and Savior Jesus Christ.

—Katherine Ludeman Eisenhut, Owner/
CEO Keisenhut Designs

We are instructed in the scriptures to call no man good. So what do you say about someone who leads you to the source of all good? As one who has devoted his entire life to the discipleship of Jesus Christ, John Pontius's testimony as written in his books has pointed me to the source of all that is good. He has blessed me to know Christ better and to be more faithful to His Church. John was a fellow sojourner and only thought of himself as such; but the amount of lives he has blessed by his willingness to speak of Christ and write of Christ will ripple throughout the eternities.

—Todd McLaughlin, Cofounder, Joseph
Smith Research Institute

John's testimony is a witness of gentle truths that are heart-felt and raise the spirit in these troubled times. With Terri's help we are again blessed to partake of sacred insights from a gifted man who continues to bless our lives even from the other side of the veil. I encourage all to ponder John's experiences and powerful teachings. Thank you, John. We love you.

—**Derek Hegsted, Fine Artist and Illustrator;**
Visual Arts Director and Teacher

What a joy it has been to read and share my feelings on John Pontius's book *Journey to the Veil II: Path of Discipleship*. This book is powerful, transformative, and apropos for our time. It has helped to clear up many questions of mine about how to seek Christ, how to hear Him, how to ask Him, and how to obey Him—plus much more. It gives me hope that I, too, can walk the path of discipleship and build Zion within my heart. What a tender mercy this book is!

—**Susan Edwards, Visual Artist and Singer/Songwriter**

What a journey I have had with my best friend, my "Bruder," as we used to call each other. I have been friends with John since 1993 and have had the distinct pleasure of reading most of his books prior to publication. What a sweet spirit filled me as I read these pages of inspired writing. John sought to have the Spirit as he shared experiences and answered questions in the first *Journey to the Veil*. In this second volume some of the most intimate writing comes forth from his pen. Some of his journal writings are given to us to ponder and rejoice with him as well as his other life stories that he tells so beautifully. John writes as if he's our best friend and lets us into his world. I loved talking with John as he shared these beautiful truths on the Unblog. The comments from his posts always touched him so deeply, as he felt like all of his readers were his best friends. Terri has done a beautiful work putting these stories together. It has been a work of love for her. I hope the reader feels the love John has for the Savior and the Church. I miss my Bruder terribly and look forward to a sweet reunion with him again.

—Shayne Holmes, Business Owner; Follower of Christ

Also by John Pontius

Visions of Glory

Following the Light of Christ into His Presence

The Triumph of Zion

Journey to Zion Series:
Fire of the Spirit
Angels of Fire

We Three Kings

Journey to the Veil

Additional books, essays, and
fireside sound tracks are available at:
www.followingthelight.org
and on the UnBlog
http://UnBlogmysoul.wordpress.com

Journey

to the VEIL II

Path *of* Discipleship

Journey to the VEIL II

Path *of* Discipleship

by JOHN PONTIUS

Compiled by Terri Pontius

CFI
An imprint of Cedar Fort, Inc.
Springville, Utah

ISBN 13: 978-1-4621-4240-8

Published by CFI, an imprint of Cedar Fort, Inc.
2373 W. 700 S., Springville, UT 84663
Distributed by Cedar Fort, Inc., www.cedarfort.com

Library of Congress Control Number: 2013032907

Cover design by Courtney Proby
Cover design © 2022 Cedar Fort, Inc.

Printed in the United States of America

10 9 8 7 6 5 4 3 2 1

Printed on acid-free paper

Contents

Contents

CONTENTS

Preface

It has been nine years since my husband, John Pontius, journeyed through the veil of this mortal life to begin his new mission on the other side. Soon after his passing, I compiled the book *Journey to the Veil*, which features selected blog postings from his website, "UnBlog My Soul," which he wrote from 2010–2012. I never actually considered publishing another *Journey to the Veil* book until quite recently. I was in prayer and received the clear impression that I was to bring the last of John's words out of obscurity.

This honestly took me aback. Being busy with family and musical projects, I did not immediately begin. But with the advent of the COVID-19 pandemic, I suddenly had more time to study John's remaining blogs in depth. I found them to be doctrinally illuminating and deeply relevant for today.

As with the first *Journey to the Veil*, I have grouped the individual blogs according to subject, not chronologically. The blogs were posted on different dates—some years apart—but each approaches the subject from a different perspective, contributing its own unique thread of understanding to the gospel tapestry.

Also, between the chapters I have included short entries from John's personal journal from 1973–2011. I confess that I had never read his journals before I started compiling this book. They were so poignant, and made me miss him all the more. But as I read, I realized that these snippets from his life illustrate a gospel path much like that which we all experience. His story is filled with the ups and downs of this mortal condition, yet powerfully illustrates that the highest blessings of the gospel are truly available to every humble seeking soul who patiently submits to the Lord's sanctification and timetable.

Many thanks to my dear nephew for his loving support and incredible assistance with this book. While this book is John's personal opinion and experiences and is in no way official doctrine, his greatest desire would be that these pages might draw you closer to our Savior Jesus Christ, within the true haven of The Church of Jesus Christ of Latter-day Saints.

—Terri Pontius

Introduction

My Dear Friends,

I rejoice in being with you all and learning from you as we continue to have marvelous discussions. I love you and truly thank God for each of you, even as my body continues to experience the challenges of cancer. Thank you for making my life a joy amid these mortal trials.

Someone at a recent fireside asked why I felt comfortable sharing sacred and personal things during firesides and on this UnBlog. It made me ponder a bit, but I think there are two reasons. The first is that when I found out my life has an expiration date of six months, I did not want to take these precious happenings and truths and gifts I have received, and the knowledge of how I received them, with me into the next life.

If God handed you a hammer, nails, and a pile of boards without much more explanation, you would assume His intent was that you use all of your gifts, and you would start to build. You wouldn't ignore the hammer and nails and try to just stack the boards into something. You also wouldn't ignore the boards and try to pound the nails into the air.

God seems to have handed me a lifetime of extraordinary spiritual experience. This is my hammer. He gave me a gift of communicating, writing, and speaking. These are my nails. And, He gave me a willing publisher and the UnBlog, which are my building materials. The way I have chosen to focus my particular gifts into service to God is to shout what I have learned from the rooftops, to make them known, to use whatever time remains on my clock to proclaim to anyone who will listen—that God lives! He loves us, and every promise, privilege, and priesthood promise or power that any man or woman has ever experienced are available to you and me according to the grace and timetable of the Father.

As I have searched the scriptures, one thing is startlingly true about the latter days: a day of miracles is coming. When it arrives, angels will be commonly seen. Signs and wonders will be over our heads and under our feet. God will "make bare his holy arm" in the eyes of the nations. Can you imagine people in the Latter-day Zion, the "City of the Living God," where Jesus Christ personally dwells, being reluctant to speak of angels or personal miracles of faith?

Somewhere between now and then we will learn to speak of and hear glorious things with no other emotion than joy and belief.

I choose to speak of great things because they are part of who I am. It is a big part of what it means to "UnBlog My Soul." Anyone who knows me knows that I do not seek for attention or worldly status; yet how blessed I feel to not take the precious things living in my soul into another world where they can't be spoken to the benefit of my children and to you, my dear siblings in Christ.

Thank you for allowing me to be your fellow traveler on this glorious path.

Hurrah for Israel!

Brother John

Chapter One

Our Glorious Foundation

A Thunderclap of Joy

As this year came into being, I had the thought enter my mind that this year was going to be filled with opportunities to meet with people, do firesides, and openly rejoice.

I lived in Alaska for thirty-three years until recently. During most of that time, the Lord kept my involvement in such things uncomplicated. Those were years of service and silence. There are people who have known and rubbed shoulders with me for thirty-three years who have no idea that I have even written a book. In that time I gave fewer than a dozen firesides, and most of those were here in Utah. One of the hardest things I did in Alaska was to be quiet—not by choice but as a matter of obedience.

It seems as if—at least for the next little while—the Lord has lifted the bushel off my little light. I find it sweet and liberating, even a little intimidating. Writing this UnBlog is very atypical of my past. I think the title "UnBlog" is even a quiet acknowledgment of the relief I feel in this new direction. I hardly feel adequate but sense that my spiritual pressure gauge is no longer red-lined.

What I know and have to say is not vast or earth-shaking. But apparently it is timely, which thrills me, because the greater majority of what the Lord has given me to know, and now apparently to say, is directly aimed at personally claiming the fullest blessings the restored gospel offers. It is about the building of the latter-day Zion and personally preparing for the return of Christ.

When it comes to timing and being prepared, that is one event you don't want to be caught clipping your fingernails by the light of a lamp about to run out of oil.

It may be that what separates me from traditional thinking is that I am apparently too unsophisticated to realize that just because Enoch, or Abraham, or Mahonri Moriancumer did something, that I can't do it too. I just believe such things. It seems perfectly reasonable to me that if Peter raised the dead, or walked on the water, that one day I will, too. And it can happen on either side of the veil, according to the Lord's will.

I wasn't always this way. Somewhere years ago, when the path was wide and comfortable, it occurred to me that not only is the gospel of Jesus Christ true, but it works. It works the same today as it did in the days of Adam, or Enoch, or Jesus Christ. The gifts and privileges and powers of those days are fully operable today. We just need to believe them and then experience them. This didn't come to me as an insight; it came to me as an observation—as experiential truth.

When spiritual pilgrims realize that the gospel actually works, their view of what is truly possible can become unlimited. These truths, as far as we understand and believe them, just simply work. As we start to believe and seek, trusting in the Lord's timetable for us, the curtain opens a little more, and we see a little more, and believe a little more—and then those things work, too. We know, because we can see and touch them.

And, now, standing upon the precipice of the latter days, we can see much further still. My faith tells me that by this same simple belief, we will arise and claim our place within these glorious things. Then those times and blessed happenings which the righteous of every generation have seen with an eye of faith, and yearned to be a part of, will burst upon us—you and me—with a thunderclap of joy.

Brother John

The Mountains Will Move

The power of the gospel of Christ isn't that it points to a glorious outcome and cheers us on. The power lies in the fact that from the moment of our birth, through every decision and trial in our lives, to every necessary enhancement to our souls, to purging our sins, to lifting us beyond our mortal abilities, to cleansing, sanctifying, and purifying—Christ not only showed us the way, but He *is* the way. It is through the grace of Christ that we can become these things, which are far more than any mortal can achieve and be on their own.

He said, "Come, follow me," not because He had a great idea and defined a pathway toward that goal but because He became "the way" by the shedding of His blood and offering salvation to us at a cost that is well within our mortal budget.

It is within our reach because God does not require perfection of us per se. He requires obedience to His voice, which is His law (D&C 88:13), and in return He sanctifies, purifies, and changes us by virtue of His grace so that we become like Him. It doesn't happen—it *can't* happen—as a result of our works, no matter how impressive they may seem to be. It is eternally beyond our ability to perfect ourselves by our works. It can only happen because we obey laws that trigger eternal gifts of grace that lift us to divine climbs.

Elder Bednar taught us in these words:

> All of our worthy desires and good works, as necessary as they are, can never produce clean hands and a pure heart. It is the Atonement of Jesus Christ that provides both a *cleansing and redeeming power* that helps us to overcome sin and a *sanctifying and strengthening power* that helps us to become better than we ever could by relying upon our own strengths. (David A. Bednar, *Ensign*, November 2007, 82; italics in original)

In other words, we have the same privileges "in Christ" as Christ had in His Father. Christ will show us all things whatsoever we should do and then empower us to do them.

The great chasm that we must cross to follow Him and to do the works that He did is that we are not able in and of ourselves to be perfect, as He was. But through His grace, we do have the ability to be perfectly and flawlessly obedient, as Christ was. The beauty and power of Christ's plan is that as we obey Him, He will provide all that we lack. He will close the great chasm we cannot cross by changing us so that we meet the standard of worthiness.

We must be obedient to Christ's voice as Christ was to the Father's voice. But don't despair! With the grace of Christ to enable us, this is well within our power. We can, in all matters of our ministry, speak every word that Christ puts to our lips and perform every service that He asks and directs us to do. And then comes the absolute power of the gospel of the Son of God: When we command such obedience of our hands, hearts, and lips, then Christ applies the atoning blood He spilt in Gethsemane and upon the cross, which cleanses, sanctifies, and perfects us so that we "in Christ" can do all the works that He did—and in time, even greater.

We will never be perfect in our own name or by our own efforts. Mortals are not engineered to have self-exalting strength. We are engineered to be humble, obey the Master, and thus let Him upgrade, cleanse, and perfect us.

I pray that we prayerfully enshrine this truth in our hearts. When we at last believe and obey, Christ delights in overlaying our failings and weakness with His perfections, and we will become perfect *in Christ*. We will then cease to struggle with spirituality. We will cease to fear and worry that we are not enough, that we can't live the higher laws, or that our faith is yet too tiny to move the mountains in our lives. When we become "perfect in Christ," we will simply hear His voice and faithfully obey, and the mountains will move.

Brother John

Saving Faith in Christ

A dear member of our family is very brilliant (I'll call him David). He has a photographic memory and a genius IQ. We have at times talked about faith and how faith is impossible for him, because he has been unsure much of his life that God actually exists. He had always felt that faith was too subjective to be believable.

However, a few years ago while visiting us in Alaska, David told me a story. He had been absorbed in studying the replication of DNA and had observed that as the double helix unwound to replicate, it tangled, just the way two spiral telephone cords being pulled apart do. Science has discovered that there is a little protein machine (for lack of a better word), an intelligent, purposeful organic device within every cell, which goes down the helix and snips it at the entangle-ment. It then stays with the strand, and once it is free, this little intel-ligent machine reconnects the strand and then goes up and down it to check for integrity. If the strand is up to specs, the little machine detaches and floats away. If the DNA is flawed, it triggers a destruc-tion sequence of that DNA strand so that it cannot create a mutation.

When David deeply considered this and the billions of other similarly intelligent "machines" that facilitate function of body and mind, in a flash it became apparent to his mind that this was of absolute intelligent design. It was just too perfect, too genius, too intricate to have resulted from random evolution.

He told me that evening he had gone for a long walk, and somewhere during that walk, he looked up and asked out loud, "God, are you there?" To his astonishment, he heard an instant reply—an audible voice that he knew for a fact was not his. It said, "Yes, I am here."

David now says, "I know without doubt that there is a God; I just don't know what He is like, or what he wants from me."

I am overjoyed with David's new knowledge of God. But his story also illustrates the three requirements for faith that the Prophet Joseph recorded so powerfully: "Three things are necessary in order that any rational and intelligent being may exercise faith in God unto life and salvation. First, the idea that He actually exists. Second, a *correct* idea of his character, perfections, and attributes. Thirdly, an actual knowledge that the course of life which he is pur-suing is according to His will" (*Lectures on Faith* 3:2–5).

It seems obvious to you and me that one must believe God actually exists to have faith. But for one struggling with believ-ing in God, it is a nearly impossible obstacle. We must have a *correct* understanding of God's attributes and perfections. As Hebrews 11:6 states, "But without faith it is impossible to please [God]; for he that cometh to God must believe that he is, and that he is a rewarder of them that diligently seek him."

We must know—not merely believe, but know—that God is a rewarder of them that seek Him. And how do we learn that for our-selves? We arrive at this understanding by our acts of faith, which are always followed by unfailing blessings from God. In that process, we see that God never fails us—that He always blesses *every time* we obey His laws. He never changes. His laws function the same forever and ever. He never asks us to serve Him or sacrifice for Him without preparing a way for us to succeed, and then to reward us a hundred-fold.

Without this essential understanding of God's attributes, one might falter at the altar of sacrifice, doubting that God would follow through, and our sacrifice be in vain. We could look at a covenant we are being asked to make, or to which we must live faithfully, and doubt that God would really keep His end of the contract.

We obtain true understanding of God's attributes through our gospel walk. We obey some law or prompting, and then year after year we observe how He always blesses us, how He is faithful and anxious to prosper and uplift us. We pray year after year, and receive answers year after year, until we no longer just believe, but we are a witness that God will faithfully bless *all* those who seek Him.

Then comes the final requirement for obtaining saving faith: an actual knowledge that the course of our life is pleasing to God.

If we are picking and choosing which promptings or which commandments we are going to obey, then this latter and greatest knowledge cannot exist in us. Only by obeying *all* of the commandments and *all* of the promptings does one come to this knowledge. And, it is only possible to obey them *all* because we correctly understand God's unfailing love, His gifted grace, and His eternal consistency in blessing the faithful.

This is where the rubber of our souls hits the road of consecration. It takes most of a lifetime to arrive at a point where we can dedicate and consecrate every act, and all of our heart, might, mind, and strength to obedience. But, when we do, then the heavens open and the Father informs us, "Ye shall have eternal life!"

> Wherefore, ye must press forward with steadfastness in Christ, having a perfect brightness of hope, and a love of God and of all men. Wherefore, if ye shall press forward, feasting upon the word of Christ, and endure to the end [in flawless obedience], behold, thus saith the Father: Ye shall have eternal life. (2 Nephi 31:20)

We call this event "having your calling and election made sure."

This same formula is evident in Nephi's blessing and subsequent promise of exaltation:

> Blessed art thou, Nephi, for those things which thou has done; for I have beheld how thou has with unwearyingness declared the word, which I have given unto thee, unto this people. And thou has not feared them, and hast not sought thine own life, but hast sought my will, and to keep my commandments. And now, because thou has done this with such unwearyingness, behold, I will bless thee forever; and I will make thee mighty in word and in deed, in faith and in works; yea, even that all things shall be done unto the according to thy word, for thou shalt not ask that which is contrary to my will." (Helaman 10:4–5)

Herein lies a great key, as we pursue *saving* faith in Christ.

Brother John

By Him and of Him

One of the comments today was that I am beginning to sound like a broken record. The funny thing is that as I was writing that post I had the words "broken record" pop into my head. I didn't know what it meant . . .

Let me ask a question. What is the most common substance in the universe?

I expect that among the first answers that popped into your mind was water, carbon, or oxygen.

The correct answer is Jesus Christ. We don't commonly think of our Savior as a substance, but the scriptures clearly say that Jesus Christ made all that exists, that it was made by Him and even *of* Him.

Doctrine and Covenants 88:41 teaches us: "He comprehendeth all things, and all things are before him, and all things are round about him; and he is above all things, and in all things, and is through all things, and is round about all things; and all things are by him, *and of him*, even God, forever and ever."

Even our own bodies are made *of* this same Christ-element, which is His creative power through the light of Christ, which because it came *from* Him, is also somehow *of* Him. This means that we are made *of* Him as well. Furthermore, Christ sustains all life because all life is a part of Him, and by His power all things remain in their proper order. Turtles don't give birth to horses, and corn seeds don't sprout into stake centers.

So, here we are, made of, by, and for Christ, hearing His voice in our hearts, depending upon His sacrifice and Atonement, dependent upon His grace for the continuation of our mortal lives and for the very hope of our eternal lives! And yet, we have trouble remembering Him and keeping His commandments—the irony being that we are surrounded by nothing so profoundly permeating as Christ and His creations.

We forget at times that Christ is not just the source of the still small voice in our heads, but He is everything else: the way, the truth, and the light. He isn't the signpost that shows the way, He *is* the way.

And here is the reason for the broken record: No truth is more important than this. Because He is all things to us, the only open door through which we may come unto Him, and to become "one" with Him, and to live the life that He lives—we must hear and obey His voice. We don't need a PhD, a brilliant IQ, or a chorus of angels to reveal the way. All we need is our grace-empowered obedience. He will change us to be like Him, and in time sit us down upon thrones in our own kingdoms of glory.

And we will praise Him forever.

Brother John

The Holy Ghost and Light of Christ

In response to several comments and questions, let's take another look at the difference between the Holy Ghost and the Light of Christ. The Light of Christ emanates from Christ and is disseminated to us through the Holy Ghost. This function of the third member of the Godhead is commonly referred to as the Holy Spirit (as an example, see Mosiah 3:19). It is also appropriately called the light of truth, the voice of Christ, the voice of truth, the spirit of truth, the word(s) of Christ, the Word, His voice, "My" voice, the voice of the Good Shepherd, the Spirit of Christ, the Spirit of God, the Spirit of the Lord, and the Light of Christ.

The function of the Light of Christ is to teach us good from evil, and right from wrong. Any time we hear or feel a prompting to choose the right, do good, be kind, express love, or serve or bear testimony, that knowledge comes from Christ.

The Holy Spirit is also the source of our conscience and is a free gift to all mankind because of the Atonement of Christ. It has the power to warn, entice, enlighten, and urge obedience. It will expand its mission to become a teacher of great eloquence as we give heed to its guiding voice.

Even in its most powerful role, the Holy Spirit generally remains a "still small voice." Even profound truths can come silently and require faith to hear and obey. Through righteous experience and obedience to the voice of the Holy Spirit, the Light of Christ becomes more powerful. It communicates greater and greater truths and in time administers the spiritual gifts such as faith, hope, prophecy, knowledge, teaching, believing, healings, and other miracles (see Moroni 10:1–34).

Bruce R. McConkie taught: "Moroni says that the gifts of God come from Christ, by the power of the Holy Ghost and by the Spirit of Christ (Moroni 10). In other words, the gifts come by the power of that Spirit who is the Holy Ghost, but the Spirit of Christ (or light of Christ) is the agency through which the Holy Ghost operates" (McConkie, *Mormon Doctrine*, 314; parenthetical comments in original).

The operation of the Holy Spirit should not be confused with that of the Holy Ghost. When the Holy Ghost speaks in His role as a revelator, the voice (knowledge, feeling, or impression) is louder and cannot easily be mistaken. The Holy Ghost communicates truth in a more powerful way, which enlightens the soul with poignant truth. When we are so blessed to enjoy profound revelation and glorious manifestations, these also come through the Holy Ghost.

This type of grand communiqué becomes an abundant part of our lives only after we have learned to and faithfully followed the lesser gift of the guiding voice of the Holy Spirit. Prior to this the Holy Ghost only speaks on inspiring occasions, and for a special witness, such as when we first gained a testimony that Jesus Christ truly is our Savior.

The Holy Ghost is also referred to as the Holy Spirit, or other terms which usually apply to the Light of Christ, due to the fact that the operation of the agency of the Holy Spirit, and that of the Holy Ghost, becomes nearly indistinguishable as one grows nearer and nearer to sanctification. But the Holy Ghost is always correctly referred to as the Comforter, the Holy Spirit of Promise, and the Spirit of God.

For the sake of clarity, throughout this UnBlog the term "Holy Spirit" refers to the Light of Christ—the Holy Ghost acting in His assigned role as the Light of Christ. Whenever the term "Holy Ghost" is used, reference is being made to the third member of the Godhead speaking in His role as a revelator.

When Jesus Christ speaks through the Holy Ghost as our conscience, He speaks to us without the requirement for us to be worthy or even qualified. The Light of Christ comes to us essentially prepaid through the grace and mercy of the Atonement which Jesus paid for by the shedding of His own blood (see D&C 88:6). Because of the Atonement, Christ can extend mercy to us and reach us via the Holy Spirit even when we don't want it or know how much we need it.

Brother John

Making Sense of It All

I had the privilege of giving a fireside last Sunday evening. It was a great blessing. I have done far fewer of them this year because of my health, so this was a sweet experience. After each fireside, I listen to people's questions about their own journey. The questions are heartfelt and sincere, and their yearning for concrete, logical answers real. It seems to be a human quality to want to make sense of our lives by use of logic. Unfortunately, logic is poorly equipped to make sense of spiritual things because God's ways are much higher than our own, and His law is light and truth, not logic as we can define it.

I have discovered that especially in spiritual things, we want to know the formula, the rules of the road, the laws, bylaws, and fine print that govern spiritual blessings. I suppose our hope is that if we can learn all of the requirements, we can check them off one-by-one and then the blessing will manifest. Or, perhaps we are trying to make sense of why we checked off every box we understood and the blessing is still somewhere before us.

One of the things that I love about the gospel of Jesus Christ is that it is extremely custom-made for each seeker. There are under-girding principles, ordinances, and requirements that are common to every journey, but when you go beyond those few basic things, there really are very few "rules" one can write down and check off. The process is very simply to "come unto Christ, and be perfected in Him" (Moroni 10:32). That purifying and perfecting process will assuredly take as many different forms as there are people seeking it.

This doesn't mean that we are left without a clear guide as we step off of the known and seeable launching pad. It means that if we have correctly prepared to step off, we will already have taken Christ as our guide, attuned our spiritual ears to His voice, and are willing to do anything He asks us to do. Here is the great safety of coming unto Christ, that we are not following a set of rules but a living, loving, enabling, and atoning Being whose work and glory it is to see that we actually arrive there. Our exaltation isn't a sideline activity He is doing; it is the only work He is engaged in. He isn't doing anything else.

Now, here is the hard part: We must let go of the handrails and the training wheels of the launch pad and trust Christ to lead us with complete safety and in the highest definition of efficiency. If we have taken the Holy Spirit to be our guide, then we can replace every question with the assurance of faith. This is a big "if," but it is one that we should never leave home without! We do not need to know why in every instance. We only need to know that it is His will. This is not blind obedience; this is obedience with our eyes open wide with wonder and acceptance, delighting in the eternal vistas that are opening before us.

Unlike some fictional deities, our God is a God of truth and does not deceive or trick us. It is impossible for anyone to take the Holy Spirit as their guide, firmly maintain their grip upon that iron rod, and then end up anywhere else than at exaltation in the fullest eternal sense—with a multitude of blessings, miracles, manifestations, visitations, powers, protections, and blessings all along the journey there.

In this we can have absolute faith because it makes sense of everything that happens along the way. It makes sense because faith and inspired trust overcome fear and doubt. The Holy Spirit whispers peace and makes of our lives a direct course seen most clearly in revelatory flashes and inspired hindsight—but straight and true nonetheless.

Brother John

I Am a Child of God

*T*hroughout my childhood, my favorite Primary song was "I Am a Child of God." Its message resonated with my little soul and gave me a sense of belonging to my family and to Heavenly Father. Its message is still sweet and comforting.

As a spiritually mature adult, however, I have found a divine sonship which is profoundly more empowering. If now I wrote a song to enthrone and teach this greater sonship, I might well entitle it "I Am a Child of Jesus." Let me explain.

Being a child of Heavenly Father is marvelous and speaks of our eternal possibilities. But it is not unique. Every living person on the earth is a child of Heavenly Father. Even those who reject and fight against Him are His children. We are told He loves them all, even when He must withhold blessings and eternal rewards. Their divine sonship or daughtership does not entitle them to anything above anyone else.

Heavenly Father sent His Son, Jesus Christ, into this world to prepare a way for us to return to the Father's presence. We come unto the Father by coming to Christ, by taking His (Christ's) name upon us, and becoming His (Christ's) spiritual sons and daughters. When we become Christ's children, we take upon ourselves Christ's name because we are His spiritual offspring—His children. He thus becomes our spiritual Father. As His children we then are entitled to His atoning sacrifice and His much-needed advocacy with the Father. As His child, we will be brought by Christ back to the Father "in His name."

Having Christ as my spiritual Father is saving and exalting. It is the means whereby my relationship with Father continues throughout eternity and whereby I eventually may become like Father—not equal, but like Him, and most importantly *with* Him.

The prayer within "I Am a Child of God" is, "Teach me all that I must do to live with Him someday." The answer to that prayer comes in the person and mission of Jesus Christ. What must I do? I must come unto Christ and be perfected in Him.

So when I want to sing of divine kinship, of exalting fatherhood, and saving sonship, I sing of Christ—whose love and grace and spiritual fatherhood will forever elevate me—so that as a redeemed son of Christ, I can live with Christ my Father and with my Heavenly Father again someday.

Brother John

Personal Journal

September 10, 1973

It has been hard, but I have come to love these years I spent [on my mission] in South Africa, and I have realized joy in the people who accepted the truths I presented to them. I was also blessed to see many of the seeds I planted sprout and become harvested by others. There I gained a great love for the gospel and for teaching it.

I have since thought that the thing that would make me happiest would be to be able to shout repentance all the remaining days of my life to the honest in heart.

February 12, 1978

During the winter of '78 we were living in a Lincoln log home [in Alaska] during a terrible snowstorm. It snowed about two feet, and the winds got up to about 120 mph for almost two weeks. We were stuck inside the house with only a fireplace for heat. At times, the temperature got to twenty-three below zero. When the winds finally abated, I dug out our four-wheel drive Scout and tried to get into town for food. It was impossible, as drifts were across the roads as deep as six feet.

I busted through some of them that were soft and then hit a hard one doing about 35 mph. It threw me up in the air quite a height. When I landed, it broke all four springs on the truck. I tried to continue on, but with the decreased clearance I got stuck in some shallow drifts.

The wind was still blowing around 60 mph. I tried to dig out, but the wind blew the snow back in faster than I could dig. After an hour of futile digging I got back in the cab, nearly frozen to death. I was nearly out of gas and knew that I was in bad trouble. I didn't expect anyone to come along for days.

I started praying for all I was worth.

While I was sitting there praying, I saw headlights coming from the opposite direction. A big new pickup was forging its way toward me! When it got within sight, I got out and told the people that the road was blocked. They pulled me out, and I made it into town and then home via another route that was not drifted. I knew it was a miracle.

The people who pulled me out were members of the Church who were just moving into the valley. They have been my friends ever since. I know I owe them and God my life.

January 27, 1979

Another great experience happened at this time. I have been in the habit of fasting whenever the Spirit instructed me to do so. This averaged about twice a week, occasionally three times. Whenever I fasted because of obedience, I received such great spiritual blessings that I could hardly wait for the next time the Spirit would instruct me to fast.

One Sunday morning as I was sitting down to breakfast, the Spirit told me to fast because I was to give a priesthood blessing for healing the sick that day. I took the first fork full of food out of my mouth and retired to my room to pray. Then I went to church where I played the organ for Priesthood, Sunday School, and Sacrament meeting. During the prelude to priesthood meeting, one of the bishopric leaned over my shoulder and asked me to come to the hospital with him after the opening exercises and give a certain brother a blessing who was suffering from kidney stones. I readily accepted, as I was already preparing for the blessing.

After I was finished on the organ I found the bishop and said I was ready. He told me that he had just sent someone else. I was sure that he had given my job away and felt bad. Just as I was walking from the church, a new member of the ward approached me and asked me if I would give his wife a blessing. Of course I accepted, and went straight to their house with my first counselor. On the way over I asked the Lord what blessing I should give her from Him. He told me to bless her to be healed immediately. I said I would.

This young woman was sick with something akin to pneumonia and looked whiter than the sheets she was lying on. She had been in bed for almost a week, perhaps longer. With the help of her husband, she walked to the living room of their small one-bedroom apartment. We had a short discussion about anointing with oil and about how the scriptures promise a worthy recipient the remission of their sins in preparation for the healing. My companion then anointed, and I gave this sister the blessing that I had been instructed to give her, rebuking the illness and commanding her to be healed and resume her normal duties.

When we removed our hands she looked exactly the same. We talked for about ten minutes, during which time she remained as weak as ever. I knew that the Lord had commanded me to give her that blessing, and it never occurred to me that He might not honor it. I just kept looking at her, waiting for it to occur. It was kind of like holding a ping pong ball under water and releasing it; you know absolutely well that it will surface, you just don't know exactly when or where.

I stood to leave and she stood to shake hands. She asked me if I was hungry and announced that she was getting some juice. She said she hadn't eaten for three days. She refused her husband's offer to get it for her. I heard things rattling about in the kitchen, and she came back out with a sandwich and a glass of juice, as well as several other things. Around her mouthful of food, she announced that she was famished and was going to eat—please excuse her. The color was back in her face. She dove into her food and we left.

I learned the next day that she was fully recovered and had been since the blessing. I KNOW God honors priesthood blessings.

Chapter Two

One Path to Every Blessing: Obedience to the Voice of the Spirit

One Path to Every Blessing

*T*hrough every UnBlog post I attempted to high-light one truth, which is that everything we hope to attain in this life or in eternity comes to us as a result of our giving up our will in obedience to the Holy Spirit of Christ.

In truth, this concept of there being only one path, and how to walk it, seems to be a hard concept to master. Even though it is simple to understand, it is difficult to enthrone in our daily lives. I have had the privilege of writing hundreds of thousands of words on this subject and explaining it hundreds of times in firesides and face-to-face visits. Very few people truly embrace how powerful this principle is, how it stands alone as our pathway to glory, and how any other course we might attempt to take cannot deliver the glorious blessings we seek.

Since there are many commandments, many life missions, and many potential blessings along the way, it seems as if there are many ways and many "laws" to obey to receive these various blessings.

In truth, there is only one path to every blessing, including the ultimate attainment of exaltation. There is only one tool we have in our hands—*which is to identify the voice of the Holy Spirit and be flawlessly determined to obey it.* This is the sacrifice of a broken heart and a contrite spirit which Christ requires of us today.

There is only one outcome of obedience: to become like Christ in your lifetime, receive of His grace, receive miracles, visions, covenants, promises and visitations, and to live your life in the embrace of God's love and guidance. Every other blessing you or

I may seek, whether it be kindness, gentleness, faith, power in the priesthood, or "oneness" with Christ, flow only from obedience to the Holy Spirit.

This kind of obedience results in just one destination, which is to be redeemed from the Fall through the Atonement of Christ and to return to Father's presence—preferably in this life. "And every one that hearkeneth to the Spirit cometh unto God, even the Father" (D&C 84:47).

Brother John

My Sheep Hear My Voice

I was about seventeen when my dad gave us kids a 1964 VW Beetle. It was the ugliest car on earth at that time and only became "cute" to later generations—which I admit I'm still not a part of. He gave the three older kids the VW as our teenage car. We paid for gas and oil, and he maintained it. It was a sweet deal.

One of the huge drawbacks of the early VW Beetles was that they had virtually no heaters or defrosters. It was very difficult to get one warm inside and almost impossible to defrost the windows. I'm told Germans still don't heat their homes, so maybe it seemed fine to them; to me it was always a frozen, miserable trip. I appreciated having transportation, but it really seemed like a bug, a cold metal insect to me. But, the little thing started every single time, had great traction in the snow, and almost never left you stranded. Did I mention that it had very poor headlights? I mean, light a candle and hold it out the window if you really want to see where you're going.

It was late one snowy afternoon with heavy fog when I was headed home from high school. The windows were frosted over. It was dark, and I could just barely identify the road enough to drive on it. I used to like to follow other vehicles when I drove that car because I could see better from the reflected light of their headlights than from my own.

Between the school and our home was a long hill. There were train tracks at two places on the hill. The upper one was a single track. The rails were rusty, and I had never seen a train there. The lower track was a double set, and there were daily trains there. The crossing was marked by a big white X. There were no lights or arms or bells. Just the white X.

I was coming down that hill, shivering and eager to get home. I could see the crossing sign up ahead and decided it was safe to cross.

I distinctly heard the Spirit whisper, "Stop."

I came to a stop and looked closely. There was no train, and I was concerned that a car would rear-end me if I stopped in the road. I put the car back in gear and started to move over the tracks.

The Spirit again said, "Stop!" a little louder. I stopped again and again decided it was safe to proceed.

I had gone a couple feet when the Spirit plainly said, "STOP! Roll down the window!" So, I stopped again because the prompting was almost audible this time. I rolled down the window and through the muffling effect of softly falling snow heard the clickity-clack-clickty-clack of a train. I switched the lights on bright, which didn't make much difference, and was utterly terrified to see train wheels. Not a train—train wheels going past my bumper no more than a few feet away. I was literally inches from driving under a train.

Time and again, I suspect for millennia before I was born, and through my few years of mortality, this one lesson has been taught to me over and over: "My sheep hear my voice."

Brother John

Voices of Revelation

As I read the comments you write on the UnBlog and speak to friends and family, a picture is forming in my mind, which is that all of us, to some degree or another, are struggling to tell the difference between true revelation and the other voices in our minds. Last Wednesday evening I met with friends in my home, and we spent most of our time talking about how to really know when we are receiving revelation.

First, let us observe that promptings, both from good and evil sources, generally sound the same, especially in the beginning. They most often come as ideas or thoughts that enter our mind and generally don't involve words. We must carefully judge the good promptings from evil ones by their content, not on how they sound.

This is the great dividing line between true revelation and everything else. If it leads us to do good, be kind, show love, give grace or mercy or kindness, if it leads us to Christ, or leads us to help others come to Christ, then it is inspired of God. The scriptures say that we may know with a "perfect knowledge" that such things are from God. The prophet Moroni wrote:

> For behold, my brethren, it is given unto you to judge, that ye may know good from evil; and the way to judge is as plain, that ye may know with a perfect knowledge, as the daylight is from the dark night.
>
> For behold, the Spirit of Christ is given to every man, that he may know good from evil; wherefore, I show unto you the way to judge; for every thing which inviteth to do good, and to persuade to believe in Christ, is sent forth by the power and gift of Christ; wherefore ye may know with a perfect knowledge it is of God. (Moroni 7:15–16)

We also hear ourselves think. The easiest way to recognize the voice of our own mind is that it is unsure. It asks questions and ponders things. For example, "Why is this happening?" "What did that mean?" "What should I do now?" are all products of our own mind. The voice of our own mind often uses the personal case such as "I am tired," "I'm confused," or "I hate that."

The voice of evil tries to get us to ignore the voice of Christ. It actually argues against it. The Holy Spirit will say, "Study the scriptures," and then the voice of opposition rails against it: "It's late. You're tired. Do it tomorrow. Better make those phone calls first." The voice of evil can rarely just give one argument, but it seems to prefer to repeatedly rail against good promptings. That railing actually is helpful in telling us the source; even temptations will most often come to us in waves, again and again, with seemingly greater urgency to act. In contrast, the Holy Spirit does not rail but whispers its divine message once and then is quiet, honoring our agency.

Another hallmark of evil is that it often tries to get us to indulge our flesh, senses, and lusts. It is always self-serving. The voice of evil is also the only one that urges us to control other people, to limit their agency, to criticize or dominate others.

In the case that we receive a prompting to do something that is on its face neither good nor bad, we must search diligently in the Spirit to know right from wrong. I believe it is far better to take the time to pray, ponder, and even fast before acting, rather than blindly obey some prompting that may be inspired of evil. I believe it is righteous to pray something like, "Father, I just had the feeling that I should . . . I am willing to do anything you ask; but I really need to know if this is from you so I don't make a mistake. Please tell me again, in a way that I can't misunderstand."

And then after your prayer, wait for the peace to come. If the peace doesn't settle upon you, it is not right for you to pursue that prompting. As I have blogged about so often, peace is something that Satan cannot imitate.

Learning to tell the difference in these voices is one of the main spiritual processes of mortality. Those who learn to hear His voice, who receive His grace, and who obey are exalted—everyone else is not (see D&C 45:45–47; 84:43–53; 93:1).

Over time, and by righteous experience, it becomes easier and easier to tell the difference in the voices. There is a definable feeling, an essence—a flavor, if you will—that accompanies revelation. With a little persistence it will all become much easier to hear, and obedience can become a habitual way of life. It never seems to get easier to obey, just easier to tell the true source of the prompting.

It is far better to humble ourselves than to be compelled to be humble. It is far better to let the Holy Spirit teach us obedience through little things, like responding to a prompting to say you're sorry or to drive the speed limit, than it is to require some huge dramatic event to penetrate our stubborn hearts and teach us to obey.

The cost of exaltation is grace-empowered obedience, and the cost of obedience is whatever it takes to teach us to hear and obey the voice of Jesus Christ.

Brother John

Still and Small

*D*ear KJ,

There is a very simple realization one can make to begin to clearly hear and recognize the Spirit. It is this: every good thing comes from God. In other words, if you have a thought, just an impression, that you should do or say something that is good, uplifts, magnifies faith, worships Christ, gives comfort, is kind, is full of service, or is even just down-home nice, then that idea came to you via revelation from Christ through the Holy Spirit. We call these things promptings, but they may be feelings, understandings, ideas, words, voices, visual images in our minds, or miraculous events. They all come from the same source.

People get confused when they try to make all "promptings" have language, words, or audible voices. True promptings generally are ideas that lack an actual voice and do not employ language. The very phrase "still small voice" labels it as inaudible. "Still" means without sound, without movement, subdued, hushed. "Small" describes something tiny, in no great amount, of minor weight or consequence, and easy to overlook.

The *law* that governs revelation and spiritual gifts is obedience—not grand obedience to vast and amazing laws, just obedience to whatever light and truth you possess, even if it is very "still." So, we start wherever we are, with whatever truth is present in our lives, no matter how it sounds—and we obey, and obey, and obey. As a direct result of obedience to this law, we receive greater and clearer revelation, our views expand, and we obey on this new level. This stairstep upward progress is how this and every law and blessing of the gospel works.

What happens is that revelation evolves according to our "heed and diligence." As we obey (heed) it becomes easier to recognize. It will take on greater content, become more plain, and be easier to recognize and follow.

This isn't to say that in time *all* revelation becomes visionary and miraculous. Even on the highest mountain peaks of prophetic insight, most promptings will be subtle.

Prolonged obedience will add occasional spoken words, sentences, even volumes (the language we keep wanting to have to frame and define revelation), and it will include visions, sudden insights, bursts of understanding, declarations of doctrine, mysteries, miracles, and angelic visitations.

But, it all starts "still."

Brother John

It Really Does Happen

Childhood seems to demonstrate that rules stop us from enjoying life to the fullest. As kids we wanted to eat cookies for every meal, and our mother told us no. When we did it anyway, she probably punished us. Rules, it became very clear to our young minds, get in the way of our happiness.

That thinking often persists as teens and beyond, until we become mature enough to see that these rules were actually saving us from unpleasant experiences and lasting consequences. As teens and sometimes adults, if we try eating cookies for every meal, we realize it can't be done without sacrificing our happiness and our waistlines—and Mother knew it all along.

I remember a particular event when I was about ten. My health-conscious parents would not buy soda pop for the family because they said it was too sweet, and they wouldn't buy potato chips very often because they weren't healthy. On that rare occasion that they did bring home a bag, it was shared by many kids and was gone very quickly.

One day I was at my cousin's house out in the country. We decided to walk to the local country store, which was several miles away, and buy potato chips and soda pop. We had a little money between us and got permission to go. We walked and walked and walked, and finally arrived at heaven—a whole counter full of potato chips, a cooler full of soda pop, and no parents to stop us. We each bought several bags of chips and a soda, and began walking home. I was hungry from the long walk and really plowed into the chips. I couldn't believe how good they tasted! I ate them all as fast as I could without stopping, washing it down with the syrupy soda. Before we got back to the house, I became increasingly more nauseated and ended up returning home with an empty stomach. My cousin did the same. It was literally a dozen years before I could eat another potato chip.

When a prompting comes to us from the Holy Spirit, it often seems to be trying to deny us some mortal form of happiness we were just reaching for. Like little children with a bag of potato chips, we don't heed the prompting to not partake until we have experienced the bilious result of disobedience a few thousand times.

Then, we realize that promptings and commandments don't limit our enjoyment of life; they protect us from unknown hazards. And far more important, they open new vistas of possibility where there were none before. Disobedience to God's plan invariably destroys freedom—in this life and in the next. But the greatest reason to school our hearts and hands to obedience is that there is an eternal world of glorious mortal blessings that can only be glimpsed by revelatory insight and obtained by obedience to the voice of Christ. As the blessings begin to flow and the heavens begin to open, and as our souls begin to expand, we finally understand why law is so liberating.

Obedience to the Holy Spirit is the Aladdin's lamp of mortality, which by continually polishing we unleash the mighty genie of all mortal blessings, the least of which is happiness, peace, and joy in this life. The greatest blessings are an assurance of our eternal reward, power in the priesthood, eternal families, miracles, visions, prophecy, knowledge, angelic visitations, and the intimate knowledge of God.

My home teacher was visiting us yesterday evening and told us of living in the same stake as President Kimball for a while. He said that in a fast and testimony meeting, President Kimball stood up and, among other things, quoted D&C 93:1: "It shall come to pass that every soul who forsaketh his sins and cometh unto me, and calleth on my name, and obeyeth my voice, and keepeth my commandments, shall see my face and know that I am." President Kimball then said, "This scripture is fulfilled more often than you might ever imagine—many times daily."

It really does happen.

Brother John

A Lesson I Will Not Need to Be Taught Twice

Since the first great step to spiritual greatness is learning to hear the voice of revelation, I invite you [readers of the blog] to leave comments on your experiences with learning this principle. I know many of you have taken the voice of Christ as your guide. It is not a difficult concept, but it can be a very challenging process. A testimony of this concept takes both experiences in obedience and ones where we fail to be obedient. I would like to hear a few of your stories. It comes to me that your testimonies and your comments at this time would serve as a pillar of strength to the rest of us in the UnBlogosphere. If you are comfortable doing so, please share with us both your successes and your learning process.

One of the hardest things to understand about revelation is that in the beginning, revelation is rarely a voice. There are rarely words. Most often it comes as ideas, thoughts, feelings, or impressions. To the spiritual pilgrim, these things all sound alike. We learn to judge these things initially less by their sound than by their *outcome*. We "search diligently in the Light of Christ" for those things that are good. After a while—probably a long while of sorting through and identifying the voice of truth—we find it has a flavor, a spiritual essence, which becomes delicious and welcome. When we begin to hear and consistently obey, the voice changes; it becomes stronger, more informative, and even begins to use words, visual images, complete sentences, or paragraphs of truth that come to us.

Many years ago, just after I had written *Following the Light of Christ into His Presence*, I was invited to speak at a fireside in a home. The gathering was mostly with friends of my younger sister. We met in this beautiful new home, and with the happy assistance of the Spirit, we began to explore this voice of revelation that we all have.

I was explaining similar principles to this group when one sister raised her hand. She said, "Last fall I put my kids to bed and retired to my own bed to read. I like to read with a scented candle burning by my bed, and have done this for most of my life." She stopped to look at her hands a moment. "That night, I had a feeling that I should not light the candle. I couldn't figure out why. I always close my door when it is lit, and I never forget to blow it out before going to sleep. The feeling came again, stronger, but I thought it was silly and lit it anyway. Then the urge came to me to blow it back out. I didn't and began to read. For some reason my reading didn't last long, and I fell to sleep with the candle still burning.

"Sometime during the night, my two-year-old came into the room, probably to ask for a drink of water or something. He saw the candle and took it back to his own room. On the way, the hot wax touched his fingers, and he dropped the candle and ran to his room. The candle's flame spread to the carpet, then the walls, and ultimately burned our home down."

She began to weep. "Do you mean to tell me that it was Jesus Christ who was telling me to not light the candle that one night? Are you telling me that it was I who burned down our home, through my stubborn disobedience to the Holy Spirit?" She was incredulous, but she desperately wanted to understand.

I asked her a few questions. "Was what the Spirit told you that night correct? Was it the truth?"

"Yes!"

"Was it good?" I asked.

"It would have been if I had listened."

"Did this experience bring you closer to Christ?" I asked her.

"Our family has rejoiced that none of us were lost in the fire. We have considered it a tender mercy that we all survived—even our kitten survived. It has definitely brought us closer to Christ," she indicated softly.

I read to her from Moroni 7, where he teaches that anything that is good, teaches us to love and serve one another, and brings us closer to Christ is inspired of God. She seemed accepting but startled that God would use such dramatic and potentially lethal means to teach her this hard lesson.

I felt the Holy Spirit move in my heart and replied, "I am very certain that prior to that night, Jesus Christ had spoken to you many times and in many ways, and that you would have eventually learned this lesson, though probably not nearly as dramatically. I don't believe Jesus Christ burned your house down to teach you this principle. I think your little son came into your room with the randomness and thoughtlessness of a child, saw the fire, and decided to play with it, contrary to his training. But, knowing that your two-year-old's lack of judgment would result in your home burning down, Jesus Christ warned you again and again, even though He knew you wouldn't obey."

"But why?" she demanded through her tears.

"To turn this most difficult event into the most powerful lesson you will ever learn."

She became very quiet. "Do you really think that learning to listen to the Holy Spirit is *that* important?" she demanded.

"It appears for you, at that time in your life, that learning this lesson was second only to sparing your life."

She wiped away her tears. "It is a lesson I will not need to be taught twice."

Brother John

The Perfect Law

There is a stunning statement in Doctrine and Covenants 88, which connects all of the doctrinal dots regarding what the Holy Spirit is, why we hear it as our conscience, and what importance it plays in our eternal hopes.

Let us first note that this voice of truth which we call the Holy Spirit comes from Jesus Christ, who is the source of all truth, and is a function of the Light of Christ: "For you shall live by every word that proceedeth forth from the mouth of God. For the word of the Lord is truth, and whatsoever is truth is light, and whatsoever is light is Spirit, even the Spirit of Jesus Christ. And the Spirit giveth light to every man that cometh into the world; and the Spirit enlighteneth every man through the world, that hearkeneth to the voice of the Spirit. And every one that hearkeneth to the voice of the Spirit cometh unto God, even the Father" (D&C 84:44–47).

One might write the information in verse 45 as an equation, like this:

Word of the Lord = Truth = Light = Spirit of Jesus Christ

In Doctrine and Covenants 93:36 we read: "The glory of God is intelligence, or in other words, light and truth." Adding to our formula above, we have:

Word of the Lord = Truth = Light =
Spirit of Jesus Christ = Glory of God

In other words, these terms are synonymous when used in this context. Since they are equal in meaning, we learn that by increasing our obedience to the Spirit of Jesus Christ, we also in that same act increase truth, light, and inspired access to the word of the Lord in our lives.

The double edge on this sword is that the Spirit of Jesus Christ is the *only* way to acquire greater truth and light. There isn't another means or method. As Moroni 7:16 proclaims, we may know with a "perfect knowledge" that anything which is good, brings us to Christ, or is loving and kind is inspired of Jesus Christ and Him alone.

In Doctrine and Covenants 88, beginning with verse 6, we find a fairly complete discussion of the Light of Christ. The inspired Word informs us that the Light of Christ is the power of the sun, the light of the moon, and the power of creation. It is the power that enlightens our minds, changing them from a cluster of red meat cells into a living, intelligent being able to hear the voice of God.

Then in Doctrine and Covenants 88:13 we receive this startling truth: "The light which is in all things, which giveth life to all things, *which is the law by which all things are governed,* even the power of God who sitteth upon his throne, who is in the bosom of eternity, who is in the midst of all things."

In other words, not only is the Light of Christ the power of God giving life to all things, but it is the *law* by which God governs all things.

To be governed is not to be controlled; it is to have law made known, and then the governed choose to obey or not. When God speaks to the elements and tells them to organize into a world, they obey and are thereby exalted (see verses 17–19, 25–26). When God commands a rock or a tree, they obey. But God's highest creation—mankind—filters it through our weakness and lusts, and most often we natural men and women disobey.

We have a tendency to think that the law of the celestial kingdom should involve temple attendance, paying tithing, consecration, sacrifice, or serving in some noble calling. The scriptures say it is simply *obedience to the Holy Spirit,* which is the voice of Christ, and the law by which He is governing our lives. Such obedience will naturally lead us through temple attendance and every needed service, but it is hearkening to the voice of Christ which fulfills the law, not the acts that we perform.

This is important because doing it backwards, which would be to serve or attend or work, work, work, hoping this "earns" us a celestial reward, will yield bitter disappointment on Judgment Day. No amount of "good works" can substitute for obedience, which is accomplished through the Atonement of Christ. The Church has its fair share of people who work themselves to exhaustion doing good things, while ignoring their families, sacred duties, quest for true spirituality, and quietly indulging their lusts while working for public notice and ego—hiding darkness behind a façade of good works.

If such working souls took the Holy Spirit to be their guide, they would be led to a thorough inner cleansing first, then purification, sanctification, and peace—and after all that, then comes service and works in whatever part of the vineyard the Lord sends us. The work may not be mighty or public or even exhausting, but it will be sweet work, pure and peaceful.

Here is the wonder, glory, and joy of this law: It is that every living being can recognize and live it. It does not require that we be one of the great and noble. It does not require that we have money or college degrees, publish books, or even be known. A humble soul who walks in the light, even though that walk may take him or her less than a mile from their birthplace, will one day sit down with Abraham in the highest reward mortals can be given.

This is the perfect and exalting law of the celestial kingdom. It is given to all the world in such majestic simplicity that it could only have come from the mind and perfect love of God.

Brother John

True Discipleship

Quite a few of you commented on your experiences with personal revelation. They are wonderful examples of this principle operating in the lives of the faithful. I selected a few of the shorter ones and invite you to read them with today's UnBlog. They are inspiring. Thank you.

A few years ago while I was serving in a bishopric in Alaska, we learned that one of our new members had been injured in a duck hunting accident. He was a young man with a new baby, a growing business, and a glow about him since his baptism a few months earlier. He remained in a hospital in the "Lower 48," and we waited anxiously for him to return. When we were finally able to meet with him we found that he had lost the use of one eye and was a little bitter about it. He didn't understand how God could let this happen to him.

We asked him to tell us how it had happened. He told the tale of accidentally crossing paths, then walking back toward his friends. A flock of pheasants flew up in front of him, and his friends turned and fired right at him. He was only able to save his one good eye because he threw up his arm in front of his face.

I asked him, "When you turned to walk toward your friends, what were you feeling?"

He said, "I was hoping a bunch of birds didn't fly up between us, and my friends shoot me."

I said, "How many times did you feel the urge to turn around and go the other way?"

He looked sheepish. "About a hundred."

"Why did you keep walking toward them when the Holy Spirit was warning you to go another way?"

He stopped with his mouth open. He opened and closed it several times. His wife began to cry and left the room. His face went pale and he sat down. "I just didn't know it was God talking to me. I've never heard that voice before. I feel like an idiot."

I sat down beside him. "No, this time you were just unsure. You're inexperienced with the gift of the Holy Ghost. Ignoring it again would make you an idiot."

The point I am hoping these true stories illustrate is that all of us walk in the light of revelation. Those who have learned to identify it have daily experiences like these. They have inspiring and joyful exposure to the Spirit, and quite often their lives are protected.

With experience, we may all learn to trust the voice of Christ. Not only can we trust it when it warns us to duck, but we can trust it when it moves us to take the scriptures with us on a business trip or to check the laundry room. *Every* time we obey, it beautifies and uplifts our souls, and blesses those whose lives we share. Even if the outcome doesn't seem particularly spectacular in the moment, you will learn that obedience is always the right choice and will never lead you astray.

True and saving faith in Christ begins when we decide, for the remainder of our existence, to rely upon His voice.

Discipleship, true discipleship, begins when we give our lives over to Him and covenant ourselves to obey every word that proceeds forth from the mouth of God—even the still, small, almost imperceptible words.

Brother John

Coin of the Realm

A psychologist friend once told me that he could have me committed because I heard voices and did what they told me. We both laughed. He was (emphasizing the past tense) a member but had fallen away because he did not accept the principle of continuous personal revelation.

This should come as no shock to anyone here. But to the world, to the Babylonian mind, this concept of hearing and obeying personal revelation is foolishness. The only reason they don't have us all institutionalized is that they view this "voice" as originating from the fleshly mind. They consider it to be the voice of our own ego (or some psycho-term I choose to forget) and therefore no more insightful or dangerous than our conscious thoughts.

So, since I'm certifiable anyway, I'm going to up the ante a bit.

Not only does this "voice" lead us in a pathway that blesses and preserves us, but accompanying it is an actual power that upgrades and changes us. Each time we obey, this upgrading influence pushes us a little closer to becoming like the origin of the voice—Christ.

To my soul, to my heart, this is the greatest aspect of obedience to the Master. It isn't just that life is happier. It is that we become stronger, more faith-filled, easier to be taught, more insightful and inspired, and our understanding of the doctrine of the priesthood evolves upward. We slowly begin to comprehend things that were invisible and mysterious to us previously. The heavens begin to open. Visions leak through. Dreams become prophetic. Our ministries become focused and powerful. Our words become His words and our works, His works.

Not only this, but even better still is that by this very small but powerful process of obedience to the voice of Christ in small daily things *we become sanctified.*

When I write principles like this I want to italicize them, bold them, underline them, and change the font color! It is so easy to miss such a simple and sublimely powerful concept. It is the steady, undeviating, daily obedience to Christ that sanctifies. If there is a great event, an overpowering grand finale, it is appended to this apparently lesser process to illuminate the blessings being gifted to the humble seeker.

It is almost impossible to walk a selfish and self-willed lifestyle, then to feel needy, kneel down and pray all through the night, and stand up the next morning a sanctified, inspired, and perfected soul. Even when there is a heralded spiritual event, almost always that person spent years prior to it by walking in obedience, struggling to overcome, and yearning for grace to pierce the veil. Then at the apex of that struggle, after long years of obedience, the veil is at last pierced during mighty prayer. This event was the end result of a long walk of faith. The very ability to pray mightily, to petition all night, and to endure with faith until it comes is a result of the slower process of years of incremental obedience.

We have a tendency to expect vast and glorious things to result from an isolated, vast, and glorious effort. Fortunately for us, it doesn't work that way. Sustained obedience is the only pathway that will bring us to Christ. Any other combination of acts, works, or sacrifices that did not originate with obedience to the voice of the Master will take us somewhere else.

The wonderful thing is, this same principle operates for every gift we hope to receive. This makes obedience the coin of the realm, which can be spent over and over and over. It purchases every gift, opens every door, and vends every blessing mankind can receive.

Every spiritual gift is bestowed upon the humble, weak, and struggling souls whose long but obedient walk has taken them to the throne of grace to receive what they seek, not upon the lollygagging sinner who suddenly decided to give Christ a try at a rest stop on the interstate to Babylon.

Brother John

A-B-C

uite often during a fireside, something I didn't plan to say will come out of my mouth. I think it is a result of the Holy Spirit striving to get me to teach in a way that will truly reach the hearts of all those present. When one of these events happens, I usually find myself upon a line of reasoning or explaining a metaphor of which I have no idea how it ends. I'm just talking. I've learned to suppress the angst of public speaking with no object other than to speak the words that the Holy Spirit puts into my mind, no matter how foolish I might look. The Lord has never let me down. It's very much a leap of faith, but it can also produce something beautiful.

In St. George last Friday, a question was asked regarding "working out your own salvation." A sister wanted to know, at what point do we depend upon ourselves to know right from wrong and to be gainfully involved in plotting our path; and when do we just depend upon the Holy Spirit to guide us?

My answer came in a metaphor.

Imagine yourself as an infant in the premortal world, and Heavenly Father puts His hands on both of your cheeks and says, "Child, the most important thing in mortality you will learn is to hear and obey my voice. Do you understand?"

We nod excitedly and say, "Yes, Father, I will obey every word that you speak to me!"

Father smiles and says, "I know you will, but it will take some time and some experience on your part to learn to hear my voice—and even more to learn to obey everything I ask of you."

"Oh, I think I'll get it faster than that! I knew this truth well. How hard can it be to learn it again in mortality?"

Father smiles knowingly. "It will be the most important thing you learn in your mortal life. It is like learning to read: You must first learn your A-B-Cs. Hearing and obeying my voice are your spiritual A-B-Cs. I will keep helping you until you learn this lesson completely."

So, we are born into mortality. We reach the age of two or three, and we know we shouldn't have done something. Father reaches out of the heavens and allows us to experience a consequence. He takes our sweet spirit face in His big, warm hands and says, "Remember your A-B-Cs." But we don't get it, because as a toddler we wanted something else so badly at that moment.

We keep growing, and the lessons continue. We disobey our earthly parents and get hurt, and Father reminds us, "A-B-Cs." But we're not listening.

We cheat on a test in junior high, knowing full well it is wrong, and get caught. Father says, "A-B-Cs," but we're still not listening. We think the message is that we should have been more careful at our cheating.

We go from experience to experience, sometimes obeying, sometimes not, until the lessons grow in drama and power. Finally we find ourselves beaten by life, unable to carry on, full of regrets, sorrows, and weaknesses that we can't seem to conquer by ourselves. We cry out in prayer and beg Father for relief. He holds our tear-stained face once more and says, "I only want you to learn to hear my voice. Remember your spiritual A-B-Cs?"

We finally get it. We finally realize we *can't* do it on our own and that the life of happiness we envisioned for ourselves while looking down upon the earth from heaven was entirely designed to teach us this one thing: to obey His voice—then every other blessing would follow.

We look up into the heavens and Father lovingly says, "Repeat after me. A . . ."

We choke back a sob and say, "A."

He whispers, "B."

We finally understand. "A-B-C!" we cry. "From this day and forever, I will obey Thy voice, Father. *I will obey!*"

Father's face is radiant with pride and joy in us. "That's right. That's the spiritual A-B-Cs of life. Now, every other blessing will follow."

Brother John

Personal Journal

March 4, 1981

We are totally involved in our Church assignments. The only one I currently hold of consequence is that of being an institute teacher. It is a powerful joy to me to teach it, as one of my gifts seems to be the power of teaching. And when moved upon by the power of the Holy Ghost to speak words of truth, my teaching can be almost eloquent at times.

In all humility, it must be stated that without the impact of the Divine, I am quite uninspiring as a teacher. This is purely a gift to me from God, and it is not a product of my own labors or study. I often marvel that I was ever given it.

May 15, 1983

I have started into a business with my father and brother in Wasilla, Alaska. It is an automotive service center called Allied Automotive. We have been doing super good. We are now working to trim our operating costs to allow us a profit margin.

We are moving to Wasilla and have our house for sale. We would like to be moved out [of Valdez] before October, which is when the baby is due. I have been in a real spiritual low since the first of the year. I hate working on Sundays, and as soon as the garage is able to support us, I plan to quit Alyeska and work at the garage.

Early April 1987

This brings me to the present time and the current disposition of my life. I injured my back in early March and have been home with a herniated disk. I have had considerable pain. On Thursday I went into the hospital for a test. Tomorrow I should know exactly what is wrong and how long I should expect to be healing. I must say that my back injury has been a blessing, in that I have been able to have many deep conversations with my wife that were necessary for our survival. This may never have occurred had I been away at work.

July 12, 1987

I might say that this is why I love the gospel so much: it is such a powerful ally! The Spirit of the Lord is there to build and support. And when you are at your rope's end, as I have been so often recently, you can call on the Lord and He will buffer for you, and give you sweet rest.

Faith is like a never-failing canteen of cool clear water in a parched, scorching desert. It is like being able to lift that canteen and drink your thirst away, and know that you will always be able to do so, and that very few people have that great strength with them. It is also almost impossible to share with your neighbor. They can watch you drinking from your magic canteen, and still not believe what you are doing.

Chapter Three

Fear No Evil:
Facing the Struggles of Mortality

Obtaining Perspective

hen I was very young, a day seemed like a year.
I can remember sitting in grade school. It took nearly a month to get to lunch and then another month before we were released to go home. I remember going home and playing for what seemed like years before dinner and bed. Summer vacation was a lifetime, and Christmas vacation seemingly lasted for years.

When I was in my teens and someone mentioned that the Church was restored 130 years ago, I couldn't imagine such an ancient event. I wondered how we even remembered such things from so long ago. One hundred and thirty years was ten times my lifetime.

When I turned fifty, I thought one hundred years ago was only twice my lifetime and not really that long ago. When I turned sixty, it occurred to me that the signing of the Declaration of Independence was only 235 years ago, only four times my lifetime, a fairly recent event in the history of the United States.

My natural man has a tendency to look back on the past and wish I had bought Microsoft stock, or taken a penny in my pocket that is known to me now to be very valuable and just saved it. I wish I had kept all of those $2 bills and never unwrapped my Erector Set, because today it would be valuable in its original box and packing.

When I went on my mission, I had an orange box filled with sequential Superman and Fantastic Four comic books from the very first issue to that date. I had bought the current ones and was given the rest of them by an old gentleman wanting someone to have his childhood collection who would keep them and value them as he had. They were all wrapped in plastic sleeves and began with issue number one. They are now worth tens of thousands of dollars per comic, and I had several hundred of them. My mother threw them all out one day while I was on my mission because she considered them junk in her closet and bad literature. I calculate she threw a million dollars in the trash can and burned it that day. She thought it was just trash.

I also look back on some events in my life and some of my decisions, and I shudder and wish I had done something far different. With most, if not all of those decisions that later revealed themselves to be destructive, I had a distinct feeling I should not do them at the time. But I just thought the decision to be trivial, like a dusty box of old comics.

I remember driving across the bridge to my childhood home in an old truck loaded with ten-gallon milk cans and having the distinct and pressing prompting to look down into the irrigation ditch to my left. But I was only thirteen years old at that time, the bridge was narrow, and I was concentrating on getting safely across. I found out about an hour later that my little brother was drowning in the ditch at that very moment, and if I would have looked right at him and seen his struggle for life, I could have jumped into the ditch and saved him. Instead, I thought steering the truck was more important.

These are things time and perspective reveal, but which we cannot know in that moment.

Now imagine God, an eternal being, who sees and is present in all of history, and who sees and is present in all of the future, looking down upon His children here on earth praying for guidance, for relief, for deliverance, and for our lives. He sees our trials from a far different perspective than we do. He knows the value of the pennies in our pockets and the potentially life-altering cost of all the stupid things we do before we do them.

He also sees the outcome of suffering and of the harsh experiences of our lives. He knows how they will shape us into the person He sees in our eternal future. I believe that most of what we view as the "harsh realities" of mortality are left in place because that very suffering is what brings us to the knowledge that saves us—just as how we let a child burn his finger in a candle he refuses to leave alone. The knowledge gained is a precious life lesson, far more valuable than temporarily avoiding the pain.

We as parents can almost always understand the foolishness of our children's infantile insistence on their own will and their own agenda, and we can see that these very things will hurt and damage them. We often let them experience these things to some degree so that they will learn and cease to be ignorant of how life really works. After it quits hurting, they will be better prepared for life. We warn them because we love them, and they often do go against our counsel anyway. When they come to us needing a Band-Aid, we nourish them and remind them that we tried to warn them, knowing their tears are forming life-saving decisions in the future.

Father does much the same thing. He warns us and then lets us damage ourselves if we insist. He lets us burn a million dollars worth of comic books, or marry the wrong person, or suffer in wrenching ways because He doesn't just understand the future. He is viewing it—and these are the very things which over time will create the glorified person He sees and loves in our eternal future.

Brother John

Life as a Four-Wheel Drive

We took a quick trip up to Zion Canyon with Terri's family and loved it. The best part for me was the opportunity to talk of gospel topics with dear people of faith. One of the challenges we Latter-day Saints seem to face is the fact that we work so hard to serve our families and our church that we don't always succeed financially and in our careers like we might have if we had been driven and single-minded about pursuing Babylon. This leaves an "I could have been rich" feeling in the pit of one's stomach.

After a conversation about how several of us "almost made it," I had this thought occur to me. Life is like a four-wheel drive vehicle. Sometimes some of the wheels spin in the mud because the circumstances of life deny them true traction. We look at the flying mud and think ourselves to be failures in that area. For some, the failure seems to be financial; for others it is health or career, fame or popularity, or opportunities we chose not to exercise in favor of something more eternally weighty—or even something trivial.

In a Christ-directed life, at the same time those wheels are spinning in the mud, there is always one wheel that is on solid ground, moving us forward. That wheel has traction because we have earnestly prayed and found guidance and inspiration on that subject, and it is the only thing that may be moving us forward at the time. This could be our family, service to God, faith, or any other aspect of life where the clear voice and will of God is known.

The point is, because that one wheel is stabilizing our whole life, all the wheels are moving in the right direction as well. It isn't possible for one part of our life to be inspired and other aspects of our lives to be out of the Lord's care—even when they feel out of control. They are moving forward in an inspired direction because we are moving forward under the Lord's tutelage. He sees the whole picture and directs our lives by giving us direction sufficient to move onward in the only path that will exalt us.

The most difficult part is to accept that we are where we should be, even when only one part of our lives is inspired and all others seem to be in flames. We want it *all* to work like magic, for every element of mortality to be illuminated by revelation and charmed by success. It doesn't seem to work that way; at least, it hasn't in my life.

One of our relatives with us at Zion's Canyon has served as a bishop; he is a fine, kind and inspired man. Yet, discouragement in his words prompted me to suggest this vision: You are what you are, and where you are, because of an inspired course in your life that prepared and empowered you to serve the Lord in the ways you have. Any other course, any other combination of successes and struggles would have taken you somewhere else. The one wheel that found traction and propelled you into this day, into this world, was the inspired one. It did not bring you here as a partial failure. All of your wheels arrived here together, even the ones that are still spinning in the mud. You arrived here *because* of the process of your life, with its many losses and disappointments, struggles, and failures. To change any part of that would deliver you to a different destination—which would be a tragedy of eternal duration.

Brother John

Unequally Yoked

Over the years I have observed that it is unusual for a husband and a wife to be equally yoked in spiritual things. Most often one or the other is more evolved and yearns for their companion to wake up and catch up.

Spiritual inequality is a result of agency, personal experiences, and the nature of the spirit we brought with us from before this world. There is no way to change this formula, and you wouldn't want to try because to do so would be infringing upon the agency of another.

However, here are several truths that can guide us when we find ourselves in this very common situation.

1. Regardless of our gender or circumstances, our companions cannot limit our spiritual growth. We can seek and obtain every blessing the Lord opens to our understanding and for which we are willing to pay the price. An uninterested, or even unrighteous companion, does not have the ability to inhibit their spouse's blessings. Their actions might delay our achievements, but they can't ultimately stop them.

   It is true that a demanding or controlling spouse might make it more difficult, but such opposition to spiritual things, when met with humble obedience to the voice of revelation, will make us that much stronger. Becoming submissive to Jesus Christ will enable us to overcome and thrive spiritually, no matter how daunting the obstacle we are facing may seem.

2. The covenants you make and the promises you have received are yours to claim. The laws governing obtaining these things are unchangeable. When you are obedient to those

laws, regardless of what your companion does, you will one day receive the associated blessings. That is not patronizing hyperbole; that is truth.

3. We must be ever aware that a huge part of our being with this person may be the Lord's way of saving them, and in that process He is purifying and sanctifying us. We must be very careful to be informed of Christ's will by listening every moment to His voice so that we don't let our desire to fly spiritually unhindered turn our life from the path whereon our mission is ordained to unfold.

4. We must never act to limit our spouse's freedom of choice or to coerce change in them. If their choices are damaging to us, or abusive, then the Holy Spirit will guide our response as we listen to revelation in preference to emotion. It may well be that the inspired action is to leave for higher ground. But it may also be to stay and complete a mission on their behalf and receive our resulting purification for doing so. In either case, this takes tremendous courage.

5. Ultimately, your spouse will find himself or herself living with a creature of the Holy Ghost—someone who is loving and forgiving, who makes inspired choices, who influences without coercion, and whose desire is only to do what is right. When they find their lives surrounded by joy in which they are not participants, they will either reject and eject, or they will repent and rejoice that you were obedient enough to stay with them through their darkest and most dangerous days.

These are difficult paths that mortals cannot navigate unaided by constant revelation. These are pathways surrounded by mists of darkness, where only the iron rod of the Word of God can lead us safely. But, the iron rod isn't leading us into the mists of darkness; it is leading us out. Remember, that glorious rod always ends at the "most desirable above all things . . . and most joyus to the soul" (1 Neph 11:22–23).

Brother John

Be Not Deceived

Someone asked an important question. She had read in the Bible Dictionary about Satan and how he can deceive us, even transforming into an angel of light. It also said Satan could quote scripture and use many means to deceive us. She said she was 100 percent committed to obedience but was concerned she might mistake a deception for a prompting or a true doctrine for a lie.

I am mostly interested in comments from you, the UnBlog family. I know you have great collective wisdom. How can someone tell for sure that they are listening to the Holy Spirit and not a deception of some sort? What say you?

While you're pondering your response, I would like to add a couple thoughts.

First, we will be judged according to the "thoughts and intents of the heart" (Hebrews 4:12). If we are *trying* to obey, then we will be judged as obedient. If we happen to get deceived on something, we'll learn and the Holy Spirit will teach us the difference. These things will not pull us down into a permanent deception. A permanent deception only happens when we allow it, when we prefer the lie to the truth. Permanent deceptions are common among mortals who do not receive the Holy Spirit; they are rare among those who do.

Second, Satan does not have as much power as we might think. Even when he tries to appear as an angel of light, there is no glory. His light might appear to be visible, but it feels like spiritual darkness. There is the chill of present evil, not the peace and love of God. Satan cannot imitate those things. Most of us can tell the difference between a plastic cup and a crystal goblet of the same shape. There is a discernible difference. If someone who was familiar with the Holy Spirit encountered it, they would instantly understand it as a deception. One of you recently referred to Moses and his discerning of Satan, who appeared and proclaimed he was also God. Moses saw that there was no glory and commanded Satan to depart.

Third, there is a very sweet feeling that fills our bodies with the presence of the Holy Spirit and a very unhappy and dark feeling when it is absent.

Fourth, a subtle deception that Satan uses against those seeking the greater blessings is spiritual imbalance. There is a razor's edge that we must carefully navigate along a straight and increasingly narrow path. If we lean too far to the right we become discouraged and smother the fires of faith and belief; yet if we lean too far to the left, we become overzealous and prideful, demanding that the Lord give us what we want, when we want it. We then become hardened when the promised blessings are not realized according to our expectations. If one continues along that insistent course a manifestation may indeed come, perhaps even an angel of light, but it is not of the Lord. The spiritual pilgrim must be as patient and trusting as a child—humble, meek, and submissive—while at the same time courageously believing and in perfect balance. Every footfall must be guided by the Holy Spirit, the scriptures, and modern prophets.

Hence, when you have the Spirit, you feel:

- Loving, happy, and at peace, even when things are not going exactly as you hoped
- Patient with the Lord's timetable for attaining spiritual blessings
- Generous and giving
- Understanding and patient
- Difficult to offend
- Not competitive with other people's success and possessions
- Like praying and going to church
- Like enjoying wholesome things and inspired entertainment
- Love of the Savior is warm in your heart, and you want to obey Him
- Whisperings of the Holy Spirit are precious to you

When you don't have the Holy Spirit with you, you feel:

- Unlovable, unloving, unhappy, irritable, and possibly depressed or frustrated, even when nothing is especially wrong
- Pushing the Lord to grant blessings according to your timetable and expectations
- Possessive and selfish
- Very little patience with other people and children

- Easy to offend
- Jealous of other people's success and possessions
- Like you don't want to pray and go to church
- Energized by loud, violent, sexy worldly entertainment, music, and movies
- That the Savior isn't important in your life
- Like promptings are a nuisance and inconvenient

So now, what say you?

Brother John

Stand in Holy Places

A few weeks ago I mentioned having an experience with seeing a dark spirit. When I asked for feedback from the UnBlogosphere, I got the most responses to date, all of them saying they appreciated the content. Some of you mentioned that you have had similar experiences and it helped to know that you weren't alone. So many of you responded that I assume most of us have had these types of experiences, and most of us were fearful and afraid we were weird or odd. The truth seems to be that it is an almost universal phenomenon of mortality.

There was about a year in my life when it seemed that Heavenly Father wanted me to understand the intense battle we are waging for our spiritual lives and allowed me some minor glimpses of dark things. I am of the opinion that spirituality is developing a sensitivity to spiritual things—and some of those things are evil.

While acknowledging their reality, I think it is very important to not seek after experiences with dark things, nor give them our undue attention. The truth is that the world of darkness is very powerful, so much so that if we toy with those things, we will be beaten. We can't survive even one round in the ring. Our only salvation is that Jesus Christ places laws between us and darkness. As long as we don't cross into the darkness ourselves, and when needed invoke the name and power of Christ, they cannot triumph over us. However, the access they have is sufficient that they are destroying the vast majority of humanity and have kept this telestial world in a state of war and bloodshed since the dawn of time.

Christ Himself dealt with dark spirits often. It was common for Him to cast them out. The New Testament attributes many physical ailments to evil spirits. In our supposedly "modern" world, we think about such things very little and may even consider it a little weird to cast out evil spirits in a priesthood blessing. I'm not sure why this is, but I'm also very sure that Christ was not mistaken in His example of how to deal with evil.

With that in mind, I want to tell you of an experience I had with a family member. This was in the early 1990s, and I had a business trip that took me near my family. I called ahead and stopped in to visit one of my sisters. She was living in a basement apartment. Her in-laws lived up above. It was a nice setting for a small family. Her husband was away on business at the time, as were her in-laws.

I have always been visually receptive to the presence of light in people's faces. I can see the Holy Spirit in the countenances of most people I meet. I can also see darkness when it is present. It is as obvious to me as various wattages of light bulbs. When I walked into her home that evening, I noticed something very odd. The left side of her face was dark, and the right side was bright. I had never seen anything like that. We sat and talked for many hours about spiritual things. She is a spiritual seeker like myself, and it was a lovely, Spirit-blessed evening. At one point I mentioned her half-darkened face.

She was surprised but said that she had been having a hard time feeling the Spirit lately and that her prayers felt like they were hitting a brick ceiling and bouncing back. I asked her if she would like to have a priesthood blessing, and she readily agreed.

During the blessing I felt impressed to command the workers of evil to depart from her, leave her home and never return. We both felt an immediate sensation of relief and light, and the Holy Spirit grew stronger.

After the blessing, we hugged and I went upstairs to go to bed. At the top of the landing, I walked right into a cold storm of evil. Whatever I had cast out had gone upstairs. I determined later that when I had cast them "out of her home" that they left her home in the basement and went to her in-laws' quarters upstairs. On this particular occasion I could actually see them, and it was not a welcome sight. They were agitated and moving around the room. I went to the guest bedroom and invoked the priesthood—several times, actually. The home grew spiritually quiet, then peaceful.

Since that evening, which was many years ago, that particular batch of tormentors has not returned to my sister's home. Her prayers and native spirituality quickly returned to normal.

It takes a lot of pondering to understand experiences like this. I've had almost seventeen years now to think about this. I believe we are in a very dangerous war and that we hardly realize it. I think we have a powerful weapon in the priesthood, which we seldom invoke for that purpose. I think the reason Heavenly Father lets us "see" these things sometimes is simply to awaken us to our perilous situation and to teach us to resist evil while it is being held back by divine law.

I also believe that as the times of Zion approach, as we grow more and more Zion-worthy, that opposition will increase. The power of evil will amplify, and this war will evolve from now-unseen to very "in-your-face." As we begin to build Zion, the balance of good and evil that exists will be tipped dramatically, and the bowels of hell will erupt all around us. Then, these small lessons in repelling evil will be invaluable. We will have already engaged the enemy, and we will be equipped both by our faith and by our enlightened perception to stand with Christ in places made holy by our presence and not be moved.

Brother John

Overcome Evil with Good

It is almost a demand of mortal thinking that we should not let people who offend or attack us "get away with it." We want our eye-for-an-eye. We want to ensure they never do it again. We want to see that justice is done and that we are exonerated. I have written many times about letting Christ lead us through the solutions of our trials; what I have not written much about is the sublime peace of letting Christ dispense whatever justice there needs to be.

When I was a young man, I learned this lesson from a brother-in-law in Alaska for whom I was working at the time. He had subcontracted a big job from a wealthy man who was building a series of condos. My brother-in-law had worked many smaller jobs for him before, but this larger job put my brother-in-law at risk for all of the materials and labor to the tune of over $50,000. This was the 1980s, and $50,000 was a lot more risk than it is now.

He and I worked for weeks and did an excellent job. When we were finally finished, the wealthy man took the money from the bank for that portion of the project, then told my brother-in-law that if he wanted any money, he would have to sue him. There was no complaint about our work; he had planned to pocket the money from the beginning. He laughed at my brother-in-law and said he was going to go buy an airplane with the money. My brother-in-law was a great tradesman, but he was not a good businessman. He had done all the work merely on a handshake. There was not sufficient paperwork for a successful lawsuit, and the rich guy had known it from the start.

I urged my brother-in-law to sue, as did his wife. He was visibly upset, financially ruined, and almost ill from the stress. He gathered his meager papers and drove to the courthouse. About an hour later he returned. He didn't say much but told us that he had been told by the Spirit not to sue the man but to let the Lord handle it. My sister (his wife) was incredulous and furious. They were going to lose their home. I lost my job. My brother-in-law lost his business, and even worse, his business credit. It was deeply devastating. When I asked him about it privately, he just said that he felt sorry for the rich man because he said that the Lord was going to handle the injustice, and God was more exacting in such things than he could ever have been. I honestly didn't understand a word of it.

A few weeks later my brother-in-law, with deep sadness, handed me a newspaper article. It was a front page story about this rich man. He had taken his whole family up in a small plane, probably the one he had purchased with the stolen money. Somewhere out over the Cook Inlet he ran into fog, lost control of the plane, and everyone in the plane was killed but him. He lived a few hours just until rescuers arrived. When they told him all of his family was dead, he died himself.

My brother-in-law wept for the guy. He said, "I was so afraid something like this was going to happen. I should have just sued him." He never got his money, and I never heard him speak of it again. He considered the debt cancelled. A short time later, another builder offered him a job that included a $50,000 open account for parts. It got his business back on its feet.

The Apostle Paul wrote to the Romans, "Dearly Beloved, avenge not yourselves, but rather give place unto [step out of the way of] wrath; for it is written, Vengeance is mine: I will repay, saith the Lord. Therefore if thine enemy hunger, feed him; if he thirst, give him drink; for in so doing thou shalt heap coals of fire on his head. Be not overcome of evil, but overcome evil with good" (Romans 12:19–21).

There is great peace in letting the Lord repay. That means letting go of the event, the anger, the injustice, and the memory of it. This is a little-understood truth that relieves us of so much negative emotion and of the telestial necessity to measure out the appropriate pound of flesh. It also repairs relationships, heals hearts, and leaves us with the Holy Spirit in our lives.

Brother John

Conquering Addiction

One of you mentioned a lifelong addiction and wondered how to finally overcome that trial and move on into the greater blessings you desire. I am inclined to believe that most of us struggle with addictions lesser or greater. Some people are addicted to anger, money, sex, control, or to being right all the time. Some are addicted to compliments and recognition, others to substances, food, or illegal activities. But, we are all struggling with this problem on some level.

Since our entire spiritual evolution operates upon the principle of allowing the Holy Spirit to direct us in the pathway designated by Jesus Christ, then as long as we remain on that path, the Lord will take us line upon line to every spiritual accomplishment and destination we desire—and empower us to go there.

Let me say it another way: If you want to be fully clean through repentance, then become flawlessly obedient to the voice of the Holy Spirit and you will succeed.

If you want to be born again, then become flawlessly obedient to the voice of the Holy Spirit and you will succeed.

If you want to have your calling and election made sure, then become flawlessly obedient to the voice of the Holy Spirit and you will succeed.

If you want to have miracles, power in the priesthood, prophetic understanding, visions, visitations of angels, and to see inside the veil, then become flawlessly obedient to the voice of the Holy Spirit and you will succeed.

If you want to overcome an addiction, then become flawlessly obedient to the voice of the Holy Spirit and you will succeed.

It is unlikely that your addiction will suddenly lose any of its persuasive pull in your life, but when the voice of addiction demands your attention, the Holy Spirit will guide you. You will know and see the correct actions and responses, and if you act with courage and obey, even when it is at great cost and discomfort, then the magic happens.

If you try to act on your own, by your own willpower, you are pitting your strength against the power of the addiction—and the fact that you even have an addiction stipulates that your strength isn't up to the task. But, when the Holy Spirit speaks and urges you to not partake, and you choose to obey, then you are triggering the gears of heaven in dispensing grace to you to add to the battle what you have always lacked.

It is the same principle Nephi 3:7 promises that the Lord always prepares a way for us to accomplish the thing which He commands us.

When acting in obedience, you are no longer alone. It will take 100 percent of your courage and strength—which will not be enough still—but by submissive obedience you invite and enable Christ to take up your cause. He will lift your burden sufficiently that you will conquer. Then, you obey again, and again, and again, until the evil that is calling you to self-destruction has no more power over you.

No matter what we are seeking, and no matter how badly we lack, the method to obtaining any blessing is everlastingly the same: identify the voice of the Holy Spirit and flawlessly obey it. Each further step will be opened to your mind, each a little more empowered by Christ. Your part in it remains the same—obey, obey, obey, obey, obey.

Brother John

Toddling Steps into Spiritual Greatness

There is a truth about spiritual growth that few people understand even after they experience it: All blessings are equally and oppositely opposed. When God grants a blessing great or small, He is also triggering some mechanism in the eternal gears of heaven that allows evil to rise to that same degree.

For this reason, when you receive a testimony of the Church, someone shortly thereafter hands you anti-literature and/or things arise in your life to prevent you from attending and serving. Sometimes family and friends militate against your decision.

For the same reason, when we get married in the temple, there are specific trials and oppositions that try to destroy our homes. If someone were to see an angel or to speak with Jesus Christ Himself, the opposition would rise up in equal and opposite power to challenge, oppose, and thereby prove we are truly worthy of that blessing. This is the reason that so many of the greats from Cain to Judas to Oliver Cowdery have fallen. They couldn't understand or endure the equal and opposite clause of eternity.

There is an important reason this opposition must arise. It is necessary for us to prove ourselves "true and faithful" on each new spiritual plane in order to turn an earthly blessing into an eternal reward. That means everything is tested. Even something as glorious as having one's calling and election made sure will be opposed. We must not only be prepared, but we must expect the opposition.

If Christmas morning worked like this, you would open a present and after enjoying it for about sixty seconds, someone would jump on you and try to wrestle the gift away. After the fight, if you successfully defended the present, you could keep it and open another. But, if you didn't fight hard enough, or gave up, or didn't value the gift enough to fight for it, then you would not only lose that gift but all the others under the tree as well. And the larger the present, the harder the fight.

If you knew this was going to happen, you would either skip Christmas altogether (apostatize, in spiritual terms) or come to Christmas morning with a baseball bat and padded clothing on, planning to fight and conquer. The truth is, Jesus Christ has already triumphed; our part is to remain continually aware of the opposition and lean upon Him as we encounter it.

That said, some of us mere mortals have a tendency to be ignorant of the laws of opposition and then judge other people as unrighteous who are pressing through the flames of refinement. We wonder what some true seekers are doing wrong to be thus oppressed, rather than seeing what they are doing right. We doubt the validity of another's trials either because we don't have that particular trial or because we doubt the validity of our own.

Yet, there is no instance in the scriptures or written history of someone rising to glorious spiritual heights who was not refined by the fire following their toddling steps into spiritual greatness.

Brother John

Fear No Evil

*T*his UnBlog has been going now for over a year. I often think of some wonderful principle or spiritual understanding I wish to share and then remember that I've already UnBlogged about it. I also know that the priceless truths of the gospel are hard to embed in someone's heart with mere words, so I don't feel too bad about repeating myself now and then.

One of the truths I have mentioned before that actually still surprises me is that "spirituality" isn't entirely like opening a door into a world filled with light. Every time I have sought, fought for, paid the price for, and obtained some new spiritual footing, it has opened the doors to equal and opposite darkness.

I believe the prototype of this phenomenon is the First Vision, when the powers of darkness tried to destroy Joseph even while the Father and Son were riding the celestial escalator to earth. They allowed it to occur. Everything must occur according to divine law, so there must be some fine print somewhere in the "Constitution of Mortal Life" that gives the powers of darkness this power of opposition to all things good.

When we triumph it will be because through the grace of God we walked through the flames, not around them. We will rejoice in the eternal day because we have experienced and rejected the world of darkness. Jesus Christ chose to descend below all things so that we could, with Him, rise above all things.

We fear no evil because Jesus Christ conquered evil and has already paid the price for our everlasting triumph. When we experience dark things on our journey into the light, our role in this divine drama is not to conquer the evil but to conquer ourselves, and by His grace conquer our pride, fears, and flaws. We are the ransomed ones, not because we are great, chosen, or reserved but because we love and obey Him.

This isn't thinking that we might someday engage and win, but rejoicing that we already have. The earth is Christ's footstool, and by the empowerment of His Atonement we are even at this moment walking fearlessly through the towering flames of opposition back into His presence.

Brother John

Personal Journal

July 22, 1989

I want to express my love for the Lord and for His tender care. I have always seen His hand in my life and have tried to live worthy of His love. I want you to know that I also love my family. I have written about our struggles and perhaps neglected to tell why I was willing to go through the things we went through. You should know that it is because I love them. They needed me to care for them and love them, and to not give up because it was hard on me.

Don't you ever forget that love doesn't give up; it keeps giving, even if the giving takes a pound of flesh from your own body. People rush into a fire to save a loved one. Why not rush into other things just as life-threatening, only much more protracted, to save a loved one? I think that the Lord can heal all wounds if you ask Him to, and then allow Him to direct your life.

December 30, 1992

This year has seen tremendous spiritual growth. I have learned so many things that it defies probability that I will be able to write them all down here.

Perhaps the greatest thing I have learned is how very possible it is to draw near to God. I have felt His presence so often and been blessed with spiritual manifestations, miracles, answers to prayers, and many other things so often that I tremble to try to express my gratitude to Him.

Prayer has become a delight. I find myself kneeling in His presence, swallowed up in the Spirit, and pouring out such eloquent words of praise and worship that it defies the ability of English to express and transcends into the tongue of angels. I have so much love for the Savior and Heavenly Father that I can scarcely contain it. It is a burning fire within me.

The other day I was sitting in sacrament meeting and felt the Spirit begin to glow all around me, and I could feel the aura of His presence. I looked around in a sort of embarrassed way to see if others were noticing the glow. No one was. But it was like being in the embrace of a total feeling of love and warmth and protection.

If I had to say in the briefest way how I came to this blessed state, I would have to echo the words of Spencer W. Kimball: "Obey the commandments, and the promptings of the Holy Spirit. That's all: Obey. Obey. Obey. Obey. There's not much more to the formula . . ."

The gospel isn't a big machine to mold celestial candidates by forcing them through a tiny opening, thus reforming each to some uniform code of perfection. It's a vast, incredibly complex, eternally loving, individually tailored means of leading individuals of infinite variety and uniqueness back home. Each child of God receives individual care, loving guidance, and undeviating love. Each has a separate set of promptings, separate revelations, separate answers to prayer, separate tragedies and triumphs. Each will be guided step-by-step along as they hold fast to the iron rod of God's word—the voice of revelation.

December 16, 1993

Today as I was walking down the hall of our home, I was suddenly stopped when a vision opened before my eyes. I saw my own life like a movie. I saw how I had wandered back and forth, and the labors of the Spirit to direct me back into the right way. I saw every major decision and the very things the Spirit had taught me, which I had sometimes ignored. I saw the path with complete plainness. Many things were made crystal clear to my mind. I saw the straight and narrow path as exactly that—a straight, simple, narrow course that every person is required to walk. It was so simple that I was stunned and thought myself ignorant or foolish for having taken so long to arrive at my present blessings. The vision immediately closed, and a loud voice said, "Write it down and publish it." I immediately knew what I should do. I have never before considered that I might write a book on a religious topic, let alone do it well enough that it would be worthy of publication. This all took less than a nanosecond and began at almost exactly 10:00 in the morning.

Chapter Four

Ask and Ye Shall Receive: The Miracle of Prayer

Mighty Prayer

t has been a hard couple of months, and I apologize for not keeping up with the UnBlog. You have all been kind and patient with me, and I thank you.

Last Sunday I taught the priesthood lesson on prayer. It was interesting because our stake president was in attendance. He is one of my favorite people because he understands the gospel so well (which means, the same way I do) and his contribution to the class is to consistently steer every discussion back to Christ.

I think there are two very powerful tools we have to bring us from our routine prayers into prayer that soars into the heavens and calls down great blessings.

This first is to take the Holy Spirit with you into prayer. The scriptures are full of examples of great people literally parting the veil with this type of prayer. The first and greatest step is to take the Holy Spirit to be your guide in your daily life. I don't believe it is possible to ignore the promptings of the Holy Spirit during the day and then suddenly reverse that for prayer at night. We must learn to "hear" the things of the Spirit in order to "pray in the spirit" (D&C 46:28, 30), and we develop our spiritual ears through the daily walk of our lives.

Once we are attuned to the voice of revelation, we can invite that grand and divine gift into our prayers. It requires kneeling and waiting, pondering and devotion, not speaking our own mind, but waiting until the revelatory voice comes. Then, feelings of worship and praise become inspired words. Such words do not always frame themselves in our native tongue but have the tendency to soar from our souls without a need to form into language. Often such non-language is beautiful, has poetic form, and sometimes has meter and melody. The scriptures refer to it as "singing the song of redeeming love" (Alma 5:26).

Prayer of this caliber is called "mighty prayer" in the scriptures. It is the precursor of everything revelatory. I believe, and it is my experience, that every profound gift from heaven begins as this type of prayer.

The second step to mighty prayer is to pray often and long. I consider it unlikely that a mortal could conquer this type of prayer without praying often and sincerely, as best we are able, for at least twenty minutes per day. When the heart is drawn out in prayer, such prayers go on throughout the day, finding surface in quiet moments, devotional thoughts, moments of repentance and consecration, whispers of gratitude and silent longing. Then when we take a whole day of informal prayer and punctuate it with twenty minutes of "mighty prayer," the heavens begin to part.

As a final thought, I want to declare most emphatically that lofty things await you. No matter where you are or what your present spirituality is, you can ply the seas of grace and arrive at mighty prayer. It isn't something you will conquer in one or two attempts but over years of effort. God wants you to dedicate and consecrate your life to finding Him so that He may heal and redeem you. Consecration isn't just a willingness to abandon "things." It's setting aside our time, devotions, and hours of prayer to find Him.

Why does He ask such devotion and dedication of us? It is because He ultimately wants to invest in us His great creative power, His power to form worlds and create universes, and to continue the work of bringing to pass the immortality and eternal life of the inhabitants of those worlds. This life is the little moment of eternity where we get to choose and demonstrate our willingness to begin to learn those very laws and perfections which define Father, Himself.

Brother John

Pleading with Father

*M*any things in life are troubling, and challenge and threaten us. Like you, I have always prayed about these things and asked for relief, blessings, insight—sometimes for years. I have learned to have great faith in prayer, and that different seasons call for different types of prayers. The Lord listens and He does answer, most often in ways I was not anticipating.

My father had an element of faith in prayer that still amazes me many years after his passing. I don't use it very often, nor did he, but it is very powerful when you do.

Ever since I can remember, Dad had great faith that Father would change the weather for him. I actually saw it happen many times throughout my childhood. When I was a young teen we had gone to work one Saturday on the stake farm. It was a cloudy day, and as we started working it began to rain. It was not only making the day miserable, but the moisture would cause the sugar beets to spoil after they were out of the ground because of the mud clinging to them. The brethren running the farm looked around and announced that we were going to stop. We had had an opening prayer a few minutes earlier and the weather was specifically mentioned. Dad leaned toward me and whispered something like, "They don't believe in the power of their own prayers." He closed his eyes. He stood there in the field as others were trudging to their cars. I knew he was praying about the weather.

I was really hoping it would keep raining.

A few cars had pulled away as the clouds grew lighter and the rain stopped. It was still threatening, but a little patch of sunshine settled over the field. People returned and we worked all day in the sun.

Many years later, Dad and Mom invited us to a picnic on July 4 at their home in Wasilla, Alaska. I got up that morning, and it was almost a monsoon outside. I called Mom and asked if the party was still on because their house wasn't big enough to feed everyone inside. She said, "Yes, the party is still on. Your dad is outside mowing the lawn."

As we drove to their home it was raining hard. A few miles out I could see one donut hole in the dense clouds. Sun was streaming through it like the Second Coming. As we got closer, I realized it was directly over Dad's house, maybe a block in size. His house and those on every side were sunny. We ate, played games, and were just done chatting when the first sprinkles hit our heads. We stood and gathered into the house as the deluge resumed.

I know that my dad had unusual faith in this thing. Maybe his was a special gift of the Spirit that few people have. But, I also know that he didn't stop praying until he received an assurance that his request, need, or desire, had been granted or declined by Father. He just needed to know God's will, and once he knew that, he would stop praying and proceed to act upon the outcome he had requested.

A few days ago I was stumped while setting up the UnBlog family reunion. We had tried and failed for months to secure a venue. All of the free venues just didn't return our calls. The commercial venues wanted large sums of money, sizable down payments, and mandatory insurance policies

I was beginning to wonder if it was going to happen at all. That evening I remembered my dad's faith and just stayed on my knees, pleading.

It went something like this: "Please Father, please, please, please, please, please, please, please, please, please, please, please, please, please, please, please, please bless me to (fill in the blank). I will accept Thy will in all things, but please, please, please, please, please, please, please, please, please, please, please, please, please, please, please, please, please, please, please ..."

You get the idea.

Like I said, I don't know why it works. I only know that it does. Sometimes the answer is "no," but it always works for me. I know, this seems a little impertinent and even demanding. But pleading, done properly, is not trying to manipulate Him; it is trying to ascertain His will, and being willing to stay on your knees until it comes. Once you have that assurance of knowing His will, then you can move forward with much greater faith.

After I had pled with Father for a time regarding the UnBlog, I received a sudden feeling of peace—not that the reunion was going to happen but that everything was going to be as Father desired it. I was done. I had my answer. He was in charge.

The very next day things changed. A sweet couple contacted me, offering valuable financial help, which made the UVU venue possible for us. We made an appointment to go walk through it and found it to be perfect. A few days after my pleading prayer, a small feeling of peace, and a willingness to surrender to anything Father intended, the UnBlog Family Reunion was suddenly fully on track.

I'm writing this UnBlog to praise Father, to thank Him for this answer, and to share with you a somewhat surprisingly powerful form of prayer. I think of it as the big guns—to be used at times when a rifle just isn't enough.

Brother John

Ask and Ye Shall Receive

I am reminded again and again how important it is to ask in prayer for the things I need. It has always been a tendency of mine to feel continually comfortable and protected by God. I have even been of the opinion at times that God already knows my needs, and voicing them can't clarify what He already knows and desires for me.

But the commandment still stands that we must ask Father in prayer for those things which we hope to receive. And here is a great key to receiving answers to our prayers:

When we receive the Spirit of Christ by obedience to His voice, we begin to become like our Savior. Through His Atonement we are upgraded, changed, cleansed, and as Mosiah 3:19 so beautifully teaches, we become a saint through the Atonement of Christ. We become as a little child—humble, meek, patient, full of love, and willing to submit to all things. As the word *willing* suggests, our will submits to His will. This process makes us not only like Christ in ways not otherwise possible, but it makes us *one* with Him.

Here is the beauty of oneness with our Savior: Not only does His will become our will, but even more incredible to understand, our will also becomes *His*. Isn't that a stunning thought? Our will becomes Christ's will! How could it be otherwise?

If through our obedient walk and years of discipleship our hopes and desires are sanctified, and our eye becomes truly single to His glory, then we are of one mind with Christ. In other words, as we become more Christlike, those things which we want, which we hope and pray for, are the very things that Christ wants for us as well. Then, when we ask according to the will of Christ, we can ask with perfect faith that we will receive that particular blessing. We can literally call down angels, open the visions of heaven, and find grace in times of need. It is this type of prayer that changes the course of our lives and serves as a never-ending conduit of Christ's grace.

But again, we must *ask* for that which we want because we are still subject to the overriding justice of God. Nobody is exactly sure how this all works, but logic suggests that if God were to give one person an unrequested blessing, then by the demands of justice, He would have to give every other person on earth the same blessing, even though they had not asked for it and had no just claim.

So when we have the humility and faith to ask, it separates us from every other living creature, simply because we exercised our agency to request the blessing. And when our will is sanctified by being in harmony with God, the real power occurs. Our requests become holy. The mainspring of heaven engages, and because we are asking in complete faith, knowing beforehand that these things are His will as much as our own, the machinery of heaven dispenses the requested blessings as a matter of divine law.

When we place ourselves in this happy circumstance, we always receive even as we ask.

Brother John

The Mystery of Godliness

Rick asked an important question in his Unblog comment about the Lord's clear promise in D&C 88:64–65: "Whatsoever ye ask the Father in my name it shall be given you, that is expedient for you; And if ye ask anything that is not expedient for you, it shall turn unto your condemnation."

As we progress in our spiritual journey, we are taken from line to line, and from precept to precept. We learn greater things, have greater spiritual power, make greater spiritual covenants directly with God, and obtain greater gifts. One of these gifts is the ability to pray and receive whatever we ask.

The previous verse (63) defines who is actually qualified to make these powerful requests that God will always honor. "Draw near unto me and I will draw near unto you; seek me diligently and ye shall find me; ask and ye shall receive; knock and it shall be opened unto you."

From this we may understand that this type of mighty prayer, where we receive all that we ask, comes to those who have diligently sought Christ and found Him, even as the temple promises that we may approach the veil and there "knock" and have the Lord open the veil and invite us in.

The same promise and the governing law to this gift are again repeated in D&C 50:26–27 where we read: "He that is ordained of God and sent forth [which is an ordination by God, by His own hands, while in His presence, as we saw in 88:63] the same is appointed to be the greatest, notwithstanding he is the least and the servant of all. Wherefore, he is possessor of all things; for all things are subject unto him, both in heaven and on the earth, the life and the light, the Spirit and the power, sent forth by the will of the Father through Jesus Christ, his Son."

These "ordained by God" are the greatest because they have been in the presence of Christ and in this case have been given the same gifts that John and the three Nephites received while they were in His presence. They are the servants of all, as is John, Enoch, and others. They are possessors of all things because their priesthood power is the "fulness" that man may receive as a mortal. They have power of life and death (even their own death because they have been translated), but these great gifts and priesthoods only operate "by the will of the Father through Jesus Christ, his Son."

Now comes the answer to Rick's question in 88:29: "And if ye are purified and cleansed from all sin [which is of course the requirement to be allowed into the presence of Christ after we have 'sought him diligently']—ye shall ask whatsoever you will in the name of Jesus and it shall be done. *But know this, it shall be given you what to ask.*"

In other words, having the power isn't permission to use it, until you have been "given what to ask."

Thus, in order to pray and receive everything you request you must walk this path:

1. Draw near unto Christ
2. Seek Christ diligently (His appearance to you)
3. Become purified and cleansed from all sin
4. Knock and enter into His presence
5. Be ordained "of" God
6. Receive the fulness of the priesthood
7. Obtain power over life and death (which may also include translation)
8. Christ will lead you to ask for many things (the order of temple prayer)
9. You ask and receive those things Christ directs you to request, and thus all things are subject unto you
10. If you ask for something other than what Christ leads you to ask for, then this thing is not "expedient" and it will turn to your condemnation for asking

Here is the bottom line: This "expedient" clause in the divine contract only kicks in after we have received full power to ask and receive. To then use this fulness of power without Christ's permission will condemn us—which means to stop our progress.

The glorious news, the almost incomprehensible wonder of this principle, is that we *can* obtain this gift, this glory, and this power while we live here in mortality. This is the mystery of godliness that is hidden from the world and revealed unto babes.

Brother John

The Tongue of Angels

*M*ighty prayer is much more than praying long or praying hard. It begins only when we bring the Holy Spirit with us into our prayer chambers and then yield our own voice to the voice of revelation. Then the Holy Spirit guides our words and leads in worship and glorying that man alone cannot achieve. It is prayer of the highest order, and few experiences ennoble and enable the children of God with equal power.

It requires some effort, time, and a suitable background in hearkening to the Holy Spirit to achieve. But when it finally happens, you will walk away a new person in Christ.

There are two overarching reasons we should press ourselves diligently to develop and deploy mighty prayer. The first is that it is a necessary and unavoidable bridge we must cross in our quest for the full blessings of the gospel. The type of veil-rending faith we seek lies at the far side of the bridge called mighty prayer.

The second reason is that, in my personal experience at least, every grand spiritual event I sought for and eventually obtained began as mighty prayer. It's almost as if the angels who are charged by God with vending the greater blessings only speak the language of the Holy Spirit. They don't seem to converse in earth-born language, and the very essence of mighty prayer is that the Holy Spirit teaches us what to say and how to say it. In mighty prayer the Spirit lifts us, sanctifies us, and dresses us in spotless spiritual white. And for that moment, for that blink of eternity, we know how to speak with the tongue of angels.

Brother John

Peace

*Y*ears ago I attended a family picnic where I was surprised to see an old family friend. He had been my dad's friend through high school and college, and had remained close to the family all the years since. By this time he was in his eighties and quite frail. He had lived a noble life, had served as a bishop and stake president, and was presently a patriarch. He seemed to glow with the Spirit, and I admired him a great deal.

I made an opportunity to talk to him and asked him a question I haven't asked anyone before or since: "What is the most important thing you have learned in your life?" He thought about it for about a minute before replying, "Except for the idea that God lives and similar gospel truths, the most important thing I ever learned is that Satan cannot imitate peace."

I don't think I understood the import of his answer then, but over the years I have pondered it many times.

The power of this pearl of great price is that Satan *can* imitate almost everything else. He can produce plausible counterfeits for happiness, elation, and even joy. He can invite feelings of devotion and can even (poorly) imitate gifts of the Spirit. But, knowing that he cannot imitate peace—and I do believe this is a true principle—gives mortals a power tool.

When we are in the struggle of mortality, when we are in doubt and in pain and praying mightily for answers, we can reserve judgment and wait to make that life-altering decision until we have obtained peace. Once we feel peace, we can act in confidence, knowing we have not been deceived because only the true Spirit brings peace. Peace is fragile and will vanish in the presence of lies and uninspired decisions. These lesser things produce the "stupor of thought" we have all experienced.

As an example, I was on assignment in one of the far-flung branches in Alaska and met an old acquaintance there. I had known her years before when we were both in the branch there. Her face was tired, and her expression was one of fatigue and sorrow. I asked her what was going on. She replied that she was trying to decide whether or not to divorce her husband. She explained some of her challenges and then asked me what I thought she should do.

Instead of answering her question, I asked her when the last time was that she had felt true peace. She said it had been years. I asked her when she had last attended church, even though we were standing in church. She indicated it had been over a year. I asked her when she had last read the scriptures, fasted and prayed, and several other similar queries. You can guess her answer; it had been at least a year, in every case.

I told her that the decision to divorce was so weighty and so potentially eternally altering for her, her husband, and her children that such a question should be answered only with divine assistance. I asked her, "Why would you make such a potentially destructive decision without divine help?"

She responded, "I have been praying, but no matter how hard I pray, I still haven't received the right answer."

I suggested that she was probably receiving an answer, just not the one she wanted to hear. She agreed that was a possibility and asked what she should do.

I suggested that she search backward in her heart to the last time she felt peace in her life, remember all the things she was doing back then, and then start doing them once again. She admitted that the last time she had felt peace was when she was attending church, searching the scriptures and praying, praying together with her husband, having family prayers, and many other spiritually critical things she had since stopped doing because her life was in such upheaval.

I promised her that when she once again felt peace in her life, she would be able to hear and understand the Lord's reply. I told her that it may not be the answer she wanted right now, but with peace in her heart she would know it was right and it would bring her the most happiness and bless her children and family. I explained that as long as she was in the Lord's will this peace would continue, no matter which way the Lord sent her.

It isn't necessary to finish that story, because it is the story of every person alive. Some have the courage to postpone the dismantling of their lives; but most don't. Others have the spiritual IQ to seek and obtain true peace—which is their rock.

But, my old friend was absolutely right: seeking peace is among the most important things one can learn.

Brother John

Praying Vocally

One of the UnBlog family asked a question: Is it good to pray vocally? Can the bad spirits hear our prayers that way? Shouldn't we pray silently for that reason?

I have asked myself the same question and arrived at this answer for myself, at least: it doesn't matter. Whether "they" can hear our prayers or not does not give them additional power over us. True prayer, whether silent or vocal, invites the Holy Spirit into the room, and evil *must* depart. Light and darkness cannot exist in the same place at the same time. On the other side of the coin, if our prayers are routine and insincere and do not invite the Holy Spirit, then "they" haven't heard anything worth hearing. So I honestly believe it just doesn't matter.

I personally find my greater prayers tend to be silent, but I have also been urged at times to pray vocally. The key is to listen and obey.

There are a few steps that one can take to develop mighty prayer.

First, let the Holy Spirit be your guide. Do this in every decision of your life. When you kneel to pray, yield yourself to the same voice that speaks daily to you of right and wrong. This is the voice of revelation and the only way to pray with power.

Second, pray, pray, pray, pray. The only way to learn to pray powerfully is to pray often and long. I personally think that praying twenty minutes every day is a minimum requirement for powerful spiritual progression.

Third, don't use these special mighty prayers to ask for things until the Holy Spirit guides you. Use them to worship, praise, and commune with Father. When the power of prayer falls upon you, praise is natural because you are suddenly in the audience with the God of heaven who loves you as dearly as if you were His only child. You will shout praises and weep because you will remember Him and love Him, and yearn to be there with Him, feeling His tender love all around you. When He then tells you what you may ask for, you will have tremendous faith in His desire to grant you these things, and you will ask with complete faith. When you ask for anything in these favored circumstances, it will have already been granted and you will know it.

Mighty prayer seems to be about 80 percent praise and 20 percent pleading.

Fourth, enjoy your mighty prayers. It is truly a glorious thing. When you reach for and obtain this mighty communion with your

Heavenly Parent, you will desire to stay and then to return often. It is a delight. Brother Joseph called fasting and prayer "fasting and rejoicing." He ought to know.

Brother John

An Unending River of Light

During my pilgrimage as a would-be saint of the latter days, through all of the deep valleys and lofty peaks, I have been blessed to experience many types of prayer. There have been many prayers that didn't leave my room and a few that forever altered my eternity.

Even looking back through the hazy glass of memory, I'm not sure I understand why some prayers are so mighty and most are not. At times I have tried to elbow my way into the heavens. I had been there before, and I wanted more to rejoice in—but most without success. The times I have succeeded in reaching far beyond conventional prayer into the vastness of mighty prayer, there have always been a few truths in operation.

First, I was in a pattern of life wherein I was seeking, deeply searching. These times have occasionally been a result of spiritual hunger; a few times they were fueled by bitter anguish and exquisite sorrow. Mostly they were driven by a sense that I yearned to be somewhere far closer to the veil.

Second, at those times I was not asking for something. I wasn't needing, begging, or pursuing relief from some mortal trial, as I usually did. I was seeking—anything, everything of God. I wasn't looking for God to see me; I was seeking to see God.

Third, I had identified the voice of revelation in my walk of life and had been as obedient to it as I was able. Mighty prayer, at least in my experience, has always begun by waiting, worshiping, listening, and then letting prayer overtake me. I was not able to do that until I understood revelation in lesser, daily things; then greater things followed. When I intellectually tried to raise my voice, I faltered. When I have occasionally obtained the voice of angels, then the heavens often parted.

Fourth, I spent a lot of time on my knees. More than anything else, this one factor seems penetrating. I was willing to pray for hours. At those times, it isn't labor. It doesn't require discipline or pillows under the knees. It is delightful. I discovered that I loved it. I loved the flow of the Spirit. I loved feeling deeply welcome. I loved feeling the Lord's delight in my small voice of worship and praise.

Fifth, when the heavens opened and I found myself surrounded by love and peace, and I knew that anything I requested I would receive, I found that I had no desire to ask for any earthly thing. The light and truth and glory that flowed through me like a waterfall at the end of an unending river of light was enough.

And if I, with my many weaknesses and human foibles, can delight in that kind of prayer, you can experience this unspeakable joy as well.

Brother John

Personal Journal

February 6, 1994

I am almost done with the book I have been writing. I have titled it Following the Light of Christ into His Presence. *It is a powerful book. I have spent hundreds of hours enveloped in the Spirit, writing by pure revelation. I have been taught marvelous things. It has truly been a glorious experience. It has also been surprisingly hard. It has required much editing and reworking.*

The parts I wrote while under the powerful influence of the Spirit flowed onto the paper effortlessly and required no editing. The parts that are rough are the parts that I wrote to tie the book together, or where I was constrained by the Spirit to write on some subject but not given the words. I had to work and rework those parts over and over again.

Dad has been helping me a lot with the book. He took my rough draft and marked it up. His comment when he handed it back was, "I can tell which parts you wrote by inspiration because they are perfect and didn't need so much as a punctuation mark. The other parts need a lot of work." He understands it by the Spirit and can even add to the truths written. He is a stake patriarch and a righteous man. I, like Nephi, have been born of goodly parents.

April 24, 1994

An older gentleman with a slight continental accent visited our high priest quorum this Sunday. He was accompanied by a taller man who was quite talkative. The shorter man said nothing at all. I asked them who they were and where they were from. The taller guy introduced himself. I have since forgotten his name. He said they traveled the world on assignment for their employer and loved to visit the Saints whenever the opportunity arose.

I taught a lesson on obeying the promptings of the Holy Spirit. After the meeting I suddenly found him standing very close to me. He looked me in the eyes. His eyes were gray and very penetrating. He had a commanding presence, and when he spoke he spoke with authority. The Spirit whispered that he was a messenger, and I listened very closely. I thought he may be one of the three Nephites or perhaps just a good man being led by the Spirit to deliver a message.

He said he was impressed with me and my teaching, that I had a great spirit about me, and I had taught what was true. He said I had handled the objections of one of the class members with kindness and love. He said I had spoken directly and precisely and had spoken the truth. He said the Lord was surely pleased with me. He asked me if I was going to be as good a man twenty years from now. I answered, "Even better." He looked away as if in thought, and replied, "Yes, you will." Then he added something to the effect that it was a great challenge, but he knew I could do it if I stuck to my present course.

He said that it was a real treat to visit the Saints from time to time, especially when he was able to feel the Holy Spirit in our meetings. He said he had been doing a lot of traveling and didn't get to visit the Saints as much as he used to. He thanked me again and walked from the room. I felt like running after him and asking, "Who are you, really?" But I didn't. He had a very happy and pleasant demeanor. He had not made a single comment during the lesson but had just smiled and listened. I have no idea who he was, but I appreciated the message.

I snapped my briefcase closed and turned to ask him a few questions, but he was not to be found in the room, hallway, or foyer. He could not have gone more than a few steps from me, but I could not find him.

May 1, 1994

My spiritual manifestations continue to grow from day to day, and I am led continually to worship and praise Heavenly Father. I rejoice all day long. The spiritual power is so strong within me that I can scarcely stand to go to work and deal with petty people and petty things. I see all these material things as mere stage props and of no eternal worth.

I was complaining to the Lord that I would prefer to be called to some great work wherein I could serve Him day and night, and leave this petty world behind. I was told, "By the sweat of thy brow shalt thou eat bread all the days of thy life." I quit complaining, but I still have this profound desire to accomplish something of eternal worth in His name.

Last Saturday I went into town to pick up a load of tires for the business. I went to the warehouse that is also a big tire store and a competitor of mine, although I hardly compete with him; I buy all my tires from him. His store is massive. It is one of five stores and is a whole city block in size. It is a multi-million dollar empire. I felt repulsed and offended by the worldliness of it all. I have NO desire for worldly wealth or power. My whole motive and joy is to serve the Lord and to await my reward at some future time. I have no other desire, and I am so grateful for this purity of motive.

This is the first time in my life that I have understood what it means to have your "eye single to the glory of God." It comes because of the refining influence of the Holy Ghost.

June 5, 1994

I have been petitioning the Lord earnestly to allow me to change the circumstances of my life so that I can serve him all day, every day. My joys and the thoughts and intents of my heart are so much removed from this world that I can scarcely stand going to work and battling with people to try to make a living. I rejoice in the fact that my heart and my eye are single to the Glory of God. I have no other purpose for living than to serve Him and bring Him joy in my service. It is a struggle, therefore, of necessity to spend my time doing things other than what my heart yearns to do. I hope that in time I may have this great wish granted. The Spirit whispers that it will be so.

July 7, 1994

Prayer continues to be a joy and delight. Satan has gained great power to tempt and lie. More so than I have ever thought possible. The other day I was told a carefully crafted lie which took me aback. I struggled with it, then rejected it and turned to the Lord for guidance. I heard this: "Well done, my son. Well done!"

I was so overjoyed! He seemed so close, and so pleased by my righteous choice that it filled me to overflowing.

Chapter Five

Not Only Is It True: Testifying of the Restored Gospel

Not Only Is It True

I have UnBlogged about this several times, but I want to say again that after years of study, seeking, research, prayer, fasting, and sacrifice, I do not find any valid reason to criticize this latter-day church. The Church of Jesus Christ of Latter-day Saints is fulfilling its latter-day calling in exactly the way Jesus Christ desires. Nothing more needs to be done. Nothing more needs to be taught. Nothing more needs to be revealed for the faithful to receive every promised blessing.

I fully understand that this telestial church is not perfect. But I also understand better than most that it is functioning exactly as it should.

The reason I say this is that I am a personal witness of the fact that every blessing mortals may seek is presently available to us because there truly is power in the priesthood ordinances and promises received within the bosom of the Church. If the Church were defective, or apostate, or strayed from the correct path, then that power would evaporate. If the Church were teaching false doctrine or perverting the true meaning, the power would evaporate. If *the* prophet was not actually *a* prophet, the power would evaporate.

I will stand up and say this for the remainder of my life and on into eternity, that I have sought and obtained, and the promises are vast and valid. All this tells me, by the exact logic used above, that our prophet is *a* prophet, and all other things are as they should be.

Do I think the Church is flawless? No.

Do I think there is nothing that could be improved? No.

Do I think doctrine is perfectly taught in every class and every sacrament meeting, or that people's pride doesn't muddle the work, or that wrongs are not perpetuated, or the truth-seekers are not at times misunderstood or persecuted? No, I have unfortunately seen otherwise.

But, I have also seen the windows of heaven open. I have seen the priesthood power manifest to raise the dead and instantly heal, and to qualify us for the visions and proclamations essential to whatever quest we are led to seek. I have seen hundreds of inspired leaders minister to and bless the humble. I have sat in counsels where the Spirit of God was so profoundly present that everything that was said and done was the will of God. I have shared in revelation that led and inspired a new bishop to correctly fill every office and officer and teacher in his new ward, from the elders quorum and Relief Society to who plays the piano for Primary. These things are the norm and the pattern of this church. If Jesus Christ, for reasons of misconduct on our part, was not leading this great work, then these things would not occur.

If anything is actually amiss it is that we, the people, live below our privilege, that we do not seek and obtain the voice of the Lord throughout our lives, and that instead of inspiration we use human philosophy and logic.

If anything is amiss, it is that many who complain about the Church or its leaders do not seek, study, and extend themselves in searching sufficiently to obtain an inspired view of what our privileges and powers truly are, and how to obtain them. Instead of seeking and obtaining them where they are actually enthroned—in the privacy of our own obedience and ordinance-powered quest— we want the Church leaders to spoon-feed us advanced spiritual concepts that we are not sufficiently evolved to hear. Then we feel cheated and disillusioned that we are not seeing visions and working the miracles we read about in the scriptures—and we blame the Church.

Another form of deception is when we run ahead of the Spirit and seek for visions and manifestations on our timetable, and not the Lord's. We must learn to diligently seek and then with patience wait upon the Lord. As Doctrine and Covenants 88:68 teaches, all these things are manifested in His own time, and in His own way, and according His own will.

The scriptures clearly teach that there is a mighty struggle that qualifies us for these gifts. Every powerful practitioner of pure priesthood power obtained their gifts after sacrifice, searching, struggling, repenting, and willingly suffering the schooling of the purification process that must precede such blessings.

But when we at long last understand the path and patiently walk it to its conclusion, then whatever flaws might exist in this divine drama of mortal errors, simply do not matter because we have obtained.

When one struggles through university and finally obtains his or her PhD, it simply does not matter anymore that the professors were boring, the classrooms too crowded, and the cafeteria too costly.

And so I repeat: not only is this Church true, but it works. It works today as in any generation of the past.

Brother John

The Ever-Present Danger

Please forgive me that it has been almost a week since my last UnBlog. This has been a chemo week. Everything nasty they say about chemo is true. I also find that having a sick body makes spiritual attunement that much more difficult. So I appreciate your patience with me, and I love you all.

I have been pondering why so many of the faithful of days past and of today who have attained a seemingly more blessed spiritual stature seem to struggle with criticizing the Church or the Brethren.

Here is the problem as I view it. Anyone who diligently studies the gospel, who fasts and prays, who studiously reads and cross-references the scriptures and inspired writings of the latter-day prophets, and who fervently seeks and asks will come to view the doctrine of Christ in a particular way—their perspective illuminated by a brighter light than most people achieve through casual Church membership. These are the greater blessings of the gospel that the scriptures invite us to seek and obtain.

The problem is that once a seeker obtains this brightly lit view, they might look back upon the pathway they just walked and feel inclined to say of others still on that path, "What's wrong with you? Can't you see there's more? Are your eyes closed like newborn puppies? Awaken from your sleep and lay hold upon these great and glorious things!"

And then what invariably follows is this: "What is wrong with the Church that these things aren't openly taught in sacrament meetings and general conference? Why did I have to acquire them through such a hard journey?"

The ever-present danger lies in the fact that nobody but the prophet has a voice authorized to say such things. Such complaints are in their very tone apostate-leaning, and set a very deceptive trap from which many cannot escape. The truth is, nothing is amiss. The Church is doing exactly what it is supposed to do: It is gloriously teaching the restored gospel of Jesus Christ to the world, administering the saving ordinances, and shepherding its fledgling members to a place where they can seek and find progressively greater truths as they are ready to receive them.

The inspired gospel system is designed by God to encourage every plateau of growth, to succor all of His children with truth, joy, and peace, and to lift and instruct them at whatever level they are at, in the nearby presence of "greater things." No mortal has the right to say, from a more blessed footing, that those upon the gospel pathway, wherever they are, are unguided or failing in some way by being there. These are upward paths and steeply heavenward climbs for us all.

Here is the great danger that has taken away salvation so many times: It is when we think we have obtained some greater light that we feel obligated to use it to point out shadows and find fault. No matter how justified we may feel, criticism and judgment of either the Church, its leaders or its members does not foster the Spirit and is simply not of God. Let Jesus Christ handle His Church and any faults there may be; and then feel the abiding peace that will flow to you.

Also, I believe we must not interpose our brighter gospel knowledge, as we suppose, into the sacred process of our family members or fellow Saints, unless acting upon a direct prompting from the Spirit to do so. Each person's process is uniquely their own, and they will find their path as quickly as their personal discipleship allows. Anything else will just slow them down.

After all, it is Christ's work and His glory, not our own.

Brother John

The Church and the Gospel

In a recent general conference, one of the Seventy gave a marvelous talk on the difference between the Church and the gospel. I would like to echo and amplify this important truth.

The Church and the gospel are both true, and they are both essential, but they are not the same thing.

The gospel is the means of salvation and the source of priesthood power, atoning grace, revelation, and blessings. It does not require a church organization or mortals to make it true. It is eternal in nature and derives its truth and power from the Atonement of Christ.

The gospel is a divine system of powers, priesthood, and principles that are indeed flawless and can never err. The gospel embraces all truth, and if we understood it fully and flawlessly, we would understand the mind of God and would share His eternal understanding of all things. The gospel can never falter or fail to deliver the promised blessings because the gospel and Jesus Christ are inseparably intertwined.

In comparison, The Church of Jesus Christ of Latter-day Saints is an earthly organization currently authorized to administer the gospel in its fulness. It is profoundly true, however, that a beautiful portion of the gospel is held by every true Christian. We praise God that we are not alone in the cause of Christ! But the Church is the only place where the authorized priesthood resides and where the ordinances are righteously performed. This is where God has called His living prophet. The Church itself has no means of actually saving us, but it is the administrator of the gospel and leads us to Christ, who saves us.

For a church to be "true," it must have the current and ongoing sanction from Jesus Christ to administer His gospel. This occurs and remains as long as the Church is organized by God and remains faithful to the laws instituted by God which govern the Church. For the Church to be "living" it must have a living prophet currently, who intimately and daily receives revelation from God to direct the Church. From 1830 to the present day, these "must have" principles have been fully functioning in The Church of Jesus Christ of Latter-day Saints.

The beauty of recognizing the difference between the Church and the gospel is that it liberates the Church from the necessity of being perfect, and it gives the Saints a correct reliance upon Jesus Christ as the source of salvation. We should first have a testimony of Jesus Christ and the Atonement, placing all of our allegiance upon Christ. Thereafter, having a testimony of the Church is of great value, as it is the authorized administrator of the gospel. We pay tithing, labor in callings, teach our children, and do all things we do because the gospel *is* "true" and the restored Church of Jesus Christ *is* its authorized and inspired vessel upon the earth.

Since the Church is administered by mortals, and mortals are inherently flawed, the Church is also unavoidably flawed. People within it will make mistakes. Doctrine will be flavored by tradition, personal philosophy, and by mortal foibles. Programs will come and go, leaders will come and go, errors will come and go, and changes in programs will come and go. The only thing that keeps the Church true is the fact that Christ is constantly and patiently shepherding it, through the living prophet, toward the gospel—which does not change.

Having this view of the Church and gospel aids us in many ways. First, we know to whom to look for our salvation. The means by which we come unto Christ each Sunday is to come to Church. But we don't depend upon the Church to save us. In other words, we absorb what the Church teaches and provides, and we love and support it. We participate in the sacred ordinances and receive the blessings of priesthood with joy. But then we go forth, studying the gospel and seeking after Christ, His grace, and His promises through our own discipleship and personal quest.

Second, it allows us to take responsibility for our own growth and our own relationship with Christ. Leaving our progression solely to what is taught in church is leaving our eternal outcome in the hands of often-inspired but flawed mortals. Without a view of the unique relationship of the gospel and the Church, if we get down the road and realize we aren't having the spiritual experiences that the scriptures teach are ours to claim, or that someone else describes, it challenges our testimony of the Church—when it should not. Such a realization should only challenge our own discipleship and inspire us to reach further into the heavens and claim these experiences for ourselves.

Third, it frees us to claim promised blessings as they come to our growing inspiration, without regard to what others are doing around us. It also frees us from wondering what is wrong with the others, or even with ourselves, when we have a grand epiphany we haven't heard another mortal describe. Without understanding this interdependence of Church and gospel we become like crabs in a fisherman's pot who pull one another back into the pot when we see someone beginning to climb. If we are not careful, the Church "norm" can become the sacred standard, instead of the gospel as it unfolds before us.

Finally, this view of the Church and gospel empowers both to function to their fullest virtue. The Church surges forward upon inspired shoulders of gospel warriors whose lives are tested and found true and faithful in all things. These warriors pay little heed to offenses given or to faults in leaders or programs. They forgive readily and serve diligently without expectation of notice or reward upon the earth because they are serving Christ foremost and serving within His Church at His request, by His direction, and for His glory.

Brother John

Into the Sunlight

I used to worry about things like, are we, as the Gentiles, rejecting the "fulness of the gospel" (3 Nephi 16:10)? Is the latter-day church moving forward fast enough? Will we ever get around to building Zion? These questions burned in my mind.

Then, something marvelous happened in my heart and mind. I was reading Doctrine and Covenants 45 regarding the condemnation under which all of us dwell for taking lightly the things we have received, when the Holy Spirit warmed my soul and simply said, "You can lift this condemnation from your own head and from your family."

It had never occurred to me that there was anything I could personally do about a sweeping general condemnation. I had felt trapped in the tide of the lack of saintliness of the Church as a whole. In that moment, I realized that the Church is only millions of individuals and that any overarching condemnation is due to what those million individuals are doing. And I was not to judge them. That being said, I—all by myself—have the ability to enjoy the full light of every blessing the scriptures promise. I learned that even though God treats us as a group, He judges us as individuals. Therefore, I am not culpable for what everyone else is doing, unless I'm doing the same things.

From that moment on I quit worrying. I began to seek and to obtain the light and blessing I had seen with an eye of faith. It was only a small leap of logic to realize that if I were stepping out of the condemnation, so were many others—perhaps millions of others. I also realized that whatever might be generally occurring, I had to do something different—more, better, with greater insight. I had to do this by choice, personal worthiness, and my personal quest.

I found this to not only be true but relatively straightforward and very available. I wouldn't say it is "easy" because it is not; but it is a straight path that was meant to be walked by the weak but obedient souls among us. It isn't a tightrope only the spiritually skillful can navigate.

I also realized that if the Lord could help me overcome those things which instigated the condemnation in the first place, I could perhaps influence others to do the same, as the Lord accorded. I could be a small light that was no longer under a bushel. I never even guessed that it would lead to writing books, giving seminars, and keeping this UnBlog. I really didn't see that coming. It's probably a good thing it was hidden from me until it occurred because it has surely done violence to my comfort zone.

The danger of 3 Nephi 16:15 is that "if they will not turn unto me, and hearken unto my voice," then God will take away the "fulness of my gospel from among them."

Therefore, by choosing for ourselves to come unto Christ and hearken to His voice, we can be insulated from the destructive events preceding the Lord's Second Coming. We can have the general condemnation lifted from our heads, receive a fulness of all that the gospel offers, and one day step into the sunlight of the latter-day glory that will become Zion.

Brother John

We Talk of Christ

As I have grown in my adoration of Jesus Christ, my language has changed from wonder to worship. I don't refer to Christ anymore as my "Elder Brother" because it so magnificently understates our relationship. He is my God, my salvation, and the lover and exalter of my soul. I depend upon Him for every part of my life. He is my only hope of exaltation.

As I have said many times, I believe there is a growing and powerful revival taking place in the present latter-day arena. Doctrine which has been known but somewhat obscure for 175 years is now commonplace, and the language of Christ is being spoken again!

When I was in the stake presidency in my previous stake, I constantly pressed to make every stake meeting and event Christ-centered. It made a difference. While in the bishopric, I always assigned sacrament meeting talks to be about Christ, and our bishopric urged people on fast day to testify primarily of Christ. It really does make a difference.

In our new Utah ward, almost every fast and testimony speaker speaks of their adoration of Christ. Little kids stand up and say first, "I love Jesus Christ," and then go on with their little testimonies of family and Joseph Smith and other things. The reason this is so is that the leadership of this ward speaks the adoring words of Christ, and the leaders of our stake also speak this way. The children's words simply mirror what they hear.

So, here is a gift we of the UnBlog possess, and one we can share. Whenever you talk, teach, or testify, have courage and speak the words of Christ. Adore Him openly, and thank Heavenly Father for the gift of His Son every time you testify. Teach your children the words of Christ so that this language becomes a part of your family culture.

This is a powerful thing because those who hear will feel the Holy Spirit warm their souls, and they, too, will open their mouths in their time. We can begin to do as Nephi taught us about 2,600 years ago: "We talk of Christ, we rejoice in Christ, we prophecy of Christ, and we write according to our prophecies, that our children may know to what source they may look for a remission of their sins" (2 Nephi 25:26).

Brother John

Unraveling the Paradox

*T*here is an odd paradox people bump into about the time they begin discovering that there is a grand eternity of mortal blessings suddenly available to them through an inspired personal quest.

It is this: When someone teaches their spiritual ears to hear the voice of the Holy Spirit, and their bodies to yield to its entic-ings, then great blessings flow. What seems to happen next is that they usually mention their new joy to several people, including people they admire spiritually. But rather than joy in their new-found blessings, they receive skepticism and doubt, and are told to be careful. Then begin the feelings of aloneness, isolation, and pon-dering why there must be a paradox between two true things—their unfolding spiritual heights and the ecclesiastical platform they were standing upon to reach them.

We naturally want to be supported in our new quest, and we want to know that this is where we are supposed to be and not off on some tangent. The paradox, which is something that seems impossible but is nevertheless true, is that while feeling new spiri-tual joys, some seekers don't feel encouraged by leaders and others in the Church; they feel dissuaded.

Here's the key. I've written about it several times on the UnBlog, but I don't mind restating it because it is so important. The Church *is* true, and it *is* functioning exactly as Jesus Christ intends. Nothing is broken. The Church administers the ordinances and bestows the gift of the Holy Ghost. From there, most of what we receive spiritually is a result of a personal quest to fulfill ordinances, keep covenants, and claim promised blessings. When we do, then vast and eternal things begin to happen. This is the correct order of things, and it is in harmony with what the scriptures and the Church teaches.

The scriptures are replete with witness to the validity of this type of spiritual pursuit. Every prophet recorded in scripture— every single one of them—was isolated, persecuted, and rejected; and yet each triumphed personally by weathering every hazard. We are blessed in that we don't experience any degree of institutional opposition today, only the words and acts of limited spiritual perception.

Great spiritual gifts and experiences are spiritually discerned, and people arrive at them at their own speed and on their own timetable. Discussing them from the pulpit won't make people understand them, because that understanding is only derived through the Spirit, not by words. In a perfect world, one where pornography wasn't more common than prophecy, these principles would be shouted from the rooftops. For now, they are deeply held within the hearts of those who seek and find.

If someone attended a university and obtained a PhD, it would be illogical to look back at another still taking basic courses and wonder what's wrong with them, or what's wrong with the university. Nor would it be logical for someone in an airplane lifting off the runway to glance back at the airport and wonder what's wrong with the people still milling around in the airport. The very fact that you are in the air proclaims the validity and inspired mission of the airport.

As I said in the beginning, it is a paradox, albeit one that faith easily unravels.

Brother John

What Is to Become of Us?

*R*esponding to "The Army of God," one of you echoed a fear and hope that I hear often:

"This outlines one of my greatest concerns about our position as the only true church. I see many men and women who are not members but who have the testimony and faith such as you described with the Korean Christians. I am so often put to shame when I compare their wonderful faith to my mini-faith. I would be interested in hearing more about your feelings of the "callings" of so many faithful who know little or nothing about the Restored Church. And why do we as a people and Church seem to have so little insight into the actual power of faith and the priesthood? We seem to be the candle covered with the bushel basket. Even more, as a Church we seem to not even recognize we have any light to broadcast to the world. No radio or TV programs to teach the gospel in power, no real member missionary effort. . . . What is to become of us?"

Let me shout words that thunder in our hearts and then around the world: Nothing is amiss! The Church is not damaged or asleep. We have all we need; everything is before us. The doctrine is pure, and the promises are being poured out.

The Christian world is indeed wholesome and good. They are leading people to Christ. The faithful, whoever they are and wherever they serve, are fulfilling the Lord's plan. No evil can ultimately triumph with those faithful to Christ of every denomination—although it surely will try.

The Lord is teaching suckling babes *and* mighty men and women in churches across the fruited plains, and profoundly in general conference, by His voice. We all hear it, millions obey, enough will partake, the ordinances will one day be received—and we will become Zion.

We will prepare a place for Christ's return, and we will end this telestial world. Then we will all sit down together with Christ for a thousand years of peace.

That's what is to become of us.

Brother John

Commenting on a Comment

*M*y *Friends,*
Thanks for taking the time to leave your comments. I am of the opinion that nothing needs to be improved in the Church. It is kind of like a medicine that successfully cures a specific disease 100 percent of the time; yet some people don't like the texture, flavor, or bottle it's in. That's just cosmetic. The higher truth is that the gospel works. The power is present. The priesthood functions. The blessings are real and being claimed. Zion will be built, and we will all rejoice.

If the Church were in fact "perfect," then this would be the Millennial day, and there would be nothing to try our faith or motivate us to look heavenward. The discomfort serves a purpose, and it is by divine design.

God bless us to always have scratchy underwear until Zion actually glows in the Millennial day.

Brother John

Living the Dream

*T*he *topic in high priest groups around the world* today was the Apostasy and Restoration. I listened to a white-haired gentleman, a former stake president, and a person whose face was aglow with righteousness bear testimony regarding these principles. It wasn't new information to me—but I did *feel.* I felt uplifted, rejuvenated, and blessed.

When I was a child I read about the ancient faithful in the Bible and Book of Mormon, and I thought that they somehow had something more powerful than we have today. I read about their miracles, faith, and blessings, and it seemed more immediate and more powerful than what I was experiencing in my life as an LDS boy.

Now that I am no longer a child, now that I have walked many miles by faith, now that I have tested the promises and sought the great blessings, now that I have asked, and sought, and knocked, now that I have seen and received and been welcomed within, I want to say with the greatest emphasis I can form into words, that not only is this gospel true, but that it works! It works today with equal power and equal privilege as it did in Enoch's day, or when Christ was alive, or when the brother of Jared climbed his holy mount.

It is all present, nothing is missing, the power is real—we *are* living the dream.

Brother John

Personal Journal

August 16, 1994

I was driving home from work from a busy, stressful day and reflecting pensively upon how futile and meaningless it all was, as I began to pray. I told Heavenly Father that I hated wasting my time and creativity on such worldly tasks while I had the potential and desire to accomplish greater things in His name. I began worshipping and praising Him in the Spirit and wishing that I could do more for His work. I told Him that I wanted to write books which might bring His children to understand His love and glory, and to teach with great power and effectiveness in convincing them to repent and worship Him. I said that in doing these things, I would also like to be able to make whatever money is required for my family, so that my energies need not be divided.

I felt a surge of joy and a divine feeling of acceptance. The Spirit said, "Just be patient." The accompanying feeling was that my request was a righteous one and would be answered with a great blessing.

August 31, 1994

The Spirit reminded me as I was going to bed to write about the time when I wrestled with an evil presence and was thereafter blessed with protection.

After I had gone to bed and had fallen asleep, I was violently attacked by a dark spirit . . . I used the priesthood to rebuke the evil, and a feeling of peace returned to the room.

I went back to bed and was filled with rejoicing and love. As I was praying and rejoicing, I had the powerful feeling of someone behind me with their arms around me. I could feel the weight of their arm across my side, and the bulge of one arm under my cheek. There was such a feeling of love and power coming from him that I felt like an infant in its mother's arms. I felt absolutely safe. So much so that I felt as if nothing, living or from the spiritual realm, could harm me. I asked to have this shield extend to my wife, who was by then asleep beside me. With my spiritual eyes I saw this shield extend to include her. I asked for it to include our whole home, and saw it extend out into the yard covering the whole

93

house. As I drifted off to sleep I remember thinking that even an atomic bomb couldn't get through such a powerful shield.

December 1, 1994

I had a marvelous revelation the other night as I was lying in bed. One of the central messages was for me to beware of the spirit of apostasy. The Spirit confirmed to me that those who presently occupy the offices in the Church are His anointed and stand righteously in their appointed callings. They are doing His will, and will remain in their office until their work is completed.

I have pondered why this information was given to me, since I have no inclination to feel critical of the Brethren. There was a time I wondered why there wasn't more effort being put into teaching the people to seek the rebirth; but I now know that all is as the Lord would have it concerning the leaders of the Church. I still expect, though, that much work remains to be done among the members.

Chapter Six

The Path of Discipleship

The Divinely Orchestrated Path

*F*or the last dozen years I was a technical writer and trainer. I produced and taught technical courses in power generation, power distribution, and controls. My field of expertise was industrial jet turbine generators. When I taught a group of technicians I began at the beginning: "This is an electron." I walked them through day after day of hands-on training: "This is a fuel control valve; it is controlled by this computer, at this digital output, by this line of software." When I was done, I tested them. The criterion for passing the course was 100 percent correct answers. Much of the test was rapid fire real-life situations and hands-on repairs. When I was done, the students were competent and qualified to troubleshoot and repair multi-million dollar turbo-generators without assistance.

When I speak at firesides and in this UnBlog, I have no idea what your background might be. I have no idea how much of the UnBlog you have read so far, and I have no idea if by describing something profound, it will come to you without introduction and thereby prejudice you against something wonderful. Even though there is a beautiful sequence to these principles, and an inspired way to acquire every gift, I have no way of knowing where your feet presently reside along the path.

The difference, of course, is that I seldom felt the Holy Spirit while teaching jet turbines and power generation. I always do when speaking and writing about sacred things. I trust that if you are reading these things that you are ready and that you will seek and find the requisite background light to implement these principles in your lives.

For those of you who may be working with spiritual baby steps, yet who have been introduced to this UnBlog by some workings of divine grace, I want to restate an indispensable principle in obtaining unmatched and even unimaginable spiritual growth: all spiritual blessings and privilege are sequentially gained. In other words, they come one at a time, in a specified order that cannot be changed.

Another way of saying this is that there is a divinely orchestrated path for your life. You must walk that path by placing every footfall where it belongs. It is not possible to skip or ignore even one step. That pathway begins with faith in Jesus Christ, then repentance, baptism, and receipt of the Gift of the Holy Ghost. From there the pathway is just as clearly defined but not by the scriptures or by convention. From there we must take the Holy Spirit as our guide and then walk the course of our life as made known moment-by-moment through divine instruction in our lives.

Most of the literature in this UnBlog is detailed instruction on how to recognize the voice of the Holy Spirit in your life. I invite you to read back through the UnBlog as the Spirit inspires you.

Taking the Holy Spirit as our guide is where the magic of the Latter-day gospel begins. This reveals the power and perfection of the plan of exaltation, wherein we can—quite easily, in fact—become fully empowered in our lives by direct and personal revelation.

The magic is that we do not have to leverage and force ourselves to newer and greater levels of perfection in order for each new blessing and privilege to become operative in our lives. As we walk in the light of this divine source of truth, these blessings simply "distill upon our souls as the dews from heaven." The divine attributes of greater faith, charity, gentleness, hope, kindness, and virtues of every color are gifted to our being by our Savior. We begin to take on the image of Christ in our countenances, becoming like He is— because He has become our guide and our master.

We begin walking the pathway of our lives with precision, gathering divine grace, inspired understanding, and sequentially obtained blessings we could not have believed, let alone obtained in any other way.

And the good news—the glorious news—is that it does not require increasingly greater degrees of perfection on our parts. Our contribution to this equation is obedience. We give up our will to His will. We school ourselves to walk in the light He reveals. We submit our will to Him, and by this token sacrifice, Christ whispers to us the pathway of our lives, one small step at a time. Then He empowers us to walk it and bestows the gifts of eternity—including every power, gift, and privilege you can read about in the scripture.

This is the heritage of the very, very obedient.

Brother John

The High Road of Faith

The universal reasoning I hear for someone choosing to not begin a quest into righteousness is fear. The object of each person's fear is different and tailor-made by the adversary to stop us in our tracks. So saying, the very definition of sanity is recognizing danger and then letting appropriate caution lead you around it.

In the matter of mortals seeking the face of God, there is a sequence whereby we may gain extraordinary courage before we face those things which we fear. It isn't reasonable to jump out of a perfectly good airplane until you have acquired and learned to trust your parachute. The sequence whereof I am speaking is the process of learning faith. I don't mean to gain faith or to exercise what faith you have; I mean to "learn" greater faith.

If a person is paralyzed by fear from starting their personal quest, then they are probably looking out the airplane door before having acquired their parachute of faith.

By learning to obey the still small voice of the Holy Spirit, which is in fact the voice of Jesus Christ, we "learn" by righteous experience that when we do what Jesus Christ is asking us to do, goodness, blessings, and peace are always the result.

This process is so simple that few recognize it. It works like this:

If, after a thousand instances of obedience to Christ we learn the blessedness that results, and then we compare this to a thousand acts of disobedience and the unavoidable pain which always follows that, we learn with surety that our only safety is in Jesus Christ and where He sends us. This is learned faith. In time, our new faith gives us sufficient courage to resume our quest with faith strong enough to consecrate everything required of us to complete our journey to the throne of God.

Courage is not an absence of fear; it is setting aside the fear we feel because faith tells us this is the right thing to do. Faith doesn't give us a perfect knowledge of what will happen, only the knowledge that it is right—and that peace and joy always follow obedience. Acting by faith alone doesn't mean that there won't be loss; it means that God repays a hundredfold.

Once upon the path as one whose discipleship is through faith cast in eternal stone, we find that this higher road *is* the pathway of joy, peace, and happiness, after all. We cease trying to fly under the spiritual radar to avoid the additional trials we suspect may be on the exacting pathway to the face of God. We rejoice in the very trials we once feared because we know that each is necessary in bringing us to where we want to be.

We wouldn't change a thing.

Brother John

Pure in Heart

It seems to me that there are two aspects of purity. The first is an absence of sin. Most of us strive all of our lives to obtain and retain this type of purity. One point here worth making over and over is that the natural man was not designed to be perfect. We all have been given "weakness" by God to make us humble and to motivate us to seek relief from Jesus Christ (see Ether 12:27). As long as we operate as a natural man, we will be forever climbing out of holes we dug for ourselves through sinful acts or omissions. It's just the natural way of this telestial world.

One abandons the natural stature and becomes a "saint through the atonement of Christ" by yielding to the enticings of the Holy Spirit, and putting off the natural man (Mosiah 3:19). Becoming a "saint" doesn't mean that we have fewer weaknesses; it means that when we approach triggering them, the Holy Spirit guides us, and by humble obedience to Christ's voice, we are empowered to not behave "naturally." In time we are dramatically changed, and have no more desire for "natural" indulgences. They are still present in our lives and available; we just don't desire them. We become "as a child, submissive, meek, humble, patient, full of love, willing to submit to all things which the Lord seeth fit to inflict upon him, even as a child doth submit to his father" (Mosiah 3:19).

Thus, through the Atonement of Christ and not by our own horsepower, we have become "saintly" and continually meek and humble; we have achieved purity from sin. We no longer even desire it, and sin loses its grip in our everyday lives.

However, there is a more difficult aspect of purity to achieve, which is to overcome the *effects* of our mortal experience. In a very real sense we are all damaged by mortality, especially by our child-hood and youth. We have all acquired false un-Christlike attitudes, beliefs, and behaviors that must be jettisoned before we can be counted "pure in heart."

These impurities are often the remnants of childhood and even more recent experience. Some "big person" tells us we're naughty, and we believe it and act it out for the rest of our lives. We experi-ence something unpleasant (like fried liver or not knowing what to say when bearing our testimony for the first time) and then vehemently avoid a repeat experience for the rest of mortality, even though both are wholesome and even valuable. We tena-ciously cling to what we have experienced as "truth" and then use avoidance, anger, resentment, hate, and even irrational behavior to give credence and credibility to these beliefs—many of which are in fact false.

It's amazing how many impure beliefs most adults are still acting upon that happened prior to their second birthdays:

"I must make people happy, or they will not like me."

"Eat all your food, or children will go hungry in India."

"Mothers yell at their kids."

"Fathers almost never come home."

"Church is boring."

"I get the most attention when I am sick, naughty, funny, cute, complimentary, disobedient, perfectionistic," or a thousand other behaviors.

The list could be endless. The point is, these falsehoods are largely invisible to us. They are the result of erroneous childhood thinking and sometimes are decisions made in moments of crisis. "I'll never do that again!" can last for a lifetime, even if you were too young to walk.

We mortals are relatively powerless to change these things, but Christ is not and has been working with us all of our lives to purify these things from our hearts.

This is the reason the Holy Spirit often prompts us to do kind acts or to say things that seem unusual, hard to say, or even impossible. Telling someone who just injured you that you are sorry may seem ridiculous, but it is probably the only way to overcome a childhood decision to pridefully hold anger and grudges inside forever. When we obey in these small things, not only do we conquer some element of uninspired knee-jerk behavior, but the Atonement of Christ begins to lift that stain from the fabric of our souls.

Why is this important? Why should I even try? What's wrong with the way I am?

The answer to these questions is found in the Bible: "The pure in heart shall see God" (Matthew 5:8). The impure in heart simply never will.

If you are reading this UnBlog, you are a seeker of great things. I consider that you either are willing to do anything it takes to claim your place at the veil and every blessing that follows, or you really, really want to be that willing and that obedient. You have an unquenchable *desire* to be willing, so to speak. It is a righteous starting place and one that every person achieves at some point.

In that quest, purity is the key that unlocks the doors of heaven and parts the veil when it is time. It is a spiritual gift that we acquire through walking the path of discipleship, by listening to the voice of the Spirit whisper words of truth to our souls, and obeying those directives.

There is an unexpected blessing that flows from this type of godly purity: it dramatically uncomplicates one's life. So much of the offense, annoyance, and anger that burbles up from the sewers of negative emotion is a product of our own impurity. People don't really cause it; we do. Someone acts like a perfectly normal impure natural man, and we feel annoyed. Someone offends us, or cheats us, or gloats over their victory at our expense, and we burble a little mortal bile.

But one who is pure in heart becomes immune to these things. He or she sees life in a pure light, from Christ's perspective. They see the offense, they know someone was being mean, but they just don't care. They feel sorry for that person's own vitriol, sorry for the pain it will cause them, and sorry for the long road that person will endure by carrying the burden.

For their own part, the pure in heart are experiencing joy in Christ and abiding peace in His love, and they honestly don't worry about such trivial things. They naturally react with kindness and forgiveness, and with sincere prayers for those who have despitefully used them. They live in a royal courtyard of divine grace and inspired happiness, which they would not leave even to inform someone that he or she had injured them. It just isn't worth the journey.

Since no impure thing can enter the presence of God, and the pure in heart *shall* see God, allowing the Holy Spirit to sanctify and purify us *is* the process of exaltation, and the highest outcome of obedience.

Brother John

Angels Will Appear

f you are like me, every time I read about something wonderful and spectacular in the scriptures, I want to know if it is happening today—and if I can do it, too. I would like someone to just stand up, raise their hand, and say, "I did that very thing last night, and this is how you do it." We universally yearn for modern evidence that such miraculous things happen in our day.

Even when we read of promised blessings that the scriptures hold out to us, we want to know if someone has actually already done it or if this was meant for someone more righteous than us. We appreciate evidence that these things are not only true but that they are happening today. We think it would build our faith and give us hope that we too might partake.

The problem is that evidence does not bring us to faith; it actually operates the opposite way. Faith brings us to evidence; faith must come first. This is always true. Inspiring us to belief is the rightful place of the scriptures. Those scriptural promises are true, and they are for you; they resonate with your spirit. Those promises give us not only faith but also the firm belief that we can and we should.

Moroni 7:36 teaches us that it is our unbelief, not our lack of faith, that limits our access to angels and every other great blessing we hope to embrace.

It is extremely significant that "angels speak the words of Christ" (2 Nephi 32:3). Isn't that thrilling to you? We hear the words of Christ through our conscience and the still small voice all day, every day. This means that we deal with angels literally all day long! It means that they are intimately involved in our progression, and we didn't even know about them.

It is of eternal consequence that angels fulfill and do the "work of the covenants of the Father" (Moroni 7:31). We rely upon these covenants for everything; we place every hope and every future joy upon the scales of the covenants of the Father. And, it is angels, those beings we interact with unknowingly but constantly, who are working to fulfill them in our lives.

Each of these amazing blessings remain dormant until we choose to believe they apply to us personally. Angels are like the Liahona that God prepared for Lehi (see Alma 37) to point a straight course through the wilderness. Even though the Liahona was actually crafted by the hand of God and was endowed with godly gifts, it still could only operate when *they* believed it could. When they doubted, it stopped. When they believed, it saved their lives.

It isn't vital that we have seen angels. What is vital is that we believe that we *will* see them when it is time. It isn't vital that we have seen visions; what is vital is that we believe that we *will* see visions when we need to. It isn't vital that we have raised the dead or worked miracles; what is vital is that we believe we *should and can and will* do these things when the voice of revelation sends us forth. Then when the still small voice instructs, we will already believe that we can, and that we should.

Then the heavens will part, the angels will appear, and the miracles will occur.

Brother John

Not as the World Giveth

I greatly appreciate your comments on peace. I read them thinking how marvelous it is to have found so many people who understand the gospel and who are spiritually evolved in their understanding and expression. I think this is part of the magic of the UnBlog—that it brings so many like-minded, seeking, and faith-filled people together.

Most all of you wrote that the peace we derive from our Savior is far different than a feeling of relief or lifting of opposition. I agree. There is a big difference.

Mark said it very well: "I believe that [true] peace can only be delivered from one source, Jesus Christ the Peacemaker himself. I am not convinced that the peace given by the Savior is the same as a feeling of intermission from a storm. Relief is different than peace. The feeling of peace given from the Savior, not as the world giveth, is unique and fully recognizable when felt, but a bit difficult to adequately describe. It's a feeling of calm, confidence and humility, light, truth and knowledge all quietly felt at once. I know the adversary and his legions cannot produce that."

I agree. There is an abiding, penetrating, and healing peace the Lord gives when we trust Him and obey Him, which often runs contrary to what is happening all around us. It is not always logical. In other words, logic and reason say we should be scared stiff, but the Spirit gives us peace that He is with us, and we are in His tender care. This is when the circumstances no longer matter; we just know that all is well, and we can view the world burning down around us with true peace.

Like you, I have experienced this many times. Some of these events were profoundly life-altering, yet the Spirit spoke peace; and even before a solution presented itself, I knew all was well.

One such circumstance I wrote about a year ago. It occurred when I chose (somewhat foolishly) to have surgery in Costa Rica to save money. We prayed about it, felt good about it, and made the arrangements. Everything went well until complications occurred after surgery and I grew desperately ill. The doctors rushed me into another emergency surgery and told Terri that I probably would not survive. I was so weak that I fully agreed—I *knew* I could not survive. It was horrifying. Not only was I extremely ill from the failed surgery, but they had given me several medicines I was allergic to, and I broke out in boils all over my body. I had difficulty breathing and my heart began acting up. My kidneys and other organs also began to shut down. I have never been in so much pain, with such debilitating weakness, either before or since. I had terrifying hallucinations, and at times felt my spirit leaving my body.

At this time, my lungs filled up with fluid and they put me on a respirator. When I awoke with the tube in my throat, I immediately realized that the respirator was not giving me enough oxygen. The tube was the size of a pencil, and it was providing only enough breath for a child.

I tried to signal to the doctors, but my arms were partly paralyzed from the medication. I couldn't speak or even write. When Terri came into the room minutes later, she saw by my eyes that I was in trouble. I pointed and gestured to get my message through. Terri tried to interpret what I was saying and finally told the doctors that she thought I wasn't getting enough oxygen. The doctors didn't believe her. They told her that all patients hate the feeling of intubation but that I would get used to it.

My vision was going dark. I knew I was in terrible trouble. Terri leaned close to my ear with tears running down her cheeks and said, "I can see you're in trouble, but I don't know how to fix it. John, I know that you can give this whole burden to Christ, and He will bear it for you. Just remember, this too will pass. Give it all to Christ."

I thought about this deeply. Her words were inspired and powerful. "This too will pass" was all I could cling to at that moment. My thinking changed, and I decided in that moment of panic to trust God. I suddenly imagined myself submerged in water as if I were diving. That little tube was the only air I had, and I became grateful for it. Peace settled upon me, and I relaxed. I considered every little puff a blessing. I waited patiently for each breath. The ever-present feeling of suffocation did not lessen for four days and nights, but I was no longer afraid.

Each day Terri tried to communicate to the staff that I wasn't getting enough oxygen. They wouldn't listen, thinking she was just an overly concerned wife. On day five, my primary doctor (who spoke English) finally returned to the ICU, and Terri told him her concerns. He stepped over to the respirator, looked at it closely, and turned pale. "Oh, look, there is a switch in the wrong position!" He flipped the switch, and suddenly I could draw a breath without the machine interfering. I gasped and gulped and sucked hard until I no longer felt suffocated or light-headed.

When the doctors fully realized what had happened, they told Terri that I would no doubt have brain damage from four days of insufficient oxygen. I didn't, though. The only reason was that I had found peace in Christ. I was able to relax and accept that He was in control, and know that "this too will pass." If I had struggled or panicked or fought, I would have required more oxygen and died or been brain damaged. If I had pulled the tube from my throat I would have not been able to breathe on my own because my lungs were still filled with fluid. Because I was at peace, that little bit of air was enough.

I believe that every circumstance of our lives can be conquered by giving the burden, fear, and solution into Christ's hands and then surrendering our own need to control the outcome. This is when the peace that surpasseth understanding settles upon us, and even in our continuing pain, we will know that "this too will pass."

Brother John

The Flight of Faith

*T*here are many things to be said about faith, most of which we have understood from childhood. The most important may be that faith grows from inspired experience. It works like this: we receive a prompting from the Holy Spirit, and when we obey we *always* experience a blessing.

That experience gives us the necessary hope to try obedience on a little higher scale, perhaps sacrificing a little to be obedient. With each act of obedience Jesus Christ blesses us and gifts us with a little more faith, and we grow by a long progression of increasingly loftier experiences into greater and greater faith.

This is referred to as receiving grace for grace. When we obey, when we dispense grace to other people, when we are more kind, more serving, more giving, and more willing to sacrifice, Christ will, in return, give us grace for our grace. Then, something profound happens: we are changed by His amazing grace; we are upgraded and sanctified by this process of His grace for our grace.

The difference is, we only have a teaspoon with which to dispense our little grace, but Christ has a dump truck. Our grace is a mere token. Even when we seem to do good things, it is because He enabled us, empowered and inspired us, and provided the way for us to do them. When we dispense grace, we willingly but imperfectly give our gifts to another. When Jesus Christ dispenses His perfect grace, it comes to us fully paid for by His blood. "For if you keep my commandments you shall receive of his fulness, and be glorified in me as I am in the Father; therefore, I say unto you, you shall receive grace for grace" (D&C 93:20).

To receive of "His fulness" is the end objective of the temple experience; the promise of the oath and covenant of the priesthood, and the greatest desire of our mortal hearts, which is to see Him and be in His presence. "Verily, thus saith the Lord: It shall come to pass that every soul who forsaketh his sins and cometh unto me, and calleth on my name, and obeyeth my voice, and keepeth my commandments, shall see my face and know that I am" (D&C 93:1).

Our faith cannot increase any other way. There is no other process. It is the 1+1=4 of the gospel of Christ. This is the only way to acquire faith powerful enough to part the veil, to work miracles, to behold angels, or any other divinely orchestrated gift.

Have you ever watched the runway lights go by as the airplane you are in accelerates into the air? Faith is somewhat like this. Each inch on the runway must be touched. Each light on the tarmac must be passed. None can be skipped. Every inch is a moment of decision, of obedience to truth. And when we obey, each inch increases our speed toward the end of the runway. When we disobey, our journey is paused and sometimes stopped entirely. No inch may be defiled and still accelerate to flight.

Then comes the flight of faith—the moment when we feel the weight lifting from our wheels. This is why every inch of the runway prior to this was precious. By the time we realize we must fly or crash, our experience and our inspired belief tells us that we *can* fly. We *can* part the veil. We *can* work miracles—because we have experienced a lifetime of inspired runway.

It is this inspired faith wrought by every moment spent on the tarmac, which now lifts our wings heavenward.

Brother John

Because of the Covenant

There is a divinely ordained law that governs the milestone event of being born again. It really doesn't matter if that rebirth process takes place over most of a lifetime, involving hundreds of acts of righteousness and slow incremental applications of atoning grace, or if it occurs as a powerful change that sweeps across one's soul, taking with it our unrighteous mindset and behavior, leaving a newly born child of Christ in its wake.

The blessings are the same in both cases—as is the act that triggers it. This is the magnificence of the Atonement of Jesus Christ, that it not only provides a pathway for us to seek and obtain these great blessings (of which being born again is actually a place to begin our journey to greater things) but that it *enables* us to actually become sufficiently Christlike to qualify for them.

The often-taught pathway of extreme discipline, eliminating each errant act and action from our walk and talk by the willpower of man—is simply not a true principle. It does not work and is not a part of the pathway to these glorious blessings of Christ's grace. This wrong pathway would require us to literally perfect ourselves in order to qualify for these blessings. The term "working out your own salvation" when viewed in this light of perfection by discipline, is not a correct principle.

The way it does work is that we submit ourselves to the will of Christ in all things—not just the big, mighty acts of self-sacrifice but in all things. We dedicate ourselves to do every good thing, the small and sometimes great things that the Spirit leads us to do every minute of every day—and then the grace of Jesus Christ changes us. Christ changes our nature and purifies our inner being. Like King Benjamin's people, we then have no more desire to do evil but to do good continually. Then, and only then, does obedience cease to be a sacrifice. It's like miraculously obtaining a deep love of exercise; it evolves from a dreaded task into a delight to our souls.

This, then, is the law: Decide and covenant, while within the embrace of the Holy Spirit, to obey Jesus Christ forevermore. It isn't some great self-immolating act that qualifies us; it is an unchangeable decision to obey.

After King Benjamin taught his people this principle and power of being born again, they were all changed and miraculously born again. His people proclaimed, "We are willing to enter into a covenant with our God to do his will, and to be obedient to his commandments, in all things . . . all the remainder of our days" (Mosiah 5:5). They were giving voice to a life-changing decision they had just made: "We are willing!"

I can almost hear his aged voice rising with the power of God, as in great joy and rejoicing he proclaimed in benediction, "And now because of the covenant which ye have made, ye shall be called the children of Christ, his sons and his daughters; for behold, this day he hath spiritually begotten you; for ye say that your hearts are changed through faith on his name; therefore ye are born of him and have become his sons and his daughters" (Mosiah 5:7).

Brother John

Gratitude in the Climb

I was thinking late last night how blessed my life is. I thought back over the past few years and felt grateful for every process of my life that has brought me to this place, to this moment of grace. Because of additional understanding recently gained, I can also see the meaning and melody of all the years prior to these last few, though until recently I could only see it with an eye of faith. My gratitude for the challenges has been admittedly slow in coming.

It seems to me that everything inspired is pushing us toward these two things: obedience and gratitude. The reason for obedience to things large (and especially the billion things small) is obvious. The laws that guide us also guard us, and obedience is indeed the coin of the realm. However, it seems less obvious why these divine forces push us toward gratitude and why gratitude is essential to our purification.

There may be many reasons, but the greatest is simply that everything God always moves us toward joy, rejoicing, miracles and revelations, and eternal vistas that can only be seen at the end of the path. Once we see how the process of our lives has brought us to true joy, then deep gratitude will follow.

Only the lives of the faithful may ever have this perspective, this vantage point of gratitude—not just for trials after we can see their value, but much more powerfully, gratitude while immersed in and during our deepest suffering.

Gratitude in this light is actually the triumph of faith. It is when faith takes our fears away and we triumph in Christ because we know there is an unfailing plan to which we gladly submit by choice.

I feel like a climber who has scaled an impossibly high mountain—mostly because it was there—and at the top found out that the everlasting vista at the end of the climb was worth the sometimes crushing process of getting there.

I also feel like my gratitude is late in coming and that these rocky cliffs and deep caverns would have not seemed so steep and dangerous had I learned gratitude years ago. So, I am shouting down the cyber canyons and listening to my voice echo through the vastness of where I've been, to warm and lift fellow climbers to the joys they don't need to wait until the summit to embrace.

Brother John

Personal Journal

December 13, 1995

This the Spirit whispers:

That which we call the "Doctrine of the Priesthood" is but a tiny glimpse of the perfect pattern of the priesthood which extends throughout all the creations of God.

The gospel is much more than we suspect. It is much broader and more perfect than the mind of man can conceive. Its perfection extends to all life, in every sphere of its creation.

November 22, 1997

The weeks since my last entry have been extremely trying. The IRS is attacking with full vigor, and demanding and making threats. I have done my best to comply with their edicts. However, great things have been happening in my life spiritually. More than at any other time in my life, I feel the veil thinning. How I rejoice in these things!

It is interesting that as my spiritual world quickly shapes itself into an invitation to penetrate the veil and speak with my beloved Master, my physical world deteriorates rapidly. Without making much comment on the matter, things do not look rosy at work. We are badly in debt, and I have been forced to take myself off the payroll to make it possible for the business to continue to function. I can't live long without income, of course. Yet, the promises of God are upon me, and I doubt nothing to be beyond His power.

Let all who read this know that my life is a complete and utter joy to me. I had never considered, nor could I have in this mortal frame, known what joy awaited me in this pursuit, and glorious journey back into the presence of God. Let all who read this know with absolute surety that this process has been worth a million times the price I have paid to achieve it. If such a price would have rendered me to atoms, yet it still would have been worth it. Let all who read this know that I am poised upon the threshold of the eternities, and the view I behold is breathtaking, vast, eternal, glorious, and more enticing than all the wealth of all the combined worlds created by the hand of God. Such joy as eclipses the ability of my mind to comprehend lies upon me as a warm blanket of infinite love.

How little I knew of the power of my request years ago when I asked Heavenly Father to show me the way to the joy the scriptures promise. It has been an exceedingly stressful and difficult journey, and still continues to be so; but it is a paltry pittance in price compared to the glorious, unthinkably fantastic promise it purchases, and the joy it brings into the heart of man. Glory be to God! And to His Son, my Savior!!!

I don't know who may read this journal, nor do I know why I may not describe it fully here, but I urge you to seek this Jesus, the face of God, to seek Him with fasting and tears until you find Him.

May 27, 1998

Many months have passed since my last entry, but a great deal has occurred. The IRS battle is only now beginning to be laid to rest. By following the urgings of the Spirit, I have found a couple of men who have helped me, and in a few days things are beginning to come to an end. For this I rejoice.

The business continues to be up and down. We are struggling to keep things going, and expanding at the same time. I have so many things going on that I am stressed to the point of breaking.

My spirituality has been up and down as well in the recent trials of life. I find it hard to keep a spiritual high when my world is crumbling around me. I suppose this is not unusual. However, I do struggle to keep going, and keep progressing. I was rereading my earlier entries, and I had to marvel at the memory of what I wrote. That had been a wonderful time, but the joy ended following a stressful family matter that arose after that last entry was made. I let my fear and sorrow sap the spiritual strength right out of me.

Now I am determined to regain lost ground, to reorder my life to obedience, and to walk in exactness once again. It is too wonderful of a way to live to long exist outside its glorious embrace.

I must confess that my joy is all in Christ, and I yearn and pray for the sweetness of His presence constantly. What joy there is in His love, what peace, and solace, and consolation! He is everything, and I count myself among the most blessed on the earth.

Chapter Seven

Navigating the Plan of Salvation

O Wretched Man

I believe Nephi spoke for all humanity when he exclaimed, "O wretched man that I am! Yea, my heart sorroweth because of my flesh; my soul grieveth because of my iniquities. I am encompassed about because of the temptations and the sins which do so easily beset me. And when I desire to rejoice, my heart groaneth because of my sins" (2 Nephi 4: 16–18).

Which of us upon a path of yearning and seeking for righteousness has not said equivalent words and mourned that we are so weak, so prone to return to the same old sins, to hear the same old temptations, and to be attracted to the same old sins and addictions? Who among us has not promised in prayer to never again— and then faltered again?

The truth is, we all have. I can say this with great certainty, not just because I have also walked this marshy path but because it is the human condition.

Let me back up a few billion years and try to make sense of what we are now experiencing.

We do not know how long we lived as spirit children in the premortal world, but it was most likely billions of years. The earth itself is billions of years old, so no matter how recently Adam was placed upon it, its creation was a very ancient event. And we as spirit children existed prior to the creation of the earth. With Joseph's permission, Sidney Rigdon wrote and taught that Christ began His ministry as our Savior 1.9 billion years prior to the creation of the Earth.

It is my belief that during all of those billions of years, we were learning and growing in ways far too magnificent for us to comprehend now. I believe we participated in the creation of the earth and everything appertaining to this earth, the sun, and the system around which it revolves. We learned how to create worlds, plant life, animals, and to sustain them upon the earth. We learned how to ignite a sun and keep it burning for millions of years. We did this because it was our heritage.

We talk about someday becoming like God over a long process of experience, obedience, and atonement. But that process began long before our birth as mortals. We saw God our Father and our Heavenly Mother do these things, and we inherited from Them the desire and capacity to do the same. We learned from Them and participated in those labors. We were those who said, "We will go down."

The telestial earth and everything about it were created to be flawed. Opposition was ordained by God. Every good thing was balanced with an evil thing. Every element of life was balanced with looming death. Every act of love was balanced by hate, good by evil, and right by wrong. All of these things we had to experience were opposed so that we could have agency and thereby demonstrate that we would obey (see 2 Nephi 2).

Father Himself described the purpose of the earth thus: "We will go down, for there is space there, and we will take of these materials, and we will make an earth whereon these [meaning, you and I] may dwell; and we will prove them herewith [via mortality], to see if they will do all things whatsoever the Lord their God (Jesus Christ) shall command them" (Abraham 3:24–25).

Because our bodies are made from the earth, they are subject to the laws of mortal opposition. The spirit within us, that eternal part of us which learned vast things, that commanded great knowledge and possessed sweeping truths and righteous accomplishment, was completely hidden by the flesh at birth. In other words, everything Nephi was lamenting as "wretched" was that part of him which was mortal.

Nephi said, "Yea, my heart sorroweth *because of my flesh*; my soul grieveth because of my iniquities. I am encompassed about [because the flesh is all-encompassing] because of the temptations and the sins which do so easily beset me."

With all of his prophetic strengths, experiences, and righteous desires, Nephi could not stop the mortal part of him from acting its ordained role to subjugate the spirit. He could not stop his mind from evil thoughts, nor his flesh from desiring sin.

As long as we are mortal, these pollutions inherent to mortality and to our flesh will not cease. But by yielding to the enticings of the Holy Spirit, we may "put off" the natural man (see Mosiah 3:19). The flesh still connects us to opposition, but in Christ we are innocent, even though the stench of opposition still surrounds us.

So, here we are on earth, unavoidably mortal, swilling in evil, and we look to Christ to deliver us. He speaks to us via the still small voice, and when we set a course for our lives of obedience to Him and repent through His name, He covers our mortal condition with His infinite grace. He counts us worthy even while the mortal condition continues. We become "perfect in Christ" because in Him, we can remain in the mortal condition, yet be counted clean.

But here's the thing we are prone to overlook: Even when He applies the atoning blood and washes us clean, He does not deliver us from the mortal condition. He forgives us of our sins but does not silence the temptations or abate the addictions. He counts us worthy and blesses us with great and glorious views, miracles and majestic love, but He does not lift us from the sewer of worldliness. The feathers of prior disobedience remain on the wind, and the mortal condition continues as long as we draw mortal breath. There is a renewing process of rebirth and rejuvenation whereby the feathers on the wind are gathered in, and the consequence as well as the accountability for past sins are wiped away. However, even when that occurs, the pull of mortality never lessens.

Too many people stop themselves in their journey because they judge themselves unworthy to proceed. Their natural man screams profane things too loudly, they think, for them to really be clean. The adversary helps them think, "If I were really forgiven, or born again, or if I were really a disciple, or if I were really a true Latter-day Saint, or a righteous father, mother, daughter or son—I would not still be tempted by these old sins. O wretched man that I am!"

Let us stop judging ourselves by our mortal condition and rather by our relationship with Christ. Let us believe that His grace

is sufficient when we humble ourselves in obedience to His voice—
even though the war rages on.

The fact that it does cannot soil the spotless white of who we
really are, through Jesus Christ.

Brother John

The Winds of Mortality

One of the questions I get asked quite often is if
pursuing a course of righteousness makes your life harder.
Does it just add trials, opposition, and pain that we could
avoid by just doing the minimum to qualify for eternal life while in
mortality?

I have considered this question for some time now. The expected
reward has to be significantly compensating for the struggle, or
people just won't do it. I'm pretty stubborn and determined in spiritual matters, but I have also wondered many times if I was just
making my life harder by pursuing the higher road.

Many years ago I was wading through a terrible time of trial
and heartache. In the midst of horrendous opposition, I had been
fasting several times weekly, and pleading with the Lord that I
might receive greater spiritual strength and to learn the path He
would have me take. One afternoon I was walking through my
home when suddenly in my mind I saw a vision of my life up to
that point. The experience seemed to go on for a long time, but no
actual time elapsed.

Through my spiritual eyes, I watched myself from above as
well as from behind. I noted that the path I should have taken,
and eventually did, was rather short and straight, and led directly
upward to the light—the end goal. Then I watched my life as I
made both good and bad decisions. The good decisions moved me
upward a little ways, but then my incorrect decisions sent me down
many long, painful paths that did not move me forward. During
those times, there was opposition, sorrow, and significant trials—
all of which I sensed were engineered to push me back onto the
straight and narrow way. I then made a series of correct decisions

by following the voice of the Holy Spirit and gained significant forward progress before allowing myself to be bumped off of the path again.

Here's the interesting thing: Even when I was on the *right* pathway, I still had trials of the same intensity—except that I was prayerful and humble, willing to learn and grow, so these trials pushed me upward instead of sideways.

I also saw that the vast majority of the trials I experienced were while I was *not* on the pathway of light and truth. During those times, my trials were grueling and exhausting; but I was given to know that they were necessary in humbling and motivating me to return to the true course.

In my little view of my life, I saw that I had traveled a hundred hard miles for every mile on the straight and narrow path. Those hundred miles were by far the hardest. By the time the vision closed up a nano second later, I had learned a great lesson that I've never forgotten.

Another metaphor of mortal life might be that life is a mighty windstorm that always blows. We are going to live our life in the biting winds of mortality, no matter if we are on the path or off. The only difference is, when we are off of the path, obeying our own will and the demands of the flesh, the pounding winds don't move us upward toward eternal life but rather blow us sideways. We are being compelled to be humble by the winds of mortality, which is a painful process with little upward movement.

When we finally humble ourselves and choose to walk the straight path, especially when we permanently declare our discipleship and our determination to obey forevermore, then the mighty winds push us *upward* along the path. Instead of humbling us with sorrow and pain, they begin to purify and gift us with faith sufficient to work miracles, see visions, and claim the greater blessings. The trials still don't end or even lessen, but the voice of revelation guides, protects, and sanctifies us throughout our wind-tossed life.

In my estimation it is actually far more difficult to experience mortality on the forbidden pathways, where the sting of mortality is not swallowed up by faith, hope, and revelatory knowledge. While traveling dark pathways we are left to ourselves, with only

Satan's buffetings as our companion . . . a lonely and difficult journey indeed.

So, I would answer the question, is life harder when we are on the path? I say no! It is approximately the same, either on or off. The glorious difference is that when we are on the straight path, we are purified by life's struggles rather than battered into submission by them. We experience the empowerment of the Atonement while on the straight path, and walk through the fiery trials with the Lord by our side, carrying us as we let Him. Our journey becomes joyful, and soon we arrive to receive the unspeakable blessings promised to those who are true and faithful in all things.

Brother John

Saved by Grace

There is a certain mindset among us in the Church that is hostile to our spiritual growth. This is that we must by our own discipline work out our own salvation—and then "after all we can do," somewhere at the end of our lives, Jesus Christ will get involved and make up for what we were not able to do during our lifetime, and in the end we will be "saved by grace."

The flaw in this thinking is that it places upon us mere mortals a burden we cannot hope to carry. We feel that we must keep every commandment, do every good thing, raise perfect families, pay our tithing, and fulfill a thousand other laws and rules, all by obedience and self-discipline, as best we can. We toil and toil and wait for the day when it is finally enough, and Jesus Christ at lasts steps in and fills in our blanks. This false belief sets us up for a lifetime of struggle that isn't going to take us where we are anticipating.

The truth of how this works is that we are given choices. We know right and wrong because of the Light of Christ, which we receive throughout our lives by grace. So, it is by grace that we even know what is good and bad. It is by grace that we know what to do. Thus it is by grace that we receive faith, truth, insight, inspiration, direction, guidance, truth, and power from the beginning to the end of our lives.

Then, when we make a right choice, such as to say we're sorry, go to church, or forgive someone who doesn't seem to deserve it, Christ dispenses more grace and we are changed. We become more like Him by His grace. We receive "grace for grace"—our grace for His grace—and we are changed in our inner man by a small degree every time we obey Christ's voice.

Thus we live by grace every moment of every day.

The falsehood is that we must be perfect, even as God is perfect, in order to be saved in the end and at last be exalted. The truth is that we are not able to self-perfect ourselves for *any* part of the journey. The real requirement is that we become obedient to Christ's guiding voice, and then He changes, upgrades, and purifies us until we are like Him—until we become "perfect in Christ."

When we come to the end of our lives, having walked in His grace, having partaken of His upgrading and empowering Atonement, we will be "saved by grace"—not in that moment alone but throughout our entire lives. Then every knee will bow and every tongue confess that Jesus is the Christ. In that great day of judgment, we will clearly see that He created us, gave us life, He sustained our lives, taught us right from wrong, and empowered us to choose the right. He forgave us when we stumbled because He loves us and we love Him. We will worship Him then and forever because we will see that we walked our entire lives in His grace—and were, "after all we can do," *saved* by Him.

Brother John

Trailing Clouds of Glory

*I*n the course of my life, I was once harshly mistreated by a local priesthood leader. Although I had always supported and served this good brother, had not done anything amiss, and my membership was never affected, it took over ten years to fully overcome the effects of his actions. Some of the fallout dangerously affected my family, one of whom quit coming to church and never returned. But, this isn't what my story is about.

When this happened, I struggled to find my course. The first time I sought the Lord in deep and hurting prayer, I heard a single instruction. The Spirit said, "Be faithful, be fearless, and be patient." At the time I could not fathom how this miniature guidance could be my answer. I wanted a battle plan, a counter attack, and an army to back me up. Instead, I was admonished to personal obedience, to jettison fear, and to just be patient.

It was the hardest thing I ever did. To be faithful when I wanted to spew venom in every direction was honestly more than my natural man could do. I prayed, begged, and fasted for the ability to obey. When the peace finally came, I clung to it like a drowning man. By the grace of God, I did as instructed and received vast blessings. Ten thousand times I swallowed my pride with a great deal of effort and walked in the light I was given.

In time, my simple instruction proved to be the only guidance I needed. This brother's actions were only a part of my Gethsemane, and soon other flames billowed around me, threatening to destroy everything I loved. In time, by being faithful, fearless, and patient (most of the time), miracles occurred, the heavens opened, and I received a hundredfold more than I had lost. Now, looking backward and considering the vastness of the blessings that flowed from this fiery trial, it was well worth the price—*and* way too harsh to want to repeat. But, still I digress.

About twenty years after this event, long after I had recovered all that had been lost, this good brother who had mistreated me passed away. Because I had chosen to be faithful, to not resist, to not fight or counter attack (like I wanted to), I retained love in my heart for this man and him for me. Before he died, he requested that I play the organ for his funeral. I readily accepted the request. I played thirty minutes before and after the service, as well as all of the congregational hymns. When it was time for the actual service, I walked off the stand and sat in the congregation. There was a lot of well-earned praise for his life and lots of music that he loved. I was enjoying the experience when something very unexpected happened.

I looked up and saw this brother walking toward me. It was apparent to me that I was seeing him with spiritual eyes, but he looked exactly as I remembered him. He sat beside me on the bench and turned to face me.

"I asked for and received permission to come back and ask for your forgiveness," he said.

I was too amazed to be gracious, I guess, and replied in my mind, "Isn't it a little too late for that?"

He shook his head. "I'm so sorry. I just did not realize until after I had died that I had injured you so severely and so unjustly. I am ashamed of what I did. I can't progress further without your forgiveness," he said with deep seriousness.

I felt tears coming to my eyes as my heart filled with the only feeling I have ever had for him. I had continued to love him through all of the nonsense that had occurred. "I was never angry at you," I said.

"I know, but I was wrong. Please forgive me," he asked meekly again.

"You have my forgiveness with all of my heart," I replied in my heart and mind.

He smiled, nodded briefly, and then vanished from my spiritual eyes. A feeling of love and peace swept through me, which remained for a long while afterward.

This event was startling and unexpected. It was unexpected because I did not feel that this brother owed me an apology or that I had yet to forgive him. But the *reason* for his coming was more startling to me than actually seeing him. I have wondered many times at the mercy that allowed him to come to me. I can only think that his great and good life justified his receiving this extraordinary and rare opportunity. But what marvels me most is that it was necessary; that somehow he could not progress without asking for my forgiveness from the other side. I have pondered this now for many years. I confess that I still don't understand it well.

More than anything else, this experience tells me that there is a very real life beyond this one; that we go back to God trailing clouds of glory and tracking the mud of mortality upon the carpets of heaven. If we are faithful and true, it appears that sometimes we are handed a broom and given the opportunity to clean up.

Brother John

The Paradox of Opposites

I have been pondering a rather obscure principle but one which I am coming to believe is responsible for most of our blessings. I have come to think of it as the paradox of opposites.

The paradox of opposites is that to gain some great blessing we must first sacrifice the mortal equivalent of it. I know this sounds odd, so bear with me a second. I hope I can explain it in an economy of words.

Jesus Christ was speaking of this principle when He said: "If any man will come after me, let him deny himself, and take up his cross, and follow me. For whosoever will save his life shall lose it: and whosoever will lose his life for my sake shall find it" (Matthew 16:24–25).

In other words, if we want *eternal* life, we must sacrifice our *mortal* life. In all but very few cases, this sacrifice isn't to our death. But it is real, and it is as the Lord may request of us personally. This may become a sacrifice of our time, talents, or all things which we are and own. (That should sound familiar.)

Consider this scenario. Suppose someone is single for reasons beyond their control, and they desperately want to be in a loving, eternal marriage relationship. They want this for personal and for eternal reasons, and the longing is gut-wrenching. How can someone in that situation gain what they righteously desire? There is the obvious prayer and fasting, and living right, and all that. But nearly forty percent of the Church today is not married, and I'll bet they have tried and tried fasting, prayer and everything else they know to do.

I don't know exactly how this works, only that it does: This is to lay our righteous desire upon the altar and and just walk away, fully trusting in the Lord to fulfill His promises in His own due time. I know it feels counterintuitive, that in order to receive a seemingly impossible but righteous gift we must give it up and walk away.

But that is why this is the paradox of opposites. It is paradoxical to sacrifice the very thing we hope to receive. It doesn't make sense to the logical mind, but it is nonetheless true.

The gospel is rich with paradoxes, like getting kicked out of the garden of Eden in order to return to God's presence, or building an ark on dry land to escape a flood, or sacrificing your son Isaac when commanded, even though all of your future blessings were promised to come through him.

Why does this work? Because the Lord repays one hundred fold of anything we righteously "forsake" in His name. It requires a great deal of faith and trust in God to make such a sacrifice. It took monumental faith for Abraham to sacrifice Isaac, but he was willing, and it even required an angel to stop him. It is a challenging principle, but it works with eternal precision.

So, how do you lay temple marriage on the altar? Of course, one would prepare spiritually by seeking the Lord's guidance in doing this. It takes some spiritual maturity to do what I will next propose. What you will do is seek and obtain your highest level of divine communion in prayer, and in this humble state you're going to say something like:

"Lord, I have desired with all my heart to obey thy commandments to be married in the temple. I will continue to take any steps you show me and will be faithful and fearless in obedience to the greatest extent of my ability. However, I have come to realize after years of tears and trying that this goal is beyond all of my abilities, wisdom, and strength. I have come to realize that it is beyond me as a mortal. Therefore, I place this righteous desire at your feet. I now surrender my will to be married, to your plan and desire for me, whatever that may be—now or in the worlds to come. I fully accept your will for me in this life, and I covenant to be obedient in any and all other ways that you show me. I will gratefully and patiently accept being single in this life, according to your will for me. I will accept being single in the next world, if that is your will for me. I will accept being a ministering angel, or any other assignment in the next life, if that is your will for me. I am giving up my will, and placing my agency—my greatest possession—upon the altar of sacrifice. I do so without expectation of reward, with a pure heart and pure desire to please and obey Thee, worlds without end."

Do you see the power of this covenantal sacrifice? You are sacrificing your will, which in this case is a righteous desire, which makes it a lamb without spot or blemish—a glorious sacrificial gift. You are doing it with faith that His will is more glorious and rewarding than anything you could want or accomplish in your own life. This invokes the "if anyone forsake homes, spouse, or family, for my sake" clause. This covenant opens the door to an eventual hundredfold reward.

The trick is that you must absolutely mean it—that you walk away with no more fear, tears, or anxiety, and you never look back. (As a natural man or woman you could never do this; but it can be achieved as a gift of the Spirit.) You never peek over your shoulder to see if the fire has fully consumed your offering. It is gone, and you rejoice in it. The burden is lifted. It is now the Lord's burden, and you are at peace. If done properly, the only possible outcome of such a sacrifice is everlasting joy and peace—and the eventual hundredfold reward.

I learned this principle through a very soul-searing experience. It lasted about fifteen brutal years. During that time I was helpless to overcome the events that seemed to be shredding my life. I prayed and fasted and did everything I knew to do—and I must say that I gained much of the spiritual maturity I now feel from those experiences. But it did not stop or even slow down the forces that were assailing me. During that time, I was often told by the Spirit how to handle the immediate situation. It was never easy, and my directive was nearly always to prostrate my needs and my desires to the needs of others. It was very humbling, humiliating, and confusing. His will for me was most often to bless and serve the very people and circumstances that were destroying my life. It was always a few inches beyond the furthest reach of my ability, and I had to struggle and pray mightily to be able to do what He asked. But, through His mercy I was enabled to do His bidding, even without resentment.

During those years, I often wondered how this could resolve my awful struggle, but I continued and eventually gained great peace in my soul. In the end, the problem just evaporated one day, and everything that I had hoped for, and a hundredfold more, just flowed into my life. I didn't struggle, work, bargain, or even pursue it. It just came to pass, and it is so wonderful now that the years of struggle seem like a small price to have paid to receive what I now enjoy.

Which of us wouldn't be willing to invest everything we have and then wait in poverty for fifteen years to see one billion dollars in our bank account? Even more so, to fill our eternal bank account?

Ours is a small price indeed.

Brother John

The Grand Prize

Years ago, I began to be called to various priesthood leadership positions. The most astonishing thing I saw, and continue to see, was how many people were struggling desperately in some aspect of their lives. What amazed me wasn't that some folks were struggling who I hadn't been aware of because they were active and putting on a brave public face. What amazed me was that *every single* ward member was struggling in some way. In a heartbeat, my perception of my ward went from "We're mostly okay" to "We are barely surviving."

Since that time, my perception has not changed. It may sound pessimistic, but I don't feel so. I find great hope in this process. Still, it is observable that we are all struggling in some way. Those who are not currently struggling, whether they realize it or not, are just between bouts. The bell will ring, and the battle will resume. Most people, including myself, struggle in silence, putting on a brave public face, while most of their wars are fought on private battlefields.

We have a tendency to equate earthly struggles to having (or not having) wealth, beauty, and fame. We look at someone who appears to have more than "sufficient for their needs" and assume they're the lucky ones. We look at those who we think have very little and assume they're living a hard life. The truth, I believe, is that struggle is universal and that wealth, beauty, and fame are actually catalysts to struggle. (In other words, they cause struggle, rather than solve it.) These powerful worldly attributes more often erect walls to oppose growth rather than perpetuate it.

The world offers up irresistible temptations, creates arrogance and pride that separate us from the Spirit, draws people into our lives who love us for the wrong reasons, darkens our children's minds, and sucks the Spirit from our lives far more efficiently than poverty, ugliness, or obscurity. The most efficient lie we believe is that the world alone offers joy and safety. A surprising commentary on wealth is that almost 100 percent of those who win large sums in a lottery find that it had destroyed their lives, and many ultimately wish they had not won it.

This expanded perspective is also why we "wizened" older people are not jealous of the young and the beautiful, because we were once the young and the beautiful and have since walked a steeply upward path away from those things to obtain the peace and spiritual safety we enjoy. Like war refugees, we prefer our lives on this side of young and beautiful, wealthy and famous.

There is only one price mortals pay for spiritual anchorage, for peace which surpasses the understanding of man, for standing upon a "sure foundation" during the storms, and a "sure knowledge" of eternal glory. This price is the 100-million-dollar check for winning the spiritual lottery of mortality, and it is two-fold. We paid the first part of it when we chose to enter mortality to allow the "mighty storm" to beat upon us. This is why we agreed to come to earth, to experience this degree of fiery opposition. Without it we were powerless to progress, and we had to choose it. We weren't sentenced to mortality; we chose it with a shout of joy—and thus made a hefty down payment upon eternity.

Second, we must pay the price to figure out that we cannot succeed by our own strength and our own genius, force of will, wealth, beauty, and personal charm. Mortality is designed specifically to beat that nonsense from our "young and beautiful" minds. When we finally have suffered enough of life to realize we cannot survive or succeed alone, then we are ready to take Jesus Christ as our sure foundation. When we cast our burdens on Him and give up trying to "work out our own salvation" by our own works, intellect, and stubborn will, when we finally know our own nothingness, then Jesus Christ steps in and becomes our strength and deliverance, hope, joy, and safety.

The trials don't end at that moment, but the struggle can. We can cease to fear and worry and doubt because the mighty opposition of mortality has "no power over you." We know in whom we trust, and we walk through the "mighty storm" without fear, only needing to place each footfall on the straight path as He guides us along. There can be far less struggle because there is only trust—and hence no fear and no eternal danger. "Thy will be done" makes the dark, thundering horizon of no consequence and gives us confidence with each guided step that peace and safety, power and truth, life and light are blossoming beneath our feet every moment of our lives.

And *that* is the grand prize.

Brother John

Stand for Truth and Righteousness

I admire people of great courage. I think of Mormon and Moroni standing with swords drawn, facing vastly superior armies, knowing they must soon die, yet with courage and confidence sufficient to motivate tens of thousands to stand with them. I think of Paul before King Agrippa after having been beaten, scourged, and bloodied for his testimony of Jesus, yet still with courage to declare the name of Christ, willing to die for the truth that was coming out of his mouth.

I have always assumed that these great ones enjoyed a unique fearlessness they had obtained through miraculous experiences, visions, or visitations. I now believe that such miraculous witnesses act upon our confidence in Christ and less upon our fear. I do not believe Moroni felt significantly less fear than those standing next to him. I just believe he felt supreme confidence that he was supposed to be exactly there, doing exactly as he was. He was willing to set aside his fear because he knew he was on the Lord's mission. His courage wasn't an absence of fear; it was a triumph of fear through faith in God, which faith came from knowing he was at that very moment doing the Lord's will.

Years ago, I was a new counselor in a bishopric and attended my first New Beginnings meeting with the Young Women. The Laurel class president stood and after a brief testimony asked, "Who will stand with me for truth and righteousness?" Every young woman except the incoming Beehives and me stood at once and shouted, "I will!" It was a stunning moment for me and for those young Beehives. They looked up at their older Sister Moroni standing there, wanting to be just like her. Then at the close of her talk, the president asked again, "Who will stand with me for truth and righteousness?" This time everyone, including the new Beehives and myself, stood and shouted, "I will!" and we all meant it. I still do.

Standing for truth and righteousness isn't by definition standing defiantly before murderous armies or mobs; it is knowing that you *should* be standing there.

Jesus was asked by Pilate, "What is truth?" Christ had actually answered that question months earlier. To His beloved and fearing disciples, He had said, "*I* am the truth." In other words, we may only know the truth of any circumstance or moment of our lives after He has revealed it to us.

Righteousness is when, after we know the truth, we act upon it with unflinching courage. Knowing the truth makes us informed; acting in obedience to truth makes us righteous. So, to declare that we will "stand for truth and righteousness" is to declare that having obtained the truth by attuning oneself to the voice of Christ, we will act upon that truth, no matter the consequence.

This is the bedrock of all spiritual greatness. This is why and how Moroni defied armies, and why and how Paul and all others like him seemed fearless and unflinching in their willingness to serve Jesus, even unto their own death. It is why Joseph did not crumple under vile persecution, false imprisonment, betrayal by his dearest friends, apostasy of those who had beheld visions with him, and even martyrdom—because he "stood for truth and righteousness" and that alone.

It is also how and why Jesus Christ wrought out the perfect atonement by the shedding of His own blood. And it is how you and I will proceed in these times of uncertainty and fear as we enter the end times, when all that we know will change. We will "stand for truth and righteousness"—and that alone.

Brother John

Personal Journal

September 20, 1998

I arose early this morning to read the scriptures before church. However, I felt as if I needed to add to my journal before studying.

It has been an interesting period of time. The stress of my life finally became so severe that I begged the Lord for relief. I knew if I didn't find some relief soon I was going to have problems. I was growing physically ill and aging rapidly.

Now, two weeks later, I rejoice that the Lord has answered my pleadings so magnificently. The IRS audit was settled. The conclusion was "no change" on the tax returns and no additional taxes due. I now have enough money to get the business through the winter, and my family crises have abated. Everything that was previously tearing at my soul has been or is in the process of being resolved.

Even so, my spiritual journey has been a bit faltering of late. I take a huge step forward and have a wonderful experience, but then it cools off rapidly. I have never been one to jerk about on my progress. It is frustrating to me. However, I think that the next few steps in my journey are glorious, and I need to make certain preparations that I am struggling with. One of these is purity of life. By that I mean, to live, think, and act with purity in all things. I am probably 96% there or more.

That last 4% has been a struggle. It is so precise in its demands that it precludes things like types of music, all TV, and many types of entertainment that I would otherwise seek and enjoy. It has proven to tax my abilities. Yet, I also realize that all these things solely come by virtue of grace and the gifts of the Spirit. So I'm determined, through the grace of Christ, to rise above all things. It is not a situation to which one (at least not I) may rise in a moment.

I am often reminded, and I understand that the blessings I seek are profound, and the opposition and effort required to achieve them is profound as well. I am only equal to the task as the Lord pours out His Holy Spirit upon me and brings me toward Him. I rejoice in the journey, as well as the point of arrival.

There is one thing I would say in conclusion. It is this: There is fantastic joy to be had in the process of righteousness. It is not only that the end result brings joy, but that the journey brings joy. If it were not so, I think no one would have the courage to seek and find it.

September 2, 1999

Much has happened since my last entry. The Lord seems to have opened the windows of heaven and poured out upon my head such unique and marvelous blessings I never before anticipated or truly even contemplated. One of these is an almost constant company of the Holy Ghost. It has had the effect of opening my mind to greater truth and of teaching me many things I had never known before.

Now, one may ask, what things? Or they may say, write these truths down!

But I can't. It isn't that type of teaching, but rather an internal, personal-to-me education in the things of righteousness. It would take more words than I could write in my lifetime to detail it all, and it would not be understandable. They are things like the nearness of the veil, the power in prayer, the use of sacred words and symbols, and other things that cannot be written. They are such things that I could not write them down if I tried. But, it truly is marvelous, and I have never been happier or more filled with the Spirit.

February 19, 2002

A few years have elapsed since I last recorded in this journal. The main reason for this is that I have been so happy, so full of the Spirit, and carried away in the process of living, loving, and rejoicing in Christ, that I have felt little need to write. It is probably folly, since the greatest blessings we receive are often whispered and then forgotten by the passage of time.

Here is what I will say: I have had marvelous blessings and spiritual manifestations in my life. I have pursued the course to the greater blessings, calling upon God to fill me with truth regarding the true course, the true destination, and the true righteousness that brings them forth. It has been a glorious adventure, and an eternally rewarding one.

Glory be to God!

March 26, 2003

While in the Provo Temple while my daughter received her personal endowments, some understanding was added to my understanding of the temple ceremony. This experience took the form of a question-and-answer session. At various points in the temple endowment the Spirit would ask me a question, then answer it.

These last few years I feel as if I am the most blessed mortal. I have marvelous prayers, and when my prayers are properly considered, I have answers every time to every request. I often hear the voice of the Spirit powerfully instructing me. I often hear words of comfort and cheer. His voice is kind and never chastises. It "upbraideth not." I could write volumes about things I have learned, seen, and heard.

I have also learned that the final step which separates man from the veil is purity. It is not purity in the sense of an absence of sin, but purity of soul, of thought, of belief, and being. It is entirely possible to be as sinless as mankind can be, and yet to harbor lies in your heart. I speak of lies like, "I'm not a lovable person," or "I'll never be as faith-filled as I want to be," or "I'm ugly," or any of a million other lies we teach ourselves and our children. The purity which the beatitudes proclaim will entitle a soul to see God is the purity of soul which makes us like children, unsullied, and unstained by false thinking. It is a lifelong process to achieve it—it is a gift of God.

Chapter Eight

Covenants and Priesthood Power

Simpleness of the Way

Quite a few years ago I had a series of earaches. Each one seemed worse than the last. I went to the doctor and got antibiotics, and every time it took longer to get better. That was back when every trip to the doctor was a bag of groceries we couldn't buy, so I delayed going each time, hoping it would just go away. It was late Sunday evening and my earache was intolerable. I decided I couldn't wait until Monday morning and was going to go to the emergency room. As I was putting on my coat the thought occurred to me to ask for a priesthood blessing. Both my father and brother were there following a family dinner. During all of this it had not yet occurred to me to ask for a blessing.

I sat on a chair in my living room. My brother anointed me and my father gave me a blessing. I was blessed to get better instantly and not need to go to the doctor. As Dad said this, my mind was still spinning with the cost and complication of going to the emergency room. I was in intense pain and apprehension.

Then Dad took his hands off of my head and said, "Well, that was a powerful blessing. I've done my part, so don't blame me if you're not healed." The statement rather startled me. I'm not sure if he meant it to be encouraging, or questioning, or what. But as soon as those words came from his lips, my ear was healed. It was so sudden that I was jolted by it. All pain left. My ear instantly opened up and I could hear from it. I opened my jaw a few times and found that everything was normal.

"I'm healed," I said rather softly. "My ear is healed." My ear was completely well and stayed that way.

As I sat there in the chair contemplating the miracle I had just experienced, all of a sudden I had a strange thought go through my mind: "Well, that was simple."

It was almost anticlimactic. A few seconds ago I was headed to the hospital, anticipating weeks of pain and months of bills I could hardly pay. Then, in that instant it was all over, and my reaction to it was that it felt "simple."

Over the years I have discovered that the joy of our Savior is to make our lives simple. In one moment we're facing some overwhelming challenge, and then in an instant it is gone—simple. In one moment we are overwhelmed with confusion and daunting challenges, and then the answer comes and it is all over—simple. One minute we are on a life-long struggle to become born again or to find the blessings of calling and election; but then a glorious moment later, and the journey is over. Simple.

It has taken me longer to realize that every time I receive a prompting, my Savior is trying to simplify my life. I receive a prompting to drive the speed limit, and by ignoring it, I complicate my life with the unfolding consequences. When I obey, nothing dramatic usually happens. But unrecognized blessings surround me with safety, and my life just seems simple. Yet whether I knew it or not, the miracle did occur. I was protected. I didn't get a ticket or have an accident, or I unknowingly avoided dangers that may have resulted from speeding that day. It has taken me years of experience to develop eyes of faith to see the "simpleness of the way."

On the flip side, nearly every time my life has imploded or exploded, there was some moment when I knew a better choice and didn't take it. "I knew that was going to happen!" has almost become idiomatic and axiomatic, we say it so often. We just rarely analyze why we know these things—because Christ tried to show us a simpler way, and we childishly insisted on proceeding with our own way.

The fact is that anytime Christ speaks to us, teaches us, or atones for us, He is simplifying our lives. Not only is this true, but the way that we hear Him—and the fact that His voice is present in every moment of our lives, embedded within the covenants we make or in the inspired priesthood blessings we receive—is simple.

We don't have to fight for it or even qualify for it. His voice is just there—simple.

He leadeth me beside the still waters—simple.

Brother John

The Lord's Priesthood Mantle

*N*ot quite ten years ago I was called as a counselor in a bishopric. Prior to that time I had served in many capacities but never in a bishopric. The stake had just created the ward and called our new bishop and his new counselors. I will remember our first bishopric meeting for a long time. We didn't have a single teacher or Young Men or Young Women leader. We didn't have Primary people, piano players, quorums, or anything else. We just sat there waiting for our poor new bishop to give us a direction. His opening statement was something like, "Don't look at me!"

We laughed and talked about many things. Finally, a thought came into my mind. "Call Brother Stevens as the Young Men president."

I opened my mouth to propose this calling when the bishop said, "What about Brother Stevens as the Young Men's President?"

I wondered at this, and said, "I feel the rightness of that calling, Bishop."

Our other counselor agreed, and the bishop assigned himself to make the calling. While he was writing, I had another thought. "Call Sister Wilson as the Young Women president."

I was just about to propose this name, when the additional thought came to me to keep quiet for a moment. After the bishop was done writing he tapped his pen on the desktop for a moment. "What do you brethren think about Sister Wilson as the Young Women president?"

I nodded and tried to say, "I was just going to propose her name," but the Spirit put on my lips, "I agree. I think she would be wonderful."

This process went on in our meetings for about a month, until the ward was fully functioning. It really didn't seem to matter how big or small the calling was or what the challenge was; I almost always heard the same prompting the bishop heard. Maybe the angels were just talking loudly in the room and I was allowed to eavesdrop.

Not long after the initial organization of the ward, we were talking about a potential calling for a ward member. I had not felt a prompting as before and for that reason doubted it was the right thing to do. My mind suddenly went back to a dozen years prior, when I had sat on a disciplinary council as a high councilor. I said, "I don't think Brother Black is ready for this calling. A dozen years ago I sat on a disciplinary council for him . . ." and the Spirit told me to shut up. It was an interesting prompting. "Stop! Be quiet!"

I closed my mouth mid-sentence. The bishop looked at me funny. I said, "I shouldn't have said that. It has no bearing on the present."

The Bishop frowned. "You know, as you said the word 'disciplinary council' I had the thought, 'He shouldn't have said that. It has no bearing on the present.' They were the same words you just used. I think the Holy Ghost just talked to me!" He seemed amazed.

I looked at him with different eyes. I realized that recognizing promptings was not what this brand new bishop had been doing these last few weeks. He had been receiving promptings and attributing them to his own intellect. He thought he was just a good organizer. The whole idea that the Holy Ghost would talk directly to him was astounding to him.

A new, fully developed thought came into my mind. I suddenly knew that teaching our humble new bishop to identify the revelation he already had was one of the reasons I was called to this bishopric. I waited a moment while the Holy Spirit warmed my soul. I said, "These last few weeks, as we organized the ward, just a few seconds before you would propose each new name, I would have the same name pop into my head. I knew it was from the Holy Spirit, and when you came up with the same name, it just confirmed that I had heard it correctly. This has happened consistently."

The Bishop laid down his pen. "Why didn't you say something? It would have helped me feel more certain about the callings to have known that."

I replied, "It wasn't necessary. The Spirit told me in each case to just concur with my bishop. I was never told to say why."

The bishop let his chair lean back as he considered this. "I think Heavenly Father has been trying to teach me how to hear the Holy Ghost. I have been having these names come into my head. Is this what the Holy Ghost sounds like, just a thought? I mean, can you trust these ideas that just pop into your head to be from the Holy Ghost?"

Our other counselor said at that moment, "I've been having some of the names come into my mind, too, but not all of them. I was wondering what was going on. I thought we were just brain-storming or something. Is that really what revelation feels like?"

They were both looking at me, and I was waiting for the Holy Spirit to put words into my mouth. After a long moment I said, "Revelation almost always feels like our own ideas. The difference is that the ideas are usually sudden, probably something or someone you wouldn't have thought of yourself, and they are accompanied by a feeling of rightness, or truth. Once you learn to recognize this revelatory process, you can identify it every time—and you can trust it every time. It is never wrong."

Our newly minted bishop wiped tears from his eyes. "I have been praying all my life to receive revelation and never felt that I could, even though I have had sudden ideas like this my whole life. Ever since I was called as the bishop I have been praying with all my heart, with great urgency, that the Lord would teach me how to receive revelation so I could truly be a good bishop and not just someone sitting in this chair."

I felt a surge of joy. I wiped tears from my eyes, too. "We have had constant revelation in this bishopric ever since the first meet-ing we held almost a month ago. Almost every decision we have made, I felt the approval of Heavenly Father." I looked at the bishop intently. "Whether you knew it or not, you are one of the most inspired bishops I have ever known."

I continued to receive confirmations as the bishop administered to his ward, but he didn't need me anymore. I would often just nod, and he would smile because he valued my accord, but he didn't need it. The Lord's priesthood mantle had settled upon him, and he was "the bishop." And in a humble, yet powerful way, he knew it.

Brother John

Words That Work Miracles

One of the joys of teaching the gospel is watching people's lives change. It is a miracle to me, sometimes as vast as raising the dead, because they transition someone from spiritual death to being alive in Christ. And I've come to learn that priesthood blessings can do the same.

I would like to tell you about someone I'll call Jake. I mentioned him in a previous post about teaching the adult institute class. I actually taught that class for nearly ten years, and loved every minute of it. During that time it was not uncommon for a sister who was attending to get excited and drag her unwilling husband to class. Jake was one of the dragged-hither ones.

The first day I met him, he told me in blunt terms before class that he did not want to be there and then proceeded to sit right next to me at the high council room table. I stood to greet the class. "I would like to welcome everyone . . ."

He interrupted loudly with, "Well, if you would like to, why don't you go ahead and do it?"

I ignored this and dozens of other snide comments during that class and for many following. Each week he ratcheted up his aggression a little. His wife apologized mightily each week, but she desperately wanted him to experience the Holy Spirit and continued to tow him forth with my blessing.

About a month into this process, I was teaching a lesson on being born again, and notwithstanding Jake's barrage of funny/rude/disruptive comments, the Spirit was present. I was remaining calm and ignoring him, when all of the sudden the Spirit put words in my mouth. To this day I can hardly believe I let them out of my lips. (Believe me, these things usually work best when you don't filter them through your own intellect.)

"Jake," I said, "we have listened to your rudeness for several months now, and I want you to stop. Your behavior is childish, aggressive, and unbecoming a priesthood holder. If you really don't want to come, just tell your wife you're staying home. If you choose to come, please act like an adult. We love you, but we want to experience the things of God without your interruptions."

I turned back to the class, the Spirit still present (which was a miracle), and I finished the lesson. Jake did not make a single wisecrack after that, but he did raise his hand and contribute several very thoughtful comments. I was rather surprised. He was the kind of person who would have actually enjoyed telling me off in public and then storming from the building with a cloud of self-justification swirling behind him.

After the closing prayer, I expected Jake to roar out of the room. He didn't. He waited until I was alone and approached me.

"Brother Pontius, you were kind of hard on me tonight," he began.

I started to apologize, but he shook his head. "No, don't apologize. I had it coming. I'm an obnoxious SOB and I know it. It takes a lot of courage to say what you did, and I really respect that. I don't respect people who just let me ride over them and say nothing at all—which most everybody does. I really am enjoying this class, so if you let me keep coming, I promise to act like an adult. And, if I don't, I give you full permission to call me out on it, just like you did tonight."

I shook his hand. "I like you, Jake," I told him. "You are welcome in my class anytime."

Jake smiled. "I can probably change that welcome over time. Very few people like me, and I know why. I just don't know how to change it. I don't go to church much because I just make people angry at me. I don't really want to do that, but I honestly don't know how to stop."

The Spirit nudged me again. "Jake, would you like a priesthood blessing?"

He thought about this for a moment and then nodded. We closed the doors to the room, his wife sat next to us, and I gave him a blessing. I was almost shocked at how profusely the Spirit poured down upon us and how freely the words flowed. The essence of the message was that Jake's aggression had served him well throughout his childhood. It had protected him. Now, with the blessing of his Savior, he was promised that his aggression was going to turn into leadership, and his innate ability to inspire and command would be essential to completing his life's mission.

By the close of the blessing we were amazed because we had each felt the profound presence of the Holy Ghost. Although the words seemed entirely improbable to the rough-hewn fellow receiving that blessing, and to the speaker of the words, the Spirit bore powerful witness that they were true. His wife wept, and Jake stood and gave me a big hug.

Jake became my very good friend, and he still is. We have enjoyed many special times together, including flying in his private plane over the pristine beauty of Alaska's wilderness. When I introduce him to friends I usually say, "This is Jake—he's an acquired taste. In time you'll love him, too." He usually laughs, then proceeds to be himself, and soon everyone understands why he's an acquired taste. But before the evening's over, they begin to love him like I do.

What is unusual about Jake isn't that he's obnoxious, nor that he's amazingly brilliant, or that he has a very high IQ and an incredible memory. It isn't even that he was kicked out of his home at a very young age, raised as an orphan, ran away several times, and was abused until he joined the Navy at age seventeen, or that he is now one of my most beloved friends. What is really inspiring about Jake is that he's become humble, teachable, even powerful. He loves the truth, and he is willing to sacrifice to follow the light he now clearly perceives. He is one of the most inspired and insightful people I know.

I have known Jake for almost twenty years now, and he has grown in every way to the stature of that blessing. He has taught me a great deal—especially not to fear to speak the words Christ puts into my mouth. Because no matter how hard or improbable they may seem, when they are *His* words, they always work miracles.

Brother John

The Extraordinary Meaning of the Sacrament

Shauna asked if the sacrament prayers are referring to the Holy Ghost or to Jesus Christ. I looked back through the UnBlog and found, to my surprise, that I had not addressed the power of the sacramental covenant.

The sacrament, what it does for us, and why we take it so often is not clearly understood by most. We have often been taught that we are renewing our baptismal covenants, and we are—in a round-about way. Unfortunately, baptism does not actually include a clearly stated covenant.

Mosiah 18 is most often given as where to find the covenants we make at baptism. We find that those people covenanted to:

> Bear one another's burdens;
> Mourn with those that mourn;
> Comfort those that stand in need of comfort;
> Stand as a witness of God in all places—even unto death;
> Be redeemed of God and numbered with those of the first resurrection,
>> that we may have eternal life.

Now let's look at today's sacrament prayers. Here we promise to:

> Eat and drink in remembrance of the body and blood of Christ;
> Witness that we are willing to take upon ourselves the name of
>> Christ;
> Always remember Him;
> Keep His commandments;
> Always have His Spirit to be with us (the crowning blessing).

We can easily see that there is little similarity between what Alma's people covenanted to do, and what we are promising through partaking of the sacrament today. They are different because this is a different dispensation.

God led Alma to place his people under a contract to support one another and to be fearless in being followers of Christ so that they would gain eternal life. But He has a greater challenge for this dispensation: We are to live so that by taking upon ourselves the name of Christ, remembering Him and keeping His commandments, we can *always* walk in the light of continuing revelation. In other words, not only must we do the things that Alma's people promised, but we must do everything that Jesus Christ, through the voice of the Holy Spirit, sends us forth to do.

Alma's covenant is rather static; it is Law-of-Moses-esque: Do these acts so that you can have eternal life.

The latter-day covenant is living, dynamic, and profound. The term "His Spirit" is referencing the Spirit of Jesus Christ. It is the Light of Christ, that which begins as our conscience, the Holy Spirit, and the still small voice. We are to become creatures of Christ, walking in continuing revelation, going forth in obedience, speaking under inspiration, serving every time we are inspired to serve, and acting as Christ would act if He were present. And all these things are done "in the name of Jesus Christ." This is the greater covenant and the higher law.

Only those in this dispensation who have taken the Holy Spirit to be their guide will survive the trials and trauma of these days and be invited to the wedding feast at Christ's coming. Consider the warning and blessings promised to those who fulfill this sacred covenant:

> For they that are wise and have received the truth, and have taken the Holy Spirit for their guide, and have not been deceived—verily I say unto you, they shall not be hewn down and cast into the fire, but shall abide the day.
>
> And the earth shall be given unto them for an inheritance; and they shall multiply and wax strong, and their children shall grow up without sin unto salvation.
>
> For the Lord shall be in their midst, and his glory shall be upon them, and he will be their king and their lawgiver. (D&C 45:56–59)

This is the extraordinary meaning of the sacramental covenant: It is that we covenant to become the wise virgins and take the Holy Spirit to be our guide, build Zion, and invite Christ to return and become our King. This is both the tragedy and the triumph of our dispensation. It is a tragedy because we scarcely understand it, and a triumph because in time, we certainly will.

Brother John

Looking at the Veil

*I*f you walk into a theater and there is a beautiful, black grand piano on the stage, what do you expect to hear?

If you walk into a theater and there is a movie screen on the stage, what would you expect to see?

If you walk into a theater and there is a trapeze and net, what do you expect to experience?

If you walk into a room and on the stage there is a large white temple veil—not a sheet of fabric representing death, but a sacred curtain that represents the veil that presently separates us from seeing and speaking with God—what would you expect the purpose of that meeting will be?

I would expect that the end object would be to teach me something about the veil. And, when I was finally standing at the veil, wearing a symbol of mortality, I would know that I was being taught that I could approach the veil in this life to speak with God and then how to enter in to actually be with God.

When we enter the temple, we sometimes become lost in the events, symbolism, clothing, words, and ceremony of it all—and we forget that in reality, we are sitting there looking at the veil.

Brother John

An Endowment

*R*ecorded in scripture and taught in the temple is the pattern to seeing God. When a person has traveled the high road of righteousness, has obtained the right to fully claim the blessings of the Atonement, and has been purified by fire, then this pattern will be repeated again on our behalf. Each account of a mortal speaking with God is a little different, but there are also great similarities.

First, we are shown a vision of the workmanship of Jesus Christ's hands. Moses saw this vision and penned the book of Genesis. Every prophet who records his personal experience with the Lord in any detail includes seeing a sweeping vision of his future ministry and quite often, of the entire history of the world—sometimes of the whole workmanship of God's hands. The list is too long to mention them all. All of the Old Testament prophets saw this grand vision: Isaiah, Jeremiah, Abraham, and Enoch, to name a few. John the Beloved recorded a portion of his vision in the book of Revelation. Lehi saw and mentioned his vision. Nephi, inspired by his father's account, saw and recorded parts of his vision in 1 Nephi. The brother of Jared saw the vision and wrote what is now the sealed portion of the Book of Mormon, purportedly the greatest literary work ever written. Mormon saw our day. Moroni wrote to us with prophetic vision because he saw and knew us intimately. Joseph Smith recorded parts of his vision in section 76.

This vision is also typified in today's temple experience. Since the actual endowment event appears to begin with a vision of all, including the creation of the earth, the temple ordinance prefiguring that same event also begins in this way.

Another consistent element of this divine experience is that we are taught and spiritually edified, and given knowledge that always eclipses what can be known by common man. Such knowledge was given to many notables such as Adam, Abraham, Moses, Daniel, Elijah, and John the Baptist. In fact, since there is only one gospel, we may safely surmise that it was given to all of the great patriarchs who entered the divine presence.

This grand vision is prefigured in this promise:

> And to them will I reveal all mysteries, yea, all the hidden mysteries of my kingdom from days of old, and for ages to come, will I make known unto them the good pleasure of my will concerning all things pertaining to my kingdom.
>
> Yea, even the wonders of eternity shall they know, and things to come will I show them, even the things of many generations.
>
> And their wisdom shall be great, and their understanding reach to heaven; and before them the wisdom of the wise shall perish, and the understanding of the prudent shall come to naught.
>
> For by my Spirit will I enlighten them, and by my power will I make known unto them the secrets of my will—yea, even those things which eye has not seen, nor ear heard, nor yet entered into the heart of man. (D&C 76:8–10)

At some point in this experience, we will be offered the chance to request a divine gift, which will be the fulness of our *actual* endowment. Although the temple ordinance is called "the endowment," it would be more correct to say it is a temple ordinance that teaches of, instructs in the laws governing, and prefigures the actual endowment. This endowment is a celestial gift that worthy men and women alike may personally request of the Lord while in His presence.

Brother John

Beyond Foundational

*There is a phenomenon in our latter-day cul-*ture that I find quite interesting. I bumped into it again two Sundays ago when I was teaching the high priests group. The lesson was on temple marriage and how to make it eternal. I chose to articulate the principle that temple marriage only has its full effect and blessing to those who actually enter into the highest degree of the celestial kingdom. Every other degree and kingdom does not offer eternal families and eternal increase. I went on to say that all ordinances, including temple ordinances, must be sealed by the Holy Spirit of Promise to be of effect into eternity.

I read multiple scriptures and statements by solid authorities to establish this principle. The point I was trying to make was that temple marriage is, in a sense, the signing of a contract that requires us to diligently seek and qualify for the celestial kingdom in order to have the ordinance of fullest value to us. This is solid and true doctrine, though I believe not well understood by many members.

One fine gentleman took exception to this and brought up an unfounded doctrine for which there is no scriptural evidence and no quotable latter-day authorities. He maintained that just the ordinance itself guaranteed us the highest degree of the celestial kingdom and that the sealer had the authority to bestow and guarantee every blessing. He spoke with loud authority.

I say he is a fine gentleman because he is presently a temple ordinance worker and a former bishop, and he loves the gospel and faithfully attends to his duties. Of course, I didn't argue. I just thanked him and went on with the lesson as if nothing had changed, and the Spirit returned. I am always of the opinion that our job is to speak the truth when prompted, not to convince anyone of it. That is the job of the Holy Spirit.

The interesting phenomenon I mentioned is that some people seem to believe that knowing the Church is "true" is the end objective of the journey. They apparently believe that after you have a "testimony" your search is over, and once you participate in the ordinances, you have "earned" exaltation. What has really happened through the ordinances is that we have, by our faithfulness thus far, been given vast promises that we must then go out and seek diligently and sacrifice to obtain.

I don't mean any of this to sound critical because this line-upon-line gospel process is the way it is supposed to work. We start from wherever our life's experience has taken us, and by belief and faith we find and embrace the truths of the gospel. Our resulting "testimony" is a triumph of faith. These things are gloriously good and foundational.

But there is so much more that builds upon this necessary foundation! There is a greater body of truth which we must obtain by diligent seeking, through greater obedience, and by hungering and thirsting after righteousness. This requires searching the scriptures, searching our souls, and earnestly searching the heavens in mighty prayer.

The scriptures testify repeatedly of the fact that those who seek *do* obtain, those who ask *do* receive, and those who knock *do* have the heavens opened unto them.

Brother John

Your Personal Temple

Years ago in a stake priesthood meeting in Idaho, I heard Elder Bruce R. McConkie ask the congregation this question: "How can you tell if you are living a life that is acceptable to God? How can you tell if you have been forgiven for a past sin you have been working to repent of?" I wrote down his answer word-for-word and have kept it all these years. He answered, "If you feel the presence of the Holy Spirit in your life, if you are receiving personal revelation, if you receive answers to your prayers—then you are in the straight and narrow way, and your sins are forgiven, because the Holy Spirit does not dwell in unholy people."

The temple is truly a place where we can receive personal revelation. Away from the cares and concerns of a telestial world, the solitude and quiet of the temple's celestial room has often been a prime location for many to hear the whisperings of a loving, giving Heavenly Father.

I remember one time several years ago when I went from an endowment session into the celestial room, I had a very strong impression to grab a Bible there in the celestial room. As I did so, I had the feeling I needed to open up to the book of Habakkuk. I could barely remember that it was a book in the Bible and thought, "Habakkuk? Habakkuk? Did we even cover that in seminary (which was decades ago)?" I found Habakkuk and was prompted to go to a specific chapter and verse—a verse which contained a perfectly worded answer to a concern I had been praying about for several days.

Besides the holy temples, there is another temple where you can receive personal revelation: yourself. The Apostle Paul wrote, "Know ye not that ye are the temple of God, and that the Spirit of God dwelleth in you? If any man defile the temple of God, him shall God destroy; for the temple of God is holy, which temple ye are" (1 Corinthians 3:16–17).

We also know the conditions under which the Spirit of the Lord will dwell within us:

Dallin H. Oaks has taught:

> The blessings available through the gift of the Holy Ghost are conditioned upon worthiness. "The Spirit of the Lord doth not dwell in unholy temples" (Hel. 4:24; see also Mosiah 2:36–37; 1 Cor. 3:16–17). Even though we have a right to His constant companionship, the Spirit of the Lord will dwell only with us when we keep the commandments. He will withdraw when we offend Him by profanity, uncleanliness, disobedience, rebellion, or other serious sins." (Dallin H. Oaks, "Always Have His Spirit," *Ensign*, Nov. 1996, 61)

The mere fact that you are receiving personal revelation means your own personal temple is functioning properly, allowing you to enjoy its attendant blessings. Conversely, if you are not receiving personal revelation, assessing the condition of your personal temple might be something to consider.

Brother John

Obtaining the Greatest Blessings

here's one other thing I'd like to mention about having "been forgiven for a past sin you have been work- ing to repent of." There is a common stumbling block that might prevent us from receiving all the blessings available, including the greatest promises prefigured in the temple.

I believe that all too often, our worst enemy is not Satan, but ourselves. President Joseph F. Smith taught: "Our first enemy we will find is within ourselves" (*Teachings of Presidents of the Church: Joseph F. Smith* (1998), 371–72).

As flawed mortals, we are prone to dwell on past mistakes and sins we have long since corrected or have taken through the repen- tance process with our bishop. We may believe that God, a being of perfect justice, is duty-bound to exact the maximum punishment for the wrongs and sins we have committed.

If you think this, if you believe this, I encourage you to stop. *God is not that kind of a being.*

If I may be so bold, could I introduce you to the Christ I per- sonally know? A very apt description comes from Elder Melvin J. Ballard, who, while serving as a missionary among the North American Indians, had a dream in which he found himself in the temple, entering one of its rooms:

"As I entered the door," Elder Ballard said, "I saw, seated on a raised platform, the most glorious Being my eyes have ever beheld or that I ever conceived existed in all the eternal worlds. As I approached to be introduced, he arose and stepped towards me with extended arms, and he smiled as he softly spoke my name. If I shall live to be a million years old, I shall never forget that smile. He took me into his arms and kissed me, pressed me to his bosom, and blessed me, until the marrow of my bones seemed to melt! When he had finished, I fell at his feet, and, as I bathed them with my tears and kisses, I saw the prints of the nails in the feet of the Redeemer of the world. The feeling that I had in the presence of him who hath all things in his hands, to have his love, his affection, and his blessing was such that if I ever can receive that of which I had but a foretaste, I would give all that I am, all that I ever hope to be, to feel what I then felt!" (Quoted by Bryant S. Hinckley, in *Sermons and Missionary Service of Melvin J. Ballard* [1949], 156)

Like His Son, our Heavenly Father has the same degree of perfect love for you and wishes and yearns for you to understand just how merciful He is. This may be why Brother Joseph once said: "Our Heavenly Father is more liberal in His views, and boundless in His mercies and blessings, than we are ready to believe or receive" (*Teachings of the Prophet Joseph Smith*, 257).

My dear friends, if you struggle to know if you have been forgiven for a past sin you have been working to repent of, please know that our Savior is more deeply eager to forgive you than you can imagine. Mortal words cannot describe the overwhelming degree of love He has for you. He longs to bless you with the maximum amount of blessings and minimum penalties that He possibly can.

To discover these boundless tender mercies for yourself, simply "ask and ye shall receive, seek and ye shall find." No blessing shall be withheld.

Brother John

Personal Journal

October 5, 2004

I'm learning many things about how my thoughts and fears shape my world. I have always thought things happen because they happen, or because something or someone else moved them. I am now of the opinion that my desires, my expectations (another way to say, my faith) seems to prefigure all that is good. My fears and negative thoughts seem to precursor all that is bad.

I'm not fully evolved in my thinking on this. I just have observed this in my life. My fears come to life, and my expectations (I just knew it was going to happen) come true—all of them. The Lord has promised that all that we desire will come to us—even if it is not the best for us! I have read books that say that we can literally shape our world and have all our desires come true by ordering our thinking, and by eliminating negatives from our lives. I am seriously examining this, even while realizing that any operation of the universe in response to our thoughts is a function of God's laws, of His grace, and of His desire to bless us.

I don't find this thinking anathema to the gospel or to my faith in any way, but it is actually complementary to it. There has to be something greater to life, to man's journey, than merely "enduring" the slings and arrows of outrageous misfortune, and then dying with a faith-filled heart. There has to be more to our connection with God's universe, with His plan for us, than merely begging for relief from overwhelming and looming destructions. There just has to be. I can't accept that we are as powerless as we have been taught.

I'll let you know what I find out. But, I WILL find out.

September 6, 2005

The Spirit whispered:

"Have greater faith in my promises. I have said that this [mini-storage] project would cause you to rejoice. This rejoicing will not be after trial, terror and torment. I do not give bad gifts. You don't need to know how this will happen, only that I said it will. I will fulfill all my promises. Have faith and let your soul be at peace."

October 13, 2006

Dear Family,

As you are all aware, I'm in the hospital with a severe liver condition caused by some dental work I had done a few weeks ago. There have been many reports of my condition, some right on, some overly optimistic. Here's what's going on.

The Dr. told me yesterday that he was finally able to say that he was "reasonably sure" I would survive. I'm feeling stronger and stronger, which means that on my best days I can get out of bed and walk around the hospital for a few minutes. The Dr. can't understand why I can even do that. He doesn't know about the power of prayer and faith.

I thank you all for your concern and for your prayers. Your love and positive energy has been a great blessing to me. I can feel the powers of heaven flowing, especially last Sunday when many people fasted for me.

Terri has been an angel. She is unfailing in her love and devotion. I think she deserves the celestial kingdom twice, one time for this gift to me.

I love all of you,
Dad (John, Grandpa)

February 4, 2009

This is the type of entry one hates to make in a journal. I am going into the hospital to have some tests. As I have been reflecting on my life these last few hours, pondering if I have done enough and if I am ready to face my own mortality, I am at peace. I have obtained the great promises, seen the visions, and dreamed the dreams. I have been taught by revelation, angels, and miracles, and been a part of the greatest truths that mortality can offer. I have loved the Lord and have served Him with all my energies—imperfectly to be sure—but with all my heart. I have a place assured, and I am content with that.

There are some things I would redo if I could, but my guess is that I would just mess something else up along the way, so I will let the deck stand without reshuffling my life or feeling "as if."

Every life in Christ ends in the final triumph, so often viewed as a tragedy.

*If this is my time, then I have had a glorious life. I have eight won-
derful and righteous children who will honor my memory and carry on
a tradition of righteousness. I am so grateful for them. Terri is the love
of my life. She will remember me and keep my love alive for the kids and
for her. It will be very hard for her, but she will do it. There are thousands
of people who know me and who will take the things I wrote and taught
and keep them alive.*

*I pray that the books I have written will be like little pebbles in an
ocean, whose waves do not diminish as they move outward, bringing the
light and truth of Christ unto untold numbers of lives. Even those who
do not read these books will be blessed when they encounter those who
have learned to live by the Spirit and walk in the light.*

*Writing has been the Lord's way of letting me have a voice, of letting
my soul rejoice in His word, in His gifts to me, and to mankind. It is His
way of letting me shout my love from the rooftops to the world.*

Chapter Nine

Zion: Our Divine Destiny

The Greatest Cause

Years ago I used to have a long commute to work in Anchorage, Alaska. I got up at 4:30 a.m., drove for about ninety minutes, and then clocked in at 6:00 a.m. I worked twelve hours with few breaks, drove home for another ninety minutes, and arrived about 8:00 p.m. I did this for years, often in very bad Alaska weather. The longest commute I had was one day when there was zero visibility and many cars were off the road. It took me five hours to get home—around midnight.

At first I listened to music on the drive, which quickly got boring. Then I listened to talk radio, which got depressing. I listened to recorded scriptures, which seemed hard to focus on for that length of time. After a few months of struggling to hang onto sanity on these long commutes, I started to pray.

Soon, I looked forward to the commute because I would begin praying as soon as the car began to move and end when I was pulling into the parking garage. Sometimes I would get so caught up with the Spirit that I didn't notice the actual driving or passage of time. This was where I learned to pray for long periods of time and to truly pierce the heavens. There were very few times when I actually asked for something. Mostly I was seeking knowledge, delighting in truth, worshiping with all of my joy, and listening very carefully.

In 1993, I had a life-altering spiritual experience. For about a year afterward I experienced what the scriptures refer to as not being able to look upon evil except with abhorrence. I was so repelled by the world and the suffering and evil therein that the very thought of it caused my soul to sicken. I remember trying to isolate myself from the world without success.

As I was driving home, the thought occurred to me to listen to the news. I hadn't heard the news for weeks, so I turned on the radio and immediately began listening to the account of Rwanda and the slaughtering that was occurring there at that very moment. The commentator quoted an American journalist as saying, "There are no devils in hell anymore. They are all in Rwanda."

I prayed and begged and begged and wept inwardly as I drove. I wanted Christ to return and nuke them all, to end the world—just to make it quit.

The Spirit came upon me and spoke to me for most of the drive home. I don't remember the actual words, but the message was this: The Lord is in control of everything that happens in this world. He is allowing these people to suffer to condemn the world, to bring about righteous punishment upon the wicked and to establish a just cause to cleanse the world by fire. This had to be done before He could judge the world in righteousness.

The Spirit also said that when these people died to fulfill His plan that He healed their wounds of heart and soul at death, and in the next life they did not look upon their sacrifice as painful or horrible but were grateful for their part in Christ's plan—a part which they had agreed to before they were born.

The Spirit commanded me, "Let not your heart be troubled." Immediately the heaviness of my soul departed and a feeling of peace and purpose replaced it. It was in that moment that I quit worrying about wars, politics, crime, or the spread of evil. I still hate it, but I'm not vexed and overwhelmed by it.

It was quite a few years later that I learned the principles regarding the building of the latter-day Zion. When I realized that Christ could not return until we build Zion and that Zion would be built only after people sought it, sacrificed for it, and reordered their lives to Zion worthiness, I realized that I could personally do something about the darkness of our world. I realized that by reordering my life to be worthy of the blessings of Zion, and actually building it in my heart, that I was doing everything I could do to end the horror and bring about the Lord's glorious day.

Now, I look at my life and every day I rededicate myself to fulfilling whatever part I may play in ending this telestial world and ushering in a greater one. This is why I labor over this UnBlog. And this is why I consider it such a glorious gift, such a miracle for a nobody like me to have the ear of so many people, who like me are willing to give everything they have or hope to ever become to the greatest cause mankind has ever undertaken—which is to arise to the stature of Enoch, to build Zion, and invite our Savior to return and reign in glory forever.

Brother John

Making the Change Voluntarily

I was quite interested in all of your responses to the last UnBlog. There really are several correct mindsets regarding last-days preparedness. One is to store and prepare like squirrels—store everything possible. I don't see anything wrong with doing that unless it causes us to feel "at ease in Zion" and overlook the essential journey it takes to obtain the Holy Spirit as our guide.

The other mindset is to faithfully proceed with physical preparations but to seek foremost to wrap ourselves in the safety of the Holy Spirit and to depend upon Christ only—not first upon our food storage and then upon the Lord, if that fails.

Perhaps in saying that I inadvertently give the impression that I am discounting physical preparation or proposing that it is not an inspired necessity. I personally have a preparedness program and hope to have more. The point I am making is that nothing can take the place of the Holy Spirit as our guide. No physical preparation will substitute or become so great and protective that we outgrow the need for the guiding hand and miracles of the Lord.

There will certainly be some among the wealthy and some governments who will dig mile-deep holes in the ground and fill them with biscuits and bullets, and the prophetic word is that they shall all perish.

The promise in Doctrine and Covenants 45:57 is that those who have taken the Holy Spirit to be their guide and have not been deceived *will* "abide the day." It is quite possible that one of those very deceptions is that food storage alone will save us. I fully expect that anyone with the Holy Spirit as his or her guide will make wise and appropriate physical preparations in executing the Lord's plan for them personally. I also expect that there will be those on the Lord's errand who do great things in preparing for their neighbors and in making preparations for places of refuge and other tasks necessary to the Lord's latter-day work.

But know this: The transition of this world from telestial to terrestrial will shake our world until there is nothing left of the telestial. In the terrestrial day there will be no hunger—which means we won't need food. There will be no disease, illness, injury, or death, which eliminates a large part of our present struggles and needs. All things will become new. The laws of nature will be altered to aid us rather than oppose us. The earth will no longer withhold her bounty, and all enmity will cease. There will be no government but Christ, and hence no conflict or war. In short, we won't need anything we presently depend upon in this telestial world.

When this metamorphosis begins, those who are clinging to something in the telestial world like wealth, power, comfort, land, politics, fame, or even food storage will not find those things to be an anchor to their souls. They will be of no worth at all. And all that telestial stuff will of necessity be destroyed so that the terrestrial may arise from the ashes.

The only way to voluntarily change from the telestial to the terrestrial is to do as the temple teaches us and consecrate everything we have to Christ. Now, this is a huge step, although a natural and joyful one as we progress spiritually. You and I both recognize that there is a vast spiritual evolution involved that such simple words can't capture. The point is that when the time comes, giving all things to Christ unfetters us from the world and provides us with true safety. We still possess those things, but we no longer depend upon them, covet them, seek safety from them, or withhold them from our neighbor. We depend upon Christ alone.

We will be like the widow who obediently gave her last meal to the prophet Elijah, and thereafter her cruse of oil never failed and her barrel of meal never wasted away. Our only safety is in giving it all away and trusting God to work the miracles that will save us.

This is the process that voluntarily brings us into the Millennial state.

Brother John

As It Was in the Days of Noah

One of the challenges of scriptures about the tribulation and Second Coming is that they are not sequential. They will speak of one event and remind us of something that must happen before "those days." Then they jump to an unknown time frame to speak of another event. This leaves us without a sequential calendar of events.

However, the Prophet Joseph left us half of the key to preparing for the Second Coming in JST, Matthew 1:41–43:

> But as it was in the days of Noah, so it shall be also at the coming of the Son of Man; For it shall be with them, as it was in the days which were before the flood; for until the day that Noah entered into the ark they were eating and drinking, marrying and giving in marriage; And knew not until the flood came, and took them all away; so shall also the coming of the Son of Man be.

The other half of the key is found in Doctrine and Covenants 115:5–6:

> Verily I say unto you all: Arise and shine forth, that thy light may be a standard for the nations; And that the gathering together upon the land of Zion, and upon her stakes, may be for a defense, and for a refuge from the storm, and from wrath when it shall be poured out without mixture upon the whole earth.

In other words, Zion is to be our ark. Just as the people of Noah's time who foolishly married and gave in marriage were unaware of the coming flood, not even aware of the true power of the ark, we of this dispensation will only be in the latter-day ark if we are inside the safety of Zion.

Joseph Smith said:

Without Zion, and a place of deliverance, we must fall: because the time
is near when the sun will be darkened, and the moon turn to blood, and
the stars fall from heaven, and the earth reel to and fro. Then, if this is
the case, and if we are not sanctified and gathered to the places God
hath appointed, with all our former professions and our great love for
the Bible, we must fall; we cannot stand; we cannot be saved; for God
will gather out His Saints from the Gentiles, and then comes desolation
and destruction, and none can escape except the pure in heart who are
gathered. (DHC 2:52)

Notice that Joseph gives two steps to be gathered to Zion. First,
we must be sanctified, and second, we will be gathered. It must
happen in that order: sanctification first, then physical safety. He
says we must be the "pure in heart" to be gathered. Why? Because
only "the pure in heart shall see God."

The reason sanctification must precede gathering is that Jesus
Christ will dwell in Zion just prior to the Second Coming. This
means that each of us must be qualified to enter His presence before
we will be admitted.

The process of sanctification is the very process of the gospel.
It is the same process we have been pursuing all of our gospel lives.
The critical difference here is that we may not have had our eye
upon the ark of Zion. We must renew our eyes to see through the
lens of Zion! If we are only trying to qualify our lives for church
callings and temple service, then we may find that the door of the
ark will be closing when we arrive to pound upon it.

The reason is the same as it was in the days of Noah. If someone
in his day was not preparing for the ark, helping to build the ark,
and with Noah, gathering the animals two-by-two, then they were
oblivious of the true purpose of the ark, and were not qualified to
enter.

With an eye upon the Zion-ark and the supreme blessings
promised in the temple, we can and will seek the face of God and
qualify ourselves for the promise and safety of Zion.

So, how do we prepare? Right now, today, we can fill our lives
with His voice, become His sheep, and take Him as our Shepherd.

We can qualify ourselves for a berth in Zion long before a single brick or stone is laid in the actual real estate of the New Jerusalem. Then, when the call comes by the living prophet, or by the voice of God we have learned to obey, we will be involved, sanctified, pure in heart, and welcome in the ark.

Brother John

The Mark of the Beast

As I have been preparing the draft for *Visions of Glory*, I have been gaining a new perspective about what the scriptures call "the mark of the beast," which one was supposed to receive in the right hand or forehead in order to buy or sell in the latter days. (Please remember that this is only my opinion. This is in no way Church doctrine, just something to consider.)

I learned that the "mark of the beast" began about ten to fifteen years ago and has been very subtle, but today it is more bold and more invasive in our lives. I understood began when we were all assigned social security numbers, and we were given the mindset that some great new order would take care of us. That was the beginning of the lie that was to become the "mark of the beast" over time.

This was the beginning of a culture, a new way of thinking, a form of political correctness that could take any truth and label it as a lie, and take any lie and relabel it as truth. One of the first things it did was to influence once-traditional Christians to partake of the new counterculture. It ridiculed traditional families, traditional marriage, traditional prayer in schools, traditional patriotism, traditional self-reliance, and traditional religion. It recast all of these things as outdated and incorrect. This culture made true and virtuous things "insensitive," "intolerant," and other labels. It took things like homosexuality and made it acceptable, modern, and natural. Pornography became an accepted expression of one's sexuality. They took basic liberties like freedom of speech and built walls around it, abridging it and excluding words and remarks from its protection. It took expressions of faith, like Christmas music and Nativity scenes, and made them "offensive" and "inappropriate." Traditional values became "stick in the mud" and unacceptable.

Through our faith and defense of what is true, we and other Christians were the power to carry the Lord's purposes forward, and thus we became the enemy. Christianity in any form was labeled bigotry, paranoia, and radical.

My current thinking is that someone accepts the mark of the beast when they knowingly buy into the lies of political correctness and all that it promotes, including abortion, homosexuality in all its deviations, sexual licentiousness, persecution of Christians, social distinction, and class envy, just to name a few. It causes its followers to merge into the world, to melt into the homogeneity of "everyone else" who believes the same. Those who have succumbed to these philosophies begin to defend and promote things which are politically correct, but which are not true in an eternal sense.

When one decides to embrace this false religion of political correctness, it changes him or her into the image of the world. The world looks upon those people as "enlightened" and "liberated," which feels good to most people. But, especially for children of the covenant along with other believing Christians, participation in the mark of the beast begins to burn into our bones and sinews. It becomes a part of us. It deafens us to the Holy Spirit, to truths as they really are, and blinds us to the work of Zion.

Zion is the pure in heart, and the mark of the beast is the exact opposite. The mark creates disunity in the name of diversity and tolerance. No longer are we God's children but citizens of the state. It creates the illusion of unity by building distrust and hatred of traditional beliefs and traditional families, which the majority of Americans presently still believe.

I have come to believe that the mark is in the right hand because it is the hand with which we make covenants with God. With the mark of the beast in the right hand, it overlays and eventually ends the blessings of covenants. The mark is in the forehead, because it is in the face and countenance in which we see the Light of Christ. It is in the face that we see the glow of righteousness and the image of God. When the mark is fully made, it creates darkness there instead of light.

The beast wants to enslave something much more important

than our bank accounts and ability to buy. He wants our enslavement to a set of beliefs that will effectively keep the Holy Spirit from purifying our hearts. The beast wants to destroy the traditional family unit, stop faith in Christ, impede religious freedom, and ultimately prevent the covenant people from building Zion.

For more than a decade now we have had the choice to either join into the new-age thinking and espouse political correctness, or to choose to be what the Lord has commanded and is guiding us to do. Where do we stand today in this growing crisis of philosophy and worldliness?

Yes, right now we can still have a job and buy at Wal-mart without selling our souls, but we must be careful to not allow the darkness of uninspired philosophy and political correctness stand between God's voice and our desire to conform to the "new normal." It is a very slippery slope, and the beast stands ready at the bottom of the hill to devour us all.

I believe the real war is a war of truth as it really is and of obedience to God's voice. We must choose to believe and stand for truth, to reject the lies, no matter how "correct" the world screams they are, and to walk a path that will prepare us for Zion. Then we will retain the "mark" of God in our right hands (for those with ears to hear) and in our foreheads so that all may see the true light that originates from the divine Lamp.

Now, what say you?

Brother John

White Light of Truth

Dear McKay,

Thanks for your questions. Yes, I do agree that either we (this dispensation) will build Zion, or God will give the privilege to someone else (in this dispensation). For that reason, we simply must not fail!

We all know that this is the last and greatest dispensation. There won't be another.

I don't have any more authority than my opinion on when things will happen. However, the spiritual call has already come to many to prepare to become Zion. The temple teaches daily how to obtain Zion, even as the world condition is deteriorating rapidly. And since we *are* the last dispensation, my faith tells me we *can* accomplish these things. When we will get around to it is the big question. Perhaps it will be accomplished by our children or grandchildren. But speaking for myself, I am not willing to push my obligations onto my posterity.

It must seem apparent to every UnBlog reader that I believe we *can* claim these privileges in our own lifetime. Even if it is not time for the physical city of Zion to be built, we can obtain the promises and stature for ourselves. This is the cause I am espousing: that we personally claim these magnificent privileges.

In all my study and research on this subject, I have come to believe that the timetable of the Lord's return is scheduled for *after* we as a people achieve the requisite worthiness, and then we will hear the call to gather and build the actual city of Zion. That means that we *can* do it because the Spirit-borne witness and call has been sounded to thousands of powerful souls. And God will not ask anything of us that He doesn't provide a way for us to do it.

So, I don't know when Christ will return; I just know that our obligation and privilege in the building of Zion will happen in this dispensation. Perhaps my part is just to sound this trumpet long and loud. The white light of truth tells me there is far more ahead for us all.

Brother John

The Condemnation upon Us All

*D*octrine and Covenants 84:54–57 is a bitter pill to swallow. The idea that all of us are under condemnation because we have taken our privileges lightly is not even debatable. It is a revealed fact.

The real question is, what can we, as individuals, do about it? The truth is, we can do almost nothing about whatever condemnation might rest upon anyone else. We can't lift any cloud that might hover over our town. We can't even change the people that are in our own home.

But, in our own universe we are the only hand upon the tiller, and we can lift whatever divine sanction might rest over us by personally repenting and correcting the acts or omissions that are fueling the sanction upon our heads. This is one of the vast definitions of agency—God does not punish one person for another's sins. If we repent and overcome whatever is initiating the condemnation, then we, personally can return to divine favor and step out of the shadow into which we were born.

What is most interesting is that we are told this condemnation rests upon *all* of us— which means that whatever it is that is causing this divine displeasure, we are all doing it. Not just a few of us, but all of us.

So, what is missing? What are we all doing that is so condemning? It almost seems impossible to accept, since most everyone I associate with in this church is full of faith and striving to walk the straightest pathway in their lives that they can achieve. It is a rather hard condemnation to understand, when viewed from the ground up.

Taking a look at it from the top down, however, gives us a little brighter view. From a ten-thousand-foot perspective (one where you can't see individuals, homes, or streets but only the broad lay of the land) one can see a startling difference between what we are and what the scriptures are asking us to become. In every gospel dispensation from Adam to Joseph Smith, there has been a specific goal, an overriding purpose, which most generations failed to achieve, namely the establishment of Zion. A few succeeded; most did not.

In our day of restoration we began, bled, and died for Zion. But then when we could not successfully establish it because of our failure to live the higher law, when we were driven from our homeland for not building Zion, we settled into our exile home in the West. We fondly called it Zion, even though we knew then, and know now, that a greater application of Zion—a far more divinely-engineered form of Zion—must be built before we have fulfilled this high commission.

In my recent book *The Triumph of Zion*, I have devoted chapters to this thought process. Please forgive me for being brief here. The fact is that Jesus Christ will not return in glory until Zion exists in its pre-millennial form and power. Until we realign our lives with this overarching commandment, we are not accomplishing the biggest part of our duties relative to this gospel dispensation—either as a people or as individuals.

If I sent employees into a far city for a season with a single command, and they did anything and everything but that task—no matter how vast their accomplishments, no matter how beautifully they adorned their temporary city—I would not consider them profitable servants but would likely fire them and find others that would actually do my bidding. In fact, this is exactly what the scriptures hint (even foretell) will happen.

The good news, the glorious news, is that the building of Zion begins when individuals look heavenward and realize that they *themselves* can establish Zion in their own lives. When they become the pure in heart, when they lay hold upon temple covenants and receive the full impact of those covenants made and realized; when they teach their families and others the principles of Zion—to seek revelation through the Spirit, to lay down their own will in obedience to the Father, to be born again, to seek the face of the Lord— then they will become Zion in the privacy of their own souls, regardless of what the world is doing all around them.

This, then, is the weight of condemnation that rests upon the children of Zion, even all. It is that this curse can only be lifted one righteous soul at a time. The Church organization is in fact guiltless. It is not under condemnation any more than a cardboard box can be under condemnation for holding something unholy. When the judgment day is finally convened, only *individuals* will be accountable for whether or not they built Zion in their own lives.

It is my conviction that the Lord is waiting for a body of people whose lives are reengineered into the Zion format, who daily experience a living flow of continual revelation, and who have been purified by the Atonement to become Zion. Then our living prophet will command us to begin to build a New Jerusalem worthy of receiving the Christ when He comes. The heavens will open, and our condemnation will evaporate like a serpentine morning mist before the warmth of the rising Son.

Brother John

Being Wise Virgins

The Savior gave us the parable of the Ten Virgins more than two thousand years ago. It wasn't until 1831 that we actually received the interpretation of that parable directly from the Lord. We've now had 180 years to figure it out.

> And at that day, when I shall come in my glory, shall the parable be fulfilled which I spake concerning the ten virgins. For they that are wise, and have taken the Holy Spirit for their guide, and have not been deceived—Verily I say unto you, they shall not be hewn down and cast into the fire, but shall abide the day. And the earth shall be given unto them for an inheritance, and they shall multiply and wax strong, and their children shall grow up without sin unto salvation. For the Lord shall be in their midst, and his glory shall be upon them, and he will be their king and their lawgiver. (D&C 45:57–59)

As I have been working on *Visions of Glory*, which discusses possible trials and glories of the days preceding the Second Coming, this message is borne out again and again: all those who have covenanted their lives to full obedience to the voice of the Holy Spirit will survive those days. They will walk in the way of divine protection, and even if the Lord's plan calls for them to leave this world of uncertainty, they will be even more powerful and more able to protect their families from their new position of glory. To be creatures of the Holy Spirit is our only safety, and it is a powerful promise because it came from Jesus Christ Himself.

In time, the earth shall be given to the "wise virgins" for an inheritance, and they will become strong because they will be changed so that the trials of the earth, death, and disease can no longer affect them. And as Doctrine and Covenants 45:58–59 teaches, their children shall grow up without sin unto salvation.

Next we are given the promise of the great Millennial condition: The Lord shall be in their midst, His glory shall be upon them, and He will be their king and their lawgiver.

There is a tendency to react to this message with fear—fear for our comfort, families, homes and safety. But the truth is that we have a perfect formula for "abiding the day." It is to take the Holy Spirit as our guide.

It is instructive that all ten of these people awaiting the arrival of the Bridegroom were called "virgins." A virgin is someone who is pure, who has not been polluted by the sin and impurity of mortality. They have worked all their lives to be pure and to do good. But, just being a "virgin" is not enough. We must also have the Holy Spirit for our guide because we ultimately cannot guide ourselves, no matter how "good" we may be.

Why isn't just being good, good enough? It is because being good is an act of compliance with law, and the law does not show us what to do, or when to duck, or where to go when these troubled times achieve their full power. Only obeying Christ's voice makes one a disciple of Christ, and only Christ can show you the pathway of safety and abundance in that challenging day.

The formula for surviving the Second Coming is this:

- Be a spiritual virgin.
- Repent, fulfill your covenants, and walk the gospel path. Never cease to ask, seek, and knock.
- Take the Holy Spirit for your guide.
- Learn to hear the voice of Christ in your heart and mind, and make a lifelong covenant to obey. Recall that in the parable, even when the foolish virgins realized their error, there was not time remaining to become "wise." It requires a lifetime to habitually take the Holy Spirit to be your guide and to amplify that voice into constant revelation. We must do this now and continue it forever. Then, you will be among the "wise," and you will have oil in your lamp.
- Do not be deceived:
  - Whatever this deception is in its fullest definition, it certainly includes the falsehood that we do not need to have the Holy Spirit as our constant companion, and our lives in constant compliance with divine will. It certainly includes the falsehood that just "doing" the gospel regimen is all that is required.
  - This deceptive thought demands that we must find our own way and plot our own course first, doing things of our own free will, and that revelation is reserved for only

those desperate moments when our intellect cannot find an escape.

- It deceives us into thinking that once the ordinances are pronounced, there is nothing more to be done but go to church and pay our tithing.

- This deception is a mist of darkness that Lehi saw obscuring the iron rod and the way to the tree of life. This is a compelling parallel, considering so many are now concerned about losing their lives in the upcoming "tribulation."

- It is interesting that so many misunderstand and are "deceived" about how to keep oil in their lamps, even though they covenant every week to "always remember Him and keep His commandments, that they may *always* have His spirit to be with them" (D&C 20:77, emphasis added).

Besides all that, it is fun to be a wise virgin, to feel the guiding hand of Christ, to walk in growing light, and to look with joy upon the changing world—rather than with terror. I am personally looking forward to the day when darkness no longer enslaves the world and evil no longer rules; when sickness and death no longer sweep the floors of mortality. To end this world of horror, to see Christ come and cleanse by fire—for this I am willing to do and be anything. And that includes working from whichever side of the veil the Lord desires.

Happy day. All is well.

Brother John

The Establishment of Zion and the 144,000

Sometime after the events at Adam-Ondi-Ahman, the Lord will begin the building of the center place of Zion, the New Jerusalem. The building of the latter-day Zion will necessitate that Zion-worthy people actually arrive at Zion. This is the beginning of the greatest gathering in the earth. Prior to this time there will have been sufficient destruction (at the end of the times of the Gentiles) that whomever the Lord designates to travel to Zion will not be arriving in Zion by modern means or modern transportation systems.

Zion and her stakes will be a refuge from the wrath which is poured out in full measure (see D&C 115:6). This necessitates that we actually be in Zion to be protected. Hence, the holy word says that the "gentiles shall flee unto Zion" (D&C 133:12).

There will be several stages of this flight to Zion. The first will be those sent by the Lord in the first wave. They will be fully prepared and endowed with power. They will begin the construction of the temple there and lay the foundations of the city. Shortly thereafter, those in Zion will be empowered and called into the 144,000. These will be high priests (and of course high priestesses, in my opinion) who will be sealed in their foreheads (which signifies the receipt of the fulness of priesthood power) and who are ordained to the "holy order of God" by His angel, and given power over the nations of the earth (see D&C 77:11).

The fulness of the Melchizedek Priesthood as available to us today, occurs through temple covenants, and bestows the full power of godliness upon mortals who keep and fulfill those covenants.

Regarding faithful sisters receiving these same great privileges in Zion, Joseph Fielding Smith taught:

> There is no exaltation in the kingdom of God without the fulness of priesthood. How could a man be an heir in that kingdom without priesthood? While the sisters do not hold the priesthood, they share in the fulness of its blessings in the celestial kingdom with their husbands. These blessings are obtained through obedience to the ordinances and covenants of the house of the Lord. (Joseph Fielding Smith, *Doctrines of Salvation*, 3:132)

The next wave of gathering will occur as the 144,000 gather the elect from out of the earth. This will be done by open display of the power of God.

The 144,000 will be translated persons, and thus will have great power to deliver and to save. Orson Pratt, an apostle and faithful friend of the Prophet Joseph, made this fascinating explanation regarding why this missionary force needs to be translated beings.

They [the Saints] will dwell in Zion a good while, and during that time, there will be twelve thousand chosen out of each of these ten tribes. . . . Chosen for what? To be sealed in their foreheads. For what purpose? So that the power of death and pestilence and plague that will go forth in those days sweeping over the nations of the earth will have no power over them. (JD, 18:25)

Pratt continued:

This [being translated] will prepare them for further ministrations among the nations of the earth, it will prepare them to go forth in the days of tribulation and vengeance upon the nations of the wicked, when God will smite them with pestilence, plague and earthquake, such as former generations never knew. Then the servants of God will need to be armed with the power of God, they will need to have that sealing blessing pronounced upon their foreheads that they can stand forth in the midst of these desolations and plagues and not be overcome by them.

In other words, we will need to be translated just to physically survive being sent forth to gather the elect out of the world. Elder Pratt continues:

When they [the servants of God] are prepared, when they have received a renewal of their bodies in the Lord's temple, and have been filled with the Holy Ghost and purified as gold and silver in a furnace of fire, then they will be prepared to stand before the nations of the earth and preach glad tidings of salvation in the midst of judgments that are to come like a whirlwind upon the wicked." (JD, 15:365–66)

If Elder Pratt is right, and I deeply believe he is, then one of the grand purposes of the temple we will build in the New Jerusalem is to bestow upon us the privilege of translation, which is the same thing as saying to make us a part of Zion. In this sealing we will become sanctified and ready to take our place in Zion and among the 144,000.

The angels are surely waiting for us to prepare to receive these gifts, that we may one day stand before the nations of the earth in the midst of swirling judgments to gather in the elect and bring them to Zion.

Brother John

I Don't Believe in Suffering

Yesterday morning I was sitting in an infusion center with a half-dozen other people my age. We chat occasionally; one lady tells jokes. Some sleep or use their cell phones. I try to read a good book.

As I was reading yesterday, a young woman walked in. She was twenty something with a cute face and youthful figure, and I expected her to sit in the folding chairs (you know, the ones for the caregivers). She didn't. She sat in the cushy patient chair as the nurse worked to get her IV hooked up. I watched her skin turn from a youthful blush to white to yellow. Then I watched her sag into her seat and close her eyes. And I decided once again, I don't believe in suffering.

In my previous stake in Alaska, I served with a friend in the stake presidency. His little grandson was born with leukemia. From less than a month old, this little guy has been on chemo, barely surviving, so filled with pain and sickness that he never learned to cry or even whimper. It is the only life he knows, and courage is his only option to have any kind of a life that isn't listless and suicidal. The grueling treatments have taken him literally to the verge of death. I remember my friend saying how they had given him a taste of ice cream for his second birthday party. Sugar was against the doctor's orders for some reason. The mother just said, "He's suffered too much," and gave him a mouth full. The little guy's eyes rolled up into his head and he cried, because he didn't know until then that life had anything sweet to offer him.

A family in our previous ward had their first son die of lung cancer when he was four. They took courage and had a second son, and then a third several years later. Their second son died of the same lung cancer at eight years old, just a year ago. Every night these parents cry themselves to sleep worrying about their only remaining son because he is turning two, and their other two sons first manifested the disease at that age. Their lives are in ruins. They have little income because the father has chosen to be with their sons instead of hiding in his job. They live with family, depend upon everyone else, and are emotionally and psychologically bankrupt.

Only the love and fellowship of the Saints seem to sustain them.

Why am I rehearsing these awful scenes? It is because these things are only a tiny tip of a planetary-sized iceberg of mortality. The news is X-rated, with horror occurring daily. Ever since its inception, this mortal world is beyond comprehension in its brutality.

All my life I have felt powerless to affect any of this. The horror spins on around me, and there has never been a way or a means whereby I could even hope to change it, so my heart eventually evolved from empathy to a deep sadness, feeling helpless as I waited upon the Lord. That is, until recently.

As I was writing *The Triumph of Zion*, it came into my soul with a thunderclap of truth that when we finally get around to building Zion, Christ will come and *He* will end this world. Then there will be a long, beautiful era of peace and safety. Babies will be born without leukemia, and young mothers will not hold their children with trembling arms, knowing they will never see them be baptized, married in the temple, or as mothers themselves.

When I realized that I could qualify for Zion all by myself, that I could be one of the many who by this choice, by this act of sacrifice and determined discipleship will be responsible for retooling this world and inviting the conquering Christ to return and purify with fire, it was then that I realized that in this small way, I *could* change this world. I can be an essential part of the end of the misery.

I also realized in that moment that if I *could*, and then *didn't*, that I would be at least partly responsible for the continuing horror that this world has always been.

Now, when I see the scenes I described above, my feelings of empathy don't evolve into sadness; they evolve into determination. They become feelings of "If I don't, who will?" Whether I'm the first, or the millionth, I am going to be within that number whose righteous walk enables the building of Zion, the return of the King of Glory, and the end of mortal pain and suffering.

I pray to God, and I offer up myself upon whatever altars exist, that this process toward Zion is quickly evolving and that you will be a part of it, too. I do believe that the Millennial day is not far away and that from whatever side of the veil I am on, I will one day see Christ standing in the clouds of heaven, His smile shining down upon those whose lives invited Him there.

Brother John

Personal Journal

May 30, 2009

Last March, Terri and I flew to Costa Rica to have the cancer removed from my colon. We chose Costa Rica because they have world-class hospitals and were about 1/10th the cost. In the end we saved about $900,000 dollars. I'm not sure it was worth it.

It was a horrendous experience. I had severe complications, and for about a week they did not believe I would survive. When I woke up after five days in a coma, I was very sick and in severe pain. The first surgery had failed, and they had kept me in a coma for two more operations. After the surgeries I would not wake up, but did a couple days later.

After the surgery I had severe delusions for five days. It was the most horrible experience of my life. In my delusions I saw people I loved get killed over and over, and I was powerless to rise and help them. I saw Terri get killed three times, as well as many other people in the most awful ways. It was absolutely real to me.

When I began to come out of it, Terri listened to each of my experiences and told me they were not real. She had to convince me by logic why they were not real. I just couldn't believe her. When I saw her that first time I was convinced she was a spirit, and she had to touch me and hold me to convince me she was not dead or injured. It took days for her to convince me that none of it had happened for real.

Because of the stress and mental trauma, I developed pneumonia, and they put me on a ventilator for four days. I was awake and felt like I was suffocating the whole time. I finally had to just give up and let Jesus Christ carry the burden of my feelings of suffocation. It was a life or death struggle. I rehearsed in my mind over and over that I was safe, and that Jesus Christ would make my body live even though I knew I was suffocating. Terri helped me a lot to give in and let Jesus worry about my life. It was horrible. Only when I was able to sleep did I get any relief. They would not let me sleep during the day. They kept urging me to breathe deeper while the machine was limiting my breath. I couldn't talk at all, but tried so hard to tell them it was impossible to breathe.

On the fourth day, I wrote on a tablet that I was suffocating and could not draw a breath, but they couldn't interpret my weak scribbles. Terri tried again to convince them that something was wrong. The doctor frowned and looked at the machine. He flipped a switch then asked if I could take a breath on my own. The machine had been set wrong for four days! I could draw a full breath by fighting against the machine. It took all my strength, but I could get a full breath once in a while. They finally removed the machine, and I almost choked to death trying to breathe again on my own, but I made it.

The one amazing thing that came from my awful experiences is that the Holy Spirit has whispered that Christ's atonement and experience in Gethsemane was somewhat similar to my delusions, in that He did not just watch and "know" the horror of the atonement, but that He was there in person. He felt the pain . . . the torture and horror of every possible pain of humanity. It was real to Him. The thought makes me physically, literally ill for Him. My experience was only over a few hours and it felt to me like weeks in hell. It is no wonder that He sweat blood from every pore.

These harsh experiences have been the most instructive of my life. I praise God for them, and for tenderly caring for me always—no matter what has been required.

June 28, 2009

I see that I have told the story of Costa Rica three times in my journal. I was going to erase some, but I think it was three times more awful than I can convey, so I will leave them in. I am doing much better, and feel my spirits and my determination rising. I told Terri today that I am not going to be defeated by this experience. I am going to succeed and be well again.

I am looking forward to the fireside in August, but feel as if I am spiritually depleted right now. I am studying the scriptures and really working to grow spiritually. I have found, to my dismay, that my spirit is attached to my body, and when it is sick, my spirit suffers. I had not even suspected this. It has been very hard for me to soar spiritually during this physical challenge. I am doing everything I know how to do to overcome this spiritually and physically.

Even so, joy is where my life is right here and right now.

December 29, 2011

For someone who writes so much, I sure don't give this journal a fair turn. During this year I gave about 35 firesides and wrote more than

300 blog entries, which add up to 400 pages of type-written text. It has been a marvelous year.

I am being a little vague because so much of my life is spiritual, and all of that is recorded in my books and in my blog "UnBlogMySoul." It may be unlikely that it is still running by the time this journal is read by anyone—if it ever is; but I have saved the entire sequence in a file called "Unblogmysoul Archive" on my computer—again doubting it has survived.

I also wrote the book Visions of Glory this year. I'm planning to publish it later in 2012. It is the visionary experiences of a new friend of mine who has died four times and each time had a near-death experience. Each experience builds upon the last until it includes his premortal childhood all the way up through the Second Coming, the Millennium, and the end of the earth. It is the most amazing thing I have ever read, or written for that matter.

He is a marvelous friend and brother in Christ. The truths that he has told me are so apropos to my own journey that they have literally lit up my life and given me another witness to those things which I already embraced as true. I know the promises that the God of heaven has given me are unchangeable, and they will all be fulfilled in His due time—no matter which side of the veil I am on. If this next year I take my last few steps in mortality, then so be it. I am willing, and I am rejoicing.

Chapter Ten

Receiving the
Unspeakable Blessings

One Can See Forever

My goal for this UnBlog is simple, but I don't know that I have ever told you. There is a "strait and narrow" path that leads to all blessings we hope to enjoy in this life and throughout eternity. Much has been written about what people think the path is and how to walk it. Mostly I agree with them. What I find myself disagreeing with is where they think it ends. Some say it ends at Christ's love, as in Lehi's dream of the tree of life. Or, they think it ends at being born again or some other blessing. My opinion—no, I have to state that differently—my *experience* is that the strait and narrow path has *no* endpoint. We don't arrive anywhere and stop; it passes through all of these blessings, moving us eternally onward and upward, without limitation. With a pure view of the pathway, one can see forever.

My goal is to push the light out toward the further and greater blessings along the path as far as mortal belief can stretch, and then push it some more. My goal is to not only shine beautiful and joyful light upon the path and how we must walk it, but to brightly illuminate *beyond* every apparent endpoint to which we have limited our belief.

And if God will bless us all, I hope to kindle within every seeking soul an overpowering reason to get there.

Brother John

One Eternal Round

n the fireside last evening, even though I had planned on saying something quite different, the words that came to my heart were this: There is only one gospel and one pathway back into the presence of God, and any person, in any dispensation, who arrives there will have traveled that path. The fact that this process never changes, and is used over and over in every generation, is part of the reason we say that God's works are "one eternal round" (D&C 35:1; D&C 3:1–2).

In 1 Nephi we read: "For he that diligently seeketh shall find; and the mysteries of God shall be unfolded unto them, by the power of the Holy Ghost, as well in these times as in times of old, and as well in times of old as in times to come; wherefore, the course of the Lord is one eternal round" (1 Nephi 10:19).

This means that when the scripture records a vision wherein the recipient saw the creation of the world, no matter if it was Adam, Moses, John the Beloved, or some other, that this was the same vision, given according to the same set of laws over and over again.

The glory of this truth is that when we identify and obey these same laws, that the same vision will unfold before us as it always has, in every generation. When and how this happens for each of us is according to the Lord's timetable; but I testify that these glorious blessings are indeed granted to the modern faithful, just as in times past.

This means that any blessing we can read about in scripture, every vision and miracle and blessing which God ever offered to them of old, is also offered to us in its fullest and richest form. Whether you realize or accept this as true or not, or believe it is intended for you personally, nevertheless it is yours to claim. Almost all of the notable and great ones of history achieved what they achieved in spite of the fact that very few, if any others, believed and achieved the same stature. Most often they stood alone.

Since the works and truths and mysteries of the gospel are available to us "in these times as in times of old," we have a tremendous opportunity and a weighty obligation to view these things with an eye of faith, and then to obtain them. Can the Jews be any less unfaithful in not recognizing Christ walking among them than we are for not seeing Christ in our day, walking among us, offering us entry to His presence and to His greatest blessings?

This one precious thing I do know, besides the fact that Jesus is the Christ, is that not only is the gospel true but that it works. It functions as it did in days of old. If we knock, seek, and obey the requisite laws, it *will* in due time bring us to the fullest blessings God has ever offered mankind.

Brother John

The Warm Blanket of Eternal Brotherhood

Before this year ends, I want to tell you about my friend Shawn. Of course, this isn't his real name. I met Shawn years ago in about 1994. I was trying to publish *Following the Light of Christ into His Presence* and was enjoying a spiritual high.

I was at work when Shawn walked in and asked if he could speak to me. I don't know that I had ever seen him before. He was nicely dressed and well spoken, and I invited him into my office. I actually thought he was a salesman!

Shawn told me he had read a manuscript copy of *Following the Light of Christ into His Presence*, which my dad had given him. He looked at me directly and asked, "Do you really believe what you have written?"

Over the next two hours we talked deeply as the Holy Spirit warmed our souls. It was one of those blessed times when the teacher learns as much as the one being taught. Shawn's words changed from doubting to hopeful. He left but returned every couple days for several months. Each time, we rejoiced in our blessings and drank the living waters. We became very good friends.

About the end of this time, Shawn came into my office and told me, "When I first read your book, and read your description of the blessings that accompany being born again, I thought you were exaggerating the blessings to encourage people to pay any price to obtain them."

I started to say something, but he stopped me.

"Last night, as I was praying I had an amazing experience. The Holy Spirit came over me, and I felt like singing and shouting praises to the heavens. I realized that I was experiencing what the scriptures call 'mighty prayer.' It went on for a long time. At the very end of it, I heard a voice tell me my sins were forgiven, like Enos in the Book of Mormon. What do you think it all means?"

I asked him what he thought it meant. (It wasn't my place to try to interpret his blessings.)

He paused here to collect his emotions. His eyes were spilling tears I don't think he was even aware of. When he looked up he said, "I guess I know what it means."

I nodded. "I think your understanding is correct," I said.

Shawn expressed his amazement and humble gratitude for this unexpected blessing. Then he said, "Now I realize that you didn't exaggerate the blessings one can receive at all. You actually understated them, because if you tried to tell the full extent of what people can obtain, nobody would have believed you."

I nodded. "Some people experience these things in a very profound way and receive these blessings suddenly, like you just did. Others receive them more quietly, and over a longer period of time, but the blessings are the same."

Shawn has been my dear friend all of these years. We have since discovered great things together, eaten fruit from the tree of life together, and rejoiced and rejoiced. We have never gone hunting together, or to a movie, or gone camping or fishing. We just share this amazing bond in Christ, which has wrapped us in the warm blanket of eternal brotherhood, and together we know in Whom we rejoice.

Shawn is presently serving as a bishop and as my best friend.

Brother John

The Order of Things

We have been talking about many spiritual events and blessings. Some of your comments have been about when and in what order these things happen. These things can be hard to piece together. It has taken me many years to realize what was happening and what the strait and narrow path actually looks like. We have discussed each of these at various times within the UnBlog. But this 30,000–foot view of things may help you better understand what is happening and where you personally are on the path:

- Obedience to the voice of Christ/Holy Spirit
  (This is the first covenant, if you have ears to hear.)
- Sacrifice (This is the second covenant.)
- Prayer
- Faith
- Repentance
- Baptism (This is the law of the gospel.)
- Gift of the Holy Ghost
- Ordination to priesthoods (essential for male pilgrims)
- Baptism of fire and of the Holy Ghost
- Being born again
- Becoming perfect in Christ
- Personal revelation
- The doctrine of the priesthood begins to distill upon our hearts as the dews from heaven.
- Temple endowment
- Where we receive the instruction on how to arrive at the veil.
- The covenant of chastity is taught here because at this point unchaste acts become eternity threatening.
- Taught by angels (as indicated in the temple)
- We obtain true power in the priesthood.
- Becoming pure in heart
- This includes the covenant of consecration.
- Calling and election made sure (becoming the elect of God)
- This is the private fulfillment of the first trip to the veil.
- Abrahamic Trial
- Second Comforter
- This is the private fulfillment of the second trip to the veil where we "enter in."
- "Endowed" from on high
- This is the request we may make of the Lord while in His presence. This is the actual endowment.

- Translation (Translation is one of many things we may ask for as our "endowment.")
- Zion/144,000 (In this dispensation, we have the privilege of asking to be a part of the building of the Latter-day Zion, which will include a call to be one of the 144,000 missionaries.)

I pray that this list may help give you gain clarity as you progress on your own spiritual journey. No matter where you are on that path, cling tightly to the iron rod—the words of Christ—with every footstep. You will arrive at each milestone just as you should, according to your faith and preparedness and the Lord's omniscient timetable.

Brother John

Obtaining the Baptism of Fire and of the Holy Ghost

*T*he question has been posed several times on the UnBlog about whether there is an actual baptism of fire that includes visible fire. Here's my take on visible fire. I am aware that some people in history and living today have experienced visible fire during the rebirth process. I do not think it is common, and I do not think it is a necessary manifestation to a pure and powerful "baptism of fire." In my own experience, there has never been an actual view of flames around me, though I was fully aware of spiritual power far greater than fire.

The key to obtaining one's own baptism of fire is quite simple. I have written this so many times that some of you are probably going to roll your eyes. Yet, it is true: the entire process is simply to learn to hear the voice of Christ in your heart and then to be flawlessly obedient. I judge that all mortals, including myself, will always fall short of "flawless" performance, but my point is not performance; it is desire. If the thoughts and intents of your heart are to be flawlessly obedient, it will be enough. The performance will follow close enough, and the Atonement will overlay our mortal flaws with a blanket of grace.

This is where the enabling and changing majesty of the Atonement is manifest: When we take whatever truth we understand and whatever light we perceive, and reorder our lives to that level of obedience, sacrificing whatever is required in that small circle of light; then the Lord changes us in that instant that our hearts turn to Him in diamond-hard desire. It doesn't happen after years of trying to prove our intent; it happens in the moment we choose to forever obey.

Then, as the light increases, a higher and higher level of desire and obedience is required to pass the angels that guard this gate. On the lowest level, we may be told to not steal a candy bar. When we choose to forever obey that law, we are changed so that the desire to steal leaves us. On the next level, we are taught to not covet the candy bar. We succeed and are changed so that we no longer covet. A further level may be to give one of our candy bars away. We obey and are changed. The next could be to give our only candy bar away. We obey and are again changed even more profoundly so that God leads us to meet our needs in other ways. When we obey, we are again changed so that our needs are met by miracles.

The greatest level may be to realize, after long experience and unfailing miracles, that anything we sacrifice to God's will we did not actually need, and that if God has asked us to give away all of our food and our water, He will change us so that we no longer need them.

This is the pathway to every glorious blessing, to incrementally climb the ladder of obedience to blessedness that exceeds the ability of man to conceive while standing below the bottom rung.

At every level, the lesson is to sacrifice the needs of the flesh in some way. Every level is greater, every sacrifice more exalting, and every change moves us nearer and nearer to when this telestial world no longer demands that we play by its rules. Then we become truly changed, born again, remade into new creatures in Christ, and changed by spiritual fire and fulfillment of temple promises in the greatest sense so that mortality is no longer our master.

Then we are truly ready to abide the day of His coming.

Brother John

Seek the Face of the Lord

As we begin discussing "Seek the Face of the Lord," it may be of value to discuss why we should even try to achieve such a high and holy gift while in mortality. One might well ask, "Why not just wait until death brings us back into the Lord's presence? And anyway, isn't seeing the Lord in this life only intended for the apostles and prophets?"

To answer, let us back up a bit. There is an ordained path that leads to the celestial kingdom. There is only one path and one way. Along that path there are specific events and ordinances we must accomplish, one by one. Although they are sometimes realized in slightly different order, one may not skip any of them and still arrive at the desired destination.

I have UnBlogged about this path many times. It is familiar to you because it is the path you have been on since you first realized you were alive. It begins with recognizing that your conscience is actually revelation from Jesus Christ and then obeying it. This path leads up through all of the ordinances of the priesthood and into the presence of God.

As members of Christ's church, we can easily name off the first half-dozen steps along this path. As we grow in understanding, we eventually recognize and begin to yearn for the "greater things" of mortality. And when we are fully evolved in the things of God, we at last realize there is no limit to what we can achieve when we are willing to live the laws and pay the price required to obtain these lofty things—in this life, according to our faith and the Lord's will.

If we hope to one day return with our families to Father and live with Him and our Savior in the celestial kingdom, we will at some point need to fully walk this pathway back into the presence of Christ. When we do, because of His position as our Savior and Redeemer, Christ will bring us back to the Father. He is the only one who can. So it seems only logical that it would be to our distinct advantage, and to the advantage of our families, to make this step sooner than later.

The reason it is so desirous to seek the face of Christ sooner than later is, first of all, Jesus Christ has commanded us to do so (see D&C 101:38; D&C 93:1). Beyond that, there are vast and glorious promises which may be obtained in this life by seeking and obtaining a face-to-face interview with Jesus Christ. The greatest of these promises involves being empowered to pass special blessings on to our posterity—to teach those we love and have stewardship over with extra power and spiritual privilege. For example, it was from this advantaged position that Alma could call down angels to arrest the decay of his son. Wouldn't you like to have that same kind of privilege?

These are without a doubt the greatest gifts and privileges we could seek in this life. We can boldly move forward to claim them—rejoicing that the Lord has commanded us to do so and that He never gives a commandment that He does not provide a way for us to accomplish— in His own time, in His own way, and according to His own will (see D&C 88:68).

Brother John

Promises Received by Faith

*L*et's discuss the supernal promises that come from unshaken faith. The all-powerful key of faith is mentioned by Moroni, when speaking of the brother of Jared, to explain why he was able to see Christ and ultimately partake of every blessing mankind is offered.

It was all a result of unshaken faith. God clearly promises that in the day that we (the Gentiles) exercise faith in Christ, even as the brother of Jared did, and become sanctified in Christ, then Christ will manifest unto us everything the brother of Jared saw (see Ether 4:7).

The reason this is significant to this day, and to you and me personally, is that the gospel is consistent. If the brother of Jared obeyed a set of laws and thus obtained certain blessings, the justice of God demands that if we obey the same laws as he did, we must likewise obtain those same blessings.

Moroni goes on in Ether 12 to discuss what he terms "the heavenly gift," which is that mortals may be called after the "holy order of God" and thus enter into the presence of God while yet mortals. He then discusses the brother of Jared, saying that "so great was his faith in God" that God could not hide his finger from the brother of Jared's sight.

Most of us easily accept that the brother of Jared had unusual and powerful faith. What we miss is the next statement of *why* he had it. Moroni tells us that it was "because of his [God's] word which he had spoken unto him, *which word he had obtained by faith*" (Ether 12:20).

Since the gospel always operates the same, and since God's path is "one eternal round," then what the brother of Jared experienced either has or will happen to everyone who seeks to approach the veil. The brother of Jared had been promised (the word which had been spoken unto him) by God that he could and actually would be admitted into God's presence.

The brother of Jared knew that God could not give empty promises, and he just simply believed it was true. This hearkens to yesterday's discussion about actually and powerfully believing the things our faith tells us are true. The brother of Jared just believed so powerfully that he had no doubt. He knew God would, when the brother of Jared properly petitioned, and according to God's timetable, appear to him and grant him the desire of his heart. This kind of mighty faith was a bestowed gift he had received line upon line, no doubt through years of meek, earnest seeking.

This is the same pedestal every soul of greatness has stood upon when they succeeded in parting the veil and conversing with Christ. They believed in a promise they had received beforehand.

Our question should be, have we also received such a promise? If we have, then can we begin to have the same caliber of faith in *our* promise that the brother of Jared had, and can our belief in time become sufficiently profound to part the veil and call forth heaven's richest gifts?

The answer is a thundering *yes!* If you have been inside holy walls, then you have been given this promise. The whole temple experience is a metaphor for our spiritual journey from before birth until we stand before our Savior at the veil. It is instruction, guidance, and promise which aligns our souls with the true North of Jesus Christ's Atonement and gifts us with faith sufficient to part the veil.

What you hear in the temple are promises meant to be spoken only at that moment. However, if we seek diligently, there is an actual real event, one that follows in a private moment, when equally significant words are repeated with eternal power. Millions have heard them. We refer to this moment as "having your calling and election made sure." These are the same words the brother of Jared heard. They contain the same promise he heard, which he believed so strongly that God Himself could not keep the brother of Jared from seeing His finger and then His whole person.

In the temple we step back and then almost immediately return to the veil to complete our journey. In the mortal world, we receive the promises of calling and election and then step back for what may be years, decades, or longer. It takes that long to realize what you just received. You have to ponder those sacred words to realize what they mean and what they are actually promising you. When the Holy Spirit finally reveals to your mind and heart what you were in fact given in that moment, then a new fire burns in the soul that the brother of Jared understood well. It is the fire of knowing—not merely hoping or believing, but knowing—that because of the promises you have received by faith, when you return to the veil, even in this life if the Lord wills it, you will be admitted.

This is not only the power of inspired believing, but it is the very reason it exists, and how to use it.

Brother John

Walking upon the Water

From time to time I think about Peter, who upon seeing Christ walking upon the water, asked Him, "If it be thou, bid me come unto thee on the water."

When Christ answered, "Come," Peter came "down out of the ship, [and] walked on the water, to go to Jesus" (Matthew 14:28–29).

There are many amazing elements to this story. Most often, what people like to observe is that when Peter heard the winds and saw the waves, he became afraid and began to sink. That being true, I think the greater point is that he actually *walked upon the water*! No matter if it was one step or ten, if he sank quickly or slowly, or if he was just afraid and his faith failed, you know what—he actually did walk upon the water. That's pretty incredible. As far as sacred history records, only Jesus Christ and Peter have ever done so.

When Christ caught him as he sank, I believe Peter's faith was restored. He had walked out there, he knew he could do it, and one can only marvel that Peter most probably walked back to the ship upon the water with Jesus.

But my point is this: unless Peter had *seen* the Master walking upon the water, Peter could not have even conceived of the idea on his own, let alone have the faith to do so.

For almost two hundred years, there has been a moratorium upon sharing grand spiritual experiences. We are told, "Those who know don't talk. Those who talk don't know." This is actually a Chinese proverb from Tao Te Ching. The rest of the proverb says, "Close your mouth, block off your senses, blunt your sharpness, untie your knots, soften your glare, settle your dust." In other words, stop talking and just listen.

How it came in this latter-day world to mean that personal and glorious spiritual experiences should never be shared, and if someone is sharing them they're always being inappropriate, is hard to tell. But, it is not true in my opinion. Those who know should talk *when inspired,* and we should not dismiss such things because of a Chinese proverb.

If Peter had been looking the other way, or stayed asleep in the boat, then his faith and belief would have never blossomed. He had to see such a thing to believe it, because belief limits us to our own definition of what is possible. The only reason he knew he could walk on water was because he saw Jesus doing it, and then he asked and received permission to do it himself.

We are not so different from Peter. When we see someone work a miracle by the priesthood, when we hear with inspired spiritual ears of a vision or great manifestation, then our faith is empowered to seek for the same. Without that witness, without seeing and knowing that someone else did these great things in the storms of their lives, we most often lack the faith to do so in ours. In fact, this is the power of the scriptures—that someone actually did seek and find the things of God before us. This is the power that is so dramatically shut off when inspired souls know, but don't talk.

Imagine a fifth Sunday in some Millennial day where Peter, now resurrected, drops in to teach the lesson. He takes the class to a nearby lake and, turning to face them, says, "Brothers and sisters, today's lesson is on walking on the water, and here is how it is done." With that, he takes ten steps upon the water, then returns and says, "Now you do it." I think all of us would go home wet from the first few tries, but like Peter, we would suddenly know that we could do it, too. We would know it because we saw Peter do it, and we would have a burning witness that the Lord wants us to do that and even greater things—to accomplish His purposes and bless His children. Very soon we would be walking on the water ourselves.

I think we are all Peters who would happily walk upon the water if we knew how. The UnBlog has taught me that I am not alone in the desire to do so. So many of us have read the scriptural promises, or believed the words of sacred ceremony, and are seeking to claim it all—sometimes without the approval of spouse, friends, or family. We desperately wish someone who actually knows how, would just speak up.

I hope you realize that you are not alone in your desires to seek and obtain greater things, those things which "eye has not seen, nor yet entered into the heart of man." But when the eye of faith does see fellow pilgrims walking upon the water, then it will enter deeply into the heart; and after some spectacular failures and serious dog-paddling, we will eventually find ourselves walking upon the waters, heedless of the storms around us.

Brother John

The Virtue That Parts the Veil

There is an almost universal misconception about translation, which is that it only occurs to perfect people. When we meet someone who is wonderful and we want to pay them a great compliment, we often gush something like, "I'm surprised you're not translated yet!"—suggesting that they are perfect enough for translation.

Many years ago, I had a humbling and glorious spiritual experience that left me pondering why that had happened to me, of all people. I knew my weaknesses, my flaws, and sins. The more I thought about it, the more it seemed like the heavens had picked the wrong person. It almost made me wonder if the experience was valid.

As these thoughts poured through my mind, I'm sure with help from our spiritual enemy, the Spirit awakened my mind and simply said, "No, you're not perfect, but you are obedient."

It was then that I realized that the Lord did not require me to be perfect to obtain the blessing I was seeking. In that case, for that blessing, He had required that I be obedient.

God does not measure us by the standard of perfection. God actually gave us our weakness (see Ether 12:27). Weakness is divinely engineered into us. As long as we are mortal, we will manifest mortal flaws. The purpose of these engineered weaknesses is so that we come unto Christ and humble ourselves. When we manifest humility through willing obedience, then His grace will make those weaknesses become strengths.

If someone knows in their heart that they should seek the blessings associated with Zion, and they set themselves up to seek perfection in this cause, they will be on a very harsh and impossible pathway that cannot be completed in mortality. The good news is that the requirement for translation is not perfection; it is purity.

We know this because the divine pattern is that persons must request this glorious gift of translation directly from Jesus Christ. This is the prototype laid forth in the scriptures. And, since "the pure in heart shall see God" (Matthew 5:8), purity becomes the virtue that parts the veil.

I have UnBlogged several times about purity. A pure person is not only obedient, but they are obedient for untainted reasons. Through the Atonement of Christ, they have become saintly and sanctified, and their desires, hopes, and motivations in everything they do are pure, including why they desire to be a part of Zion.

Here is the key: Translation has a purpose; it is not just winning the spiritual lottery. You can easily find what that purpose is by studying the people of Enoch and ascertaining what the core desire of their hearts was. It was this desire of maintaining a righteous Zion society that motivated God to take up their entire city into heaven. They could not accomplish this righteous desire in the dispensation wherein they were born, so God extended their lives elsewhere to give them the ability to fulfill this desire when the last dispensation finally came. They have been working to that end all this time.

John the Beloved and the three Nephites likewise stated this same pure desire of preparing the world for the Millennial Zion as their reason for requesting translation. We can likewise seek and obtain these glorious gifts, waiting patiently upon the Lord for them to manifest, if in our seeking we find that the desire of our hearts is that same pure desire which all have requested who have entered into the Zion condition.

Brother John

Sacrifice and Calling and Election

*There is an everlasting relationship between sac-*rifice and laying hold upon the greater blessings. Why sacrifice is required can only be understood when looking upon mortality from a spiritually profound height. The whole purpose of this life is to prove us, or to teach and then test us, to see if we will "do all things whatsoever the Lord their God shall command them" (Abraham 3:25).

The purpose for this test and the object of it (obedience) is understood when we realize that the ultimate outcome of mortality is to receive "all the Father hath." This gift is not one of things and stuff. It is the gift of the creative power. When you can create anything through the vast powers of godhood, you have everything God has. The beauty is that everyone who qualifies can have *everything* in concert with everyone else. The promise, as extraordinary and impossible as it sounds (that more than one person can have "everything") can be fully endowed.

God Himself obeys the laws He enacted into being (justice, agency, creation and the work of exalting others). He requires that anyone who receives His creative power must be eternally willing to live the same laws that He does—hence the overarching and undergirding demands that we learn to obey. We can be gifted with kindness, love, and willing service. But eternally inviolate agency demands that those who would become gods must choose, demonstrate and set in eternal stone their unending obedience to the same laws God obeys.

The only way to learn, demonstrate, and establish in the record of heaven that we possess that level of obedience is through the sacrifice of all things.

Joseph Smith explained it this way in *Lectures on Faith*:

> Let us here observe, that a religion that does not require the sacrifice of all things never has power sufficient to produce the faith necessary unto life and salvation; for, from the first existence of man, the faith necessary unto the enjoyment of life and salvation never could be obtained without the sacrifice of all earthly things. It was through this sacrifice, and this only, that God has ordained that men should enjoy eternal life; and it is through the medium of the sacrifice of all earthly things that men do actually know that they are doing the things that are well pleasing in the sight of God.
>
> *When a man has offered in sacrifice all that he has for the truth's sake, not even withholding his life, and believing before God that he has been called to make this sacrifice because he seeks to do his will, he does know, most assuredly, that God does and will accept his sacrifice and offering, and that he has not, nor will not seek his face in vain.* Under these circumstances, then, he can obtain the faith necessary for him to lay hold on eternal life. (Joseph Smith, *Lectures on Faith*, 6:7; italics added by John)

Thus it is by willing sacrifice that we obtain "the actual knowledge" that we will obtain eternal life. This actual knowledge is a revelation of unmistakable power, which informs the obedient seeker that his or her calling and election is made sure.

Joseph further left us this inspired explanation:

After a person has faith in Christ, repents of his sins, and is baptized for the remission of his sins and receives the Holy Ghost, (by the laying on of hands), which is the first Comforter, then let him continue to humble himself before God, hungering and thirsting after righteousness, and living by every word of God, and the Lord will soon say unto him, Son, thou shalt be exalted. *When the Lord has thoroughly proved him, and finds that the man is determined to serve Him at all hazards*, then the man will find his calling and his election made sure. (*Teachings*, 150; italics added by John)

As we deeply consider and bask in these glorious things, I wish to add these words of hope. This supernal gift of being called and elected is not reserved for the greatest of the great, or the best of the best. These vast promises and this process of obtaining all that the Father hath is held out to *all* who desire it and who are willing to sacrifice to obtain it.

Why is it that we, flawed and imperfect as we are, can *all* do it? It is because our little and big sacrifices engage the mighty gears of the Atonement, and Jesus Christ changes us, upgrades and polishes, purifies and sanctifies us. His divine grace and power accomplish it all—we mere mortals do not. But He does it in return for our willingness and determination to obey His will.

This is the process of sanctification. It is a demanding course for sure, and will try anyone who pursues it to the utmost of their faith and courage. We must patiently wait upon the Lord and submit to His unique timetable, never trying to run faster than the Spirit accords. This is a process we must faithfully endure on the pathway to exaltation. We must emerge through the flames of purification, not around them.

The glorious, wondrous, and healing truth that operates within these flames of purification is that the process is infused with *joy*. Miracles happen, the heavens open, angels attend, the veil is thinned, and the doctrine of the priesthood distills upon our souls as the dews from heaven.

It is above all, the ultimate mortal existence.

Brother John

Personal Journal

Terri's note: Selected details have been omitted from this entry. Please note that this was John's personal journey. Each person's experiences will be unique to him or her.

December 13, 1993—late at night

Tonight I have had the most beautiful experience of my life. I had retired to bed early and took myself to prayer. Many trials and problems were weighing on my soul, including the saddest thing that had ever happened to me in my life. . . .

After a time of deep spiritual struggle, I felt an unusual power in prayer and soon found my heart flying high in praise and worship. Time seemed to stand still as I prayed and praised and poured out my heart to Heavenly Father.

After a time, I lay in my bed and soon found my heart drawn out again in the most fervent prayer. Praise seemed as natural as breath, and worship as sweet as the greatest gift of God. I prayed and felt my spirit soaring to previously unimaginable heights. I felt myself humbled beyond the dust, as lowly as the most insignificant speck of dust, yet so grateful to be that speck of dust—so unworthy, yet so profoundly blessed that in spite of being so insignificant, yet I was at the center of Heavenly Father's infinite love and unimaginable caring.

I basked and bathed in it. I felt it light every fiber of my soul and body. I felt life flowing into me and the aura of His presence enveloping and surrounding me until it burned like encircling flames of fire within and without. I prayed that this would never end, and poured out my love to Him in words that transcended speech, eclipsed poetry or song, and entered a realm that is most holy and spoken only with the tongue of angels, and sung in the songs of redeeming love. . . .

This went on for a long time until I felt as if I would be consumed by it. At that time the Savior's voice came to me and spoke unimaginable peace to my soul. It said, "Be of good cheer, and fear not, for all that is glorious and good is yet attainable, and will not be withheld from thee, my son." The thought of my being His son was so profound that it caused me immense joy. I pondered upon it and my soul flew like a winged angel because of it. I am His son. The mightiest and holiest, and most significant, loving and holy being of all existence—I'm HIS son. I have a birthright. I am a prince in an incomprehensibly wonderful and glorious kingdom. I AM HIS SON! I wept to think of what this meant. My heart gloried in it and was magnified beyond belief by it. I soared beyond human understanding at the implications of it.

Then a voice came to me which sounded like the voice of eternity, and pronounced a blessing upon me of the most profound significance. I wish God would give me the words again to write them. I am withheld though by the sacredness of them, and by the eternal power and implications of them. I am commanded to write, but not given the words. . . .

I was promised so much—eternal life, blessings that are beyond human comprehension . . . glimpses of eternal majesties, eternal blessings so significant that human understanding bends under the weight of them. . . . I was stunned by these words and scarcely could take them in. I struggled to understand, and only felt the soaring light of truth so bright and penetrating that it deferred fullest comprehension until another time. I joyfully acquiesced to His love, and without the slightest reluctance, accepted His gifts by faith alone, content to wait upon further light and knowledge to be given later in the temple of God. . . .

I was told that my experiences and trials in this life would not diminish my ability to accomplish all that was required of me. . .

I scarcely had time to ponder these things when more came to me and I felt the infinite and unspeakable love of Father surround my soul and fill me with fire and prophecy. I felt as if I would fly away, as if I would be lifted from my bed and carried away on wings of angels to the throne room of God. I yearned for it and ached for such blessings. Yet I was left gently unto myself so that only the warmth of His love surrounded me. . . .

I was left to ponder these things, until after a few long minutes, the warmth and burning returned and the voice again repeated much of the promised blessings about my posterity, the importance of returning to the temple, and the importance of writing down these things for future generations. . . .

During this glorious event, and close to the end of it I saw two visions. . . . After that, while I lay upon my bed I was commanded to arise and write these things down, that they would be had by future generations of my children, and perhaps others. . . .

As I have been writing these things, I have felt the fire within my soul for the third time, making complete God's promise of confirming all His works with three witnesses. I am left weak and speechless, at the same time filled, drained, almost without the ability to think of anything other than my utter astonishment and joy!

I end this glorious night with these words: I love you, my beloved and most loving Father. And with all my soul do I pledge my life unto Thee. Even so—Amen.

Chapter Eleven

Saying Goodbye

Love and UnRegrets

My Dear UnBlog Friends and Family,
I regret to tell you that my health continues to take a tumble. Until I can begin to feel strong enough to get off the pain medication, I am not going to be able to continue writing Unblogs as frequently. I am not shutting down the UnBlog as of now but am giving myself an unavoidable rest. In the meantime, I invite you to continue to read the archives of 500–plus UnBlog articles. Each of them is a part of my soul and my life's work in bearing testimony of the reality and profundity of the promises of our Savior in these latter days.

I have truly loved writing the UnBlog. It has had the effect I needed to complete my work, that of giving me a way to open my heart and soul so I could bear witness to the precious things I have known and seen through the Spirit of God. I began writing it because I felt compelled to record these things so that they were not lost to my posterity after my life ended. It has evolved way beyond that. I never suspected that so many people would become involved or that it would be viewed by so many thousands of truth-seekers in these last two years. You have been a great blessing to me. Your words and prayers have uplifted me and made these last years sweet.

I consider that my life would not have been complete without these last two years of writing the UnBlog, giving firesides, meeting so many of you, and of writing *Visions of Glory*. Now, no matter how much longer Father leaves me in this sphere, I have completed the course. Through His mercy and grace, I have run the good race and fought the good fight. I have seen what lies before me, and it is far more than I could have ever wished for. I admit that I'll be glad to move forward unhampered by a desperately ill body. But, much more than that, I will rejoice to see this telestial world evolve into the Millennial day, and to be there with each of you when it happens.

I mentioned regrets in the title, only to remind me to say I have no regrets. There are things I would like to have done better, or sooner, or more often. But I honestly would not change any event or trial or struggle that has brought me to here, to now, and to this great knowledge of things as they are.

Love and tears mix so easily. My love to you all. I leave you my everlasting confessions of love for Terri, my wife, my friend, my teacher, and my true and eternal companion. Nobody knows her sacrifices in my behalf, and probably never will. But it is only because of her kind ministrations and spiritual strength that I have been able to make it through each day. She has lifted me in her arms and in her confessions of love and spiritual unity. As much as a mortal man and a woman may, I believe we have truly become one.

I also want to confess my love for all my children. Each of them holds a precious, irreplaceable place in my soul. Each of them has brought me love and given me an opportunity to grow. My special love and deepest apology go to Jessica, whose young heart bore the heaviest burden of actually watching the day-to-day struggles.

My warmest love and eternal gratitude to you all,

John Pontius

Appendix

The Challenge of the Book of Mormon

Expanded by John M. Pontius from a talk by Elder Hugh B. Brown and the teachings of Dr. Hugh Nibley.

1. Write a history of ancient Tibet covering a period of 2200 B.C. to 400 A.D. Why ancient Tibet? Because you know no more about Tibet than Joseph Smith (or anyone else) knew about ancient America.

2. You must be 23 years of age.

3. You must have no more than three years of formal education and must have spent your life in a backwoods farming community.

4. Your book must be over 500 pages and over 300,000 words in length.

5. Your history must be written on the basis of what you know already. There was no library or published works on ancient America for Joseph Smith to reference, so you must use none for your book. There is to be no research of any kind.

6. Other than a few grammatical errors and corrections, you must make no changes in the text. The first edition you dictate to your secretary must stand forever.

7. As you dictate to your secretary you may not make corrections to your text. You may not ask to have the last sentence or paragraph reread. When you stop for a break, even for days, you may not reread your manuscript to pick up where you left off.

8. This book is to contain the history of two distinct and separate nations, along with histories of different contemporary

nations or groups of people. You must describe their religious, economic, political, and social cultures and institutions. You must cover every phase of their society, including the names of their coins, weights, and measures.

9. You must change your style of writing, word choice, and phraseology many times to make the book appear to have been written by several authors, since you will claim that many ancient authors contributed to the book, each with his own style and word print. After publication, computer analysis must determine that there are multiple authors of your book, and that none of your book resembles either your own writing, or writers from the period in which you live.

10. You will weave into your history the religion of Jesus. Christ, the pattern of Christian living, and the Mosaic law.

11. You must claim that your narrative is not fiction at all, but a true and sacred history.

12. You must include in your book 54 chapters dealing with wars, 21 historical chapters, and 55 chapters on prophecy and visions. Everything you write regarding visions and prophecies must agree meticulously with the Bible without being able to reference it. You must write 71 chapters on doctrine and exhortation, and here again, you must check every statement against a flawless memory of the Bible (since you can have no resource documents) or you will be proven a fraud. You must write 21 chapters on the ministry of Christ, and everything that you claim He said and did, along with every testimony you write in your book, must agree with the New Testament— even though you may not reference it.

13. Many of the facts, claims, and ideas and statements given as truth in your writings must be entirely inconsistent with the prevailing beliefs of the world. Some of your claims must prove to be the direct opposite of the prevailing worldly beliefs, but eventually be proven true with the passage of time.

14. Included in your narration will be authentic modes of travel; whether or not those ancient people used fire; descriptions of their clothing, crops, animals, roads, war strategies, mourning customs, and types of government. You must invent about

280 new names that will stand up under scrutiny through the years as to their historical roots and derivations.

15. You will have to properly use figures of speech, similes, metaphors, narrations, expositions, descriptions, oratory, epic, lyric, logic, and parables. Although uneducated, you will have to mimic ancient writing styles and format, including subtle chiastic and poetic structures.

16. You must invite the ablest scholars and experts to scrutinize your text with care, and you must strive diligently to see that your book gets into the hands of those eager to prove it a forgery, and those who are most competent to expose every flaw in it.

17. Through investigation, scientific and historical evidence, and archeological discovery for the next 175 years, your critics must verify your claims and prove detail after detail to be true; for many of the details you put into your book are still buried beneath the soil of Tibet and won't be discovered until after your death.

18. You must publish it to every nation and people, declaring it to be the word of God and another witness for the Lord Jesus Christ. Those who read it must come closer to Christ as they do so.

19. The book must not contain any absurd, impossible, or contradictory statements. Your history must not contain any statement that will contradict any other statement elsewhere in the volume.

20. Many theories and ideas as to your book's origin must arise, but after an examination of all the facts, the theories all must fail. You have claimed that your knowledge has come from a divine origin, and this claim must continue to stand as the only possible origin and explanation. The strength of this explanation must not decrease as time passes, but actually must increase, to the point of being the only logical explanation.

21. Your record is to fulfill many Bible prophecies, even the exact manner in which your book shall come forth—to whom delivered, its purpose, and its accomplishments.

22. You must call down from heaven an angel in the middle of the day and have him bear witness to four honest, dignified

citizens of your community and the world. The witnesses must remain steadfast in their testimony, not for any profit or gain, but under great sacrifice and severe persecution, even to their death beds. You shall put their testimony to the test by becoming enemies to these men, and yet have them never recant their words.

23. Thousands of great men, intellectual giants, national and international personalities, and scholars for the next 175 years must accept your history and its teachings even to the point of laying down their lives rather than deny their testimony of it.

24. You must include in your record this bold promise: "And when ye shall receive these things I would exhort you, that ye would ask God, the Eternal Father, in the name of Christ, if these things are not true; and if ye shall ask, with a sincere heart, with real intent, having faith in Christ, He will manifest it unto you by the power of the Holy Ghost."

25. Millions must bear record to the world for the next 175 years that they know your record to be true because they put your promise to the test and found it to be so, by the power of the Holy Ghost.

26. Over 80,000 salesmen at a time must be so convinced of the truth of your book that they gladly give up two or more years of their lives to take it to all parts of the world for distribution. They will not only pay their own way during these two years, but return bearing testimony that their time spent is one of the highlights of their lives. They must receive nothing for their journey and efforts but the joy of having shared your book with others.

27. Your book is not only to raise the standards of millions of people, but is to be written in such a way that many of those people become the great moral, ethical and dynamic marvels of their day.

28. To substantiate your claims, you must for the next twenty years watch those friends who follow you, your family, and your dearest loved ones to be persecuted, driven time after time from their homes, beaten, tortured, starved, frozen and killed. Tens of thousands must undergo the most extreme

hardships in your presence just because they believe your claims concerning the origin and content of what you have written to be true.

29. You must gain no wealth from your work, but often lose all that you have. Like those who believe your false claims, you must submit yourself to the most vile persecution. After 20 years of this, you must give your own life in a brutal manner for your testimony concerning your book. All this you must do willingly and without remorse, maintaining to the death your false claims.

30. Start right now and produce this record, which covers 2700 years of history, doing it not in the peaceful atmosphere of your community, but under the most trying of circumstances, which includes being driven from your home several times, and receiving constant threats upon your life. After your book is completed, talk a friend into mortgaging his farm to raise the money to have it printed.

31. Do this all in under 90 working days.

Mysteries of God

Talk given by John M. Pontius at the "UnBlog Family Reunion" on September 1, 2012, at Utah Valley University, where 550 people were in attendance.

Thank you very much, Terri and Faith, Heather and Sister Collier, for that beautiful music. It's a long time been one of my favorite pieces of music. And I think the reason is because it so appropriately describes my life. Everything that I have ever received that was sweet or beautiful or uplifting or that enhanced and beautified my hope of eternal things, all came from my Savior Jesus Christ. And these words, "O Divine Redeemer, I pray thee, grant me pardon, and remember not, remember not, O Lord, my sins. Save in the day of retribution, from death shield thou me, Oh my God. Oh, Divine Redeemer. Have mercy. Help me my Savior!"

I think that the thing that occurs to me as I hear these songs is that we're all beggars at the feast. Every one of us who comes up and partakes of the blessings of the gospel of Jesus Christ who receives any outpouring of grace, any dispensation or miracle of the Atonement, arrived there not by our own merits, but by grace and by the Atonement of Christ. And so we're all beggars. And even when you are standing there partaking of the feast and you think, "I now have the right to eat at this table," if you look down, you'll see that you're still wearing the beggar's clothes.

In the process of my life, there are two things I've learned that I think are of the greatest significance to me. The first is that Jesus is the Christ. This I know in every fabric of my being. I know it because the Holy Spirit has borne witness to me, and I know it because of more tangible means. But the second part of my testimony that is of most worth to me is that the Church of Jesus Christ as it presently is constituted, is complete; that it is not perfect, but that it functions perfectly. That every blessing that God has ever bestowed upon any mortal in any dispensation of the world, or that you can read about in the scriptures, or that you can learn about by personal revelation, or is accounted to in the lives of the living people that we understand and love—everything is available to me and to you to search after to seek and obtain. There is nothing that you can't accomplish.

I think this is the message that I have labored hard through my writings, and through the Unblog, and through the books that I've published, to bring out that there's nothing you cannot do. If you can read in the scriptures of someone who saw angels, who talked with angels, who had revelations, who had visions, who saw the history of all of the earth from the beginning to the end of time, these are things that you, as you presently are in your present situation and your present gender—know that if you are bold and seek, you can obtain these things. There is nothing that you can't do. If you can read in there about people who have had a personal interview with Jesus Christ, you can too.

Think about the three Nephite disciples, if you wish, about John the Beloved, about Alma, about Helaman, about the brother of Jared, Lehi, Nephi—any person who has been favored of the Lord to have these glorious things occur in their lives, and which are recorded as their great accomplishments in mortality—these things are common to mankind. They are not unique. They're not unique in the sense that God offers them to any person who will pay a similar price as the brother of Jared paid.

This is 2 Nephi 26:33: "He inviteth all to come unto him and partake of his goodness; and he denieth none that come unto him, black and white, bond and free, male and female; and he remembereth the heathen; and all are alike unto God."

I get questions very often from sisters, and what they want to know is—whether it's a little bit of an indictment against "our kind"—they want to know if their husband has no interest in spiritual growth and in obtaining the greater blessings of the gospel, can they go forward and accomplish these things regardless of what their spouse chooses to do? And the answer is yes, they can. The Lord may urge them and inspire them to pace themselves in such a fashion that they bring their spouse along with them. But there is no limitation on what male or female can do. If you go through the temple and you think carefully about what's happening there, it's absolutely equal. All of the ordinations, all of the promises, all of the priesthoods, all of the privileges and the approach to the veil to receive promises unspeakable—those things are shared equally. And if there is ever a situation where one gender is favored over the other, it's our sisters.

Nephi said, "I will go and do the things that the Lord commands because I know that he will give no commandment unto the children of men save he shall prepare a way for them to accomplish the thing which he commands." And if you take that as an eternal truth—not just a statement of getting the brass plates—if you take that as an eternal truth, what it's telling you is that God does not put your feet upon a path that you are incapable of walking. It means that He won't reveal to you a truth that you aren't capable of living. It means that He won't give you a commandment that you can't obey; it means that He won't give you a prompting that is beyond you to fully accomplish. It means that He won't reveal to you and give you a testimony of a doctrine or a principle or a promise or a truth that you are not capable of fully and absolutely obtaining for yourself.

I want to bear testimony to you that this is true. It came to me in my early teens and twenties that it seemed to me like the people in the Book of Mormon and the people in the New Testament were living a different gospel; that they had somehow a different or a greater promise or a greater communion with Jesus Christ; they heard revelation better, that there were greater manifestations before. And it just simply is not true. It is the same gospel of Jesus Christ that we live now with the same set of promises, with the same set of open doors, with the same set of covenants, the same power in the priesthood, and there is nothing yet to be revealed. Nothing remains missing. There isn't anything that the prophet needs to add to our lexicon of truth in order for us to lay hold upon every single blessing that we can aspire to. God is withholding none.

The question is, how? I mean, it's wonderful to talk in hyperbole, which is what that is. But I want to get down to some nuts and bolts. And the reason that I've invited these gentlemen to speak to you is because in my eyes—and I don't know how much they'll choose to tell you about their lives and the things that they've accomplished—but in my eyes, they exemplify the journey of the common man to uncommon greatness. They are those who have cried, "O Divine Redeemer, I pray thee, grant me pardon and remember not my sins." And because of that, they have reached far beyond their own expectations and found that there really is no limit to what God, what our Savior, Jesus Christ, enables mortal man to achieve.

So the question is how, how can we do this? How can we go from common man, which we somewhat incorrectly consider ourselves to be? How can we go from common man to uncommon Latter-day Saint? There is a very specific way that you can do that. Alma 12:10–11 says, "And therefore, he that will harden his heart, the same receiveth the lesser portion of the word; and he that will not harden his heart, to him is given the greater portion of the word, until it is given unto him to know the mysteries of God until he know them in full." Now this promise is not given to prophets only or to stake presidents or area authorities only. This is a promise given to all of mankind—that he and she who will not harden their heart, they can receive the greater portion of the word.

Now, to understand what the greater portion is, let's talk for a moment about what the lesser portion is. The lesser portion is the things that are not mysterious, because he says that to understand all of the mysteries of God is to have the greater portion. So you've got the portion that everybody understands. That is that—and I'm speaking of Latter-day Saints now—that is that Jesus is the Christ, Joseph Smith restored the latter-day gospel, the Church is true, the temple is true. You should pay your tithing, you can go to the temple and be sealed for time and all eternity. You can serve as a bishop or a Relief Society president. You can have children that are married in the temple, and you can serve when you're 99.9 years as a greeter in the temple and then die. That's basically the lesser portion of the word. And the reason that's the lesser portion is not because it isn't saving or because it isn't exalting. It's not because it isn't absolutely essential or that people who go there and have all of that will not qualify themselves for the celestial kingdom. That's all true.

But there's also a greater portion of the word. Do you know what that is? That's all the things that you read happening in the scriptures. It's that we can have revelation, we can have visions, we can have miracles, we can walk on the water, we can move mountains. We can have a personal interview with Jesus Christ. You can have your calling and election made sure; you can be born again. I'm absolutely not getting these in order at all, but it is the greater things that we read about people doing in the scriptures.

Now, why is it written in the scriptures? To bear record of the fact that this greater body of truth exists. So how do you go from having the portion of the word that is commonly had, the lesser portion as Alma describes it, to laying hold upon this greater portion, to having these miracles happen in your life? Well, Alma actually describes it. He says those who do not harden their hearts.

Doctrine and Covenants 29:7 says, "And ye are called to bring to pass the gathering of mine elect; for mine elect hear my voice and harden not their hearts." So do you understand what that says? This, then, is the pathway. The greater portion of the word lies within the straight and narrow way. And that is that when we hear the voice of the Lord, however it comes to us—whether it's a still small voice or a whispered truth or an angel standing in front of you with a drawn sword, or the prophet of God standing up in general conference, or a profound moment of study in the scriptures. It simply doesn't matter how it comes to you, but when you hear the voice of the Lord, if you harden not your heart and do that thing with all of the energy of your being, with all of the courage of your convictions, with all of the strength of your testimony, with all of your heart and your might and your mind, then you are, by definition, the elect of God. And if you aren't at that moment, you will be. This is how you make that transition. This is how you go from enjoying the lesser things which are grand and glorious in their scope—and they're exalting—this is how you go to laying hold upon the greater things. "For mine elect hear my voice and harden not their hearts."

I remember as a child reading the account of Nephi after they had landed in the new world, that they lived in the land of Nephi and they had some strife with their brethren the Lamanites. And there's an account in there about how the Lord said unto Nephi, "Take the people that will follow you and depart into the world and separate yourself from your brethren in the night . . . and all those who would hearken unto the voice of the Lord did, pick up their tents and follow me into the wilderness." And I thought, wow, the Lord must have had a PA system or some other magical, powerful, profound thing that we don't have today—so that all those people heard his voice—because it must have just thundered out of the sky one afternoon and said, "If you want to be my people, follow Nephi." I really believed that.

And now having lived a few years within the whisperings of the Spirit myself, I know that what happened was that sometime in the quiet discourse of their lives, that a still small voice, a tiny movement, a prompting, an understanding of truth and light and right and wrong and all those things that you and I possess simply distilled upon their souls that they should follow Nephi. There was no PA system. There were no flashes of lights or angels standing outside their hut or anything that was magnificently profound, like I had thought. It simply was the still small voice, and they knew that Nephi was a prophet. The Lord bore witness to the words of His prophet; and they simply picked up the things that they could carry and left. And that's how you lay hold upon the greater things.

Alma 12:10: "And therefore he that will harden his heart, the same receiveth the lesser portion of the word; and he that will not harden his heart . . . is given the greater portion." In other words you just simply do what the Lord asks you to do. I suspect that except for those of you who came here kicking and screaming, that most of you are here because you felt a deep burning, a spiritual witness that this was the place for you to be tonight. And that's hearkening to the word of the Lord; that's receiving a prompting and acting upon it. "He that will not harden his heart, to him is given the greater portion of the word, until it is given unto him to know the mysteries of God until he know them in full" (Alma 12:10).

Now what is the fulness of the mysteries of God? Well, the greatest mystery and the fulness that you can receive is when you actually stand in His presence. And then, as we are taught over and over in the scriptures, the very first thing that He does after you're done hugging him and kissing His feet is that He shows you this vision of the creations of His hands and the workmanship of His hands. Sometimes, as Moses saw and John the Beloved and others, He shows them everything from the beginning of time to the end of time.

This is the 76th section of the Doctrine and Covenants, beginning at verse five: "For thus saith the Lord, I the Lord am merciful and gracious unto those who fear me, and delight to honor those who serve me in righteousness and in truth unto the end. Great shall be their reward and eternal shall be their glory." We're not talking about people who have passed away. He was talking about living people. "And to them—living people—and to them will I reveal all mysteries."

What's one of the grand mysteries of the universe? What color are the Savior's eyes? If you can tell me that, then you know one of the greatest things that you can possibly know, because only people who have been in His presence actually know. And those are the mysteries. "And to them I will reveal all mysteries."

What's another great mystery? How do you invite an angel to come into your room? There's a way and it works. How do you qualify yourself to be visited by translated people? There's a way, it's a mystery, but it's only a mystery because people have to search it out and learn it by personal revelation; and when you know what that mystery is, and when the timing of the Lord is correct, you can all do all of those things. That's the reason that the scriptures even exist, because people had these grand experiences and the Lord instructed them to write them down so that this generation and everyone that followed them could have this testimony that these things were within the grand and glorious promises of the gospel.

This is verse 7: "And to them will I reveal all mysteries, yea, all the hidden mysteries of my kingdom from days of old and for ages to come, will I make known to them the good pleasure of my will concerning all things pertaining to my kingdom. Yea, even the wonders of eternity shall they know."

How are you going to know wonders of eternity? You're going to sit there and watch the movie—as Moses did, as Enoch did, as the brother of Jared did, as John the Beloved did, as every person who has had this personal interview with Christ—they're shown the wonders of eternity. And it says, "And their wisdom shall be great, and their understanding reach to heaven, and before them the wisdom of the wise shall perish (this is verse 9) and the understanding of the prudent shall come to naught. For by my Spirit will I enlighten them."

So how do you experience the Spirit of the Lord? It's when He tells you to stay a little longer on your knees. It's when He prompts you to have family prayers. It's when He tells you to tell your wife that you're sorry. That's when you're walking past and she's doing the dishes and the Spirit says to roll up your sleeves and jump in there and do them for her. That's when you hear that still small, annoying whisper to go to your home teaching yet again. It's when you're reading the scriptures and the Spirit says, "This is what this means to you." And not just hearing the words, but knowing them and internalizing them and taking them into your soul and allowing them to re-weave the fabric of your being. That's how His Spirit changes us. It's by the Atonement. When we obey Him, not only does He teach us, not only does He enlighten us, not only does He infuse us with truth, but He *enables* us.

Let's say that a person is having an awful time with cursing. I grew up on a farm—*dang it*. And I learned how to swear, and I was pretty good at it. I mean, we never used the name of the Lord in vain, but everything else was fair game. And, we actually had a dog who thought its name was Dammit. We said, "Come here, dammit." And it learned that that was what his name was. And there are other animals that had unsavory names because that's what we called them. But so in the course of your life, having learned that having actually created physical pathways—my friend Spencer down here would be able to tell you which things get rewired when you form a habit—and having rewired my brain to those things, when the Spirit says to me, "That was not appropriate, say you're sorry, repent of that, don't use those words again"—and I hearken to the voice and I pinched those sounds off before the air actually forms vibrations in my lungs—then He enables me. He changes me. He takes those actual pathways in my brain and He rewires them into a divinely inspired way so that I no longer have the desire to do and to speak evil.

Swearing is unsavory and undelightful to me now, whereas I used to think that it was hilarious that our dog came when you called him "Dammit."

So, "By my Spirit will I enlighten them and by my power will I make known unto them the secrets of my will." Now, if we could look into the eternal scheme of things, if we could just drop the veil of mortality right now and every one of us could look beyond the physical world and see what is actually taking place in the real world, we would see that we are surrounded by angels. If there are 500 mortals here, there's probably 10,000 angels here—and they aren't all good ones.

We would see that the workmanship of God is going forward in a mighty battle. We would see that the War in Heaven that was begun before we were born was not won, but is still fully engaged. We would see that we are the object and the prize of the battle. We would see that this war is not being waged for the earth or for real estate or for money or for possessions; it's being waged over you and me. We are the prize. We are the treasure chest that the war is being fought to obtain.

And we would see that before we were born we were brilliant, intelligent, powerful, masterful, majestic, glorious, nearly god-in-stature beings who could company with deity, who could command by the voice of authority from our Savior worlds to come into being. We not only understood algebra and calculus and statistics and quantum math, we understood how to create life. We understood how to make a sun ignite. We understood how to move a planet from Kolab to the outer reaches of existence. We understood the Atonement of Christ. We understood God the Father; we had embraced Him. We understood Jesus Christ; we'd fought with Him.

When we were born, we in a sense died to that. We forgot all. We forgot not only who God is, but we forgot who we are. That's some of the most tragic forgetting—we've forgotten our own majesty. And we come down here and we think that, you know, John Pontius is this body that's broken and ill and that has these certain number of friends and these certain responsibilities and this testimony and these shoes and those socks and this car. And that isn't John Pontius at all. Those are the present mortal trappings that I've been surrounded with. But *John Pontius* is something entirely different. And so is every one of you! And if we could drop the shield of mortality, you would most probably find the closest person to you and you would fall to the ground and attempt to worship them because they would be more glorious than anything you could imagine.

I had an amazing experience years and years ago. I was teaching an institute class and there was one sister who came month after month—I'm just going to call her Lynnette—and she was a lowly woebegotten creature. She was dirty. She smelled bad. She had very bad teeth. She had been in trouble with the law. She had been in a divorce. She had kids in prison. She wouldn't talk, she wouldn't look up. She just felt like her life was worth nothing to anyone for any reason. But she would sit in the back of the room. And I, as I quite often do, I would say, "Well, I know there's a scripture somewhere in the 76th section that says this or that; and she would whisper, "76 verse 10." And I go, "Oh that's right." Or I'd say, "I seem to remember a statement by John Taylor that goes like . . ." and she would start quoting it.

And I knew that inside of this insignificant-looking and self-defacing person, there was this beautiful thing somehow. And I determined that I was going to draw her out and make her actually say something in this group of people, this group of like ten friends that would illustrate to her own thinking that she was of worth. And so I said, "I want everyone in this room to say one sentence about how Jesus Christ has changed their life. I'm going to start here, and every single one of you are going to have that turn." And she immediately buried her head in her scriptures like this, and didn't want to say anything.

And as it progressed around the room and it came her turn, my vision was changed, and I was transported to a place. I was taken into a vision, and I was standing in this beautiful garden—it was a sunken garden, and there were steps going up out of it and there were fountains and beautiful flowers and shrubbery. And it was just the most glorious setting that I can imagine. I was standing down in the center of this thing. And as I looked up, I realized there was a woman walking towards me—and she was the most magnificent thing I have ever seen. She was glorious. She was like looking at the sun walking towards me. She was pure, she was divine, she was radiating knowledge and confidence, and I could tell that she loved me—just in a brotherly-sisterly kind of way. I watched her, wondering if I should be falling to my knees and worshiping her, because she was a goddess and I knew it. As she walked up to me, she said, "You don't recognize me, do you? And I said, "No." And she said, "I'm Lynette from your institute class."

And the vision closed up. A total of no time had elapsed, and she was still looking down; and then she looked up at me and went like this (shaking head). And so I went past her and asked the next person to contribute. I wanted her to learn something that day, but who really learned something was me. I learned that the least among us is sufficient that we would worship them if we really knew who they are.

And this is you and me. Lynette is not unique. Every person here has that kind of premortal glory. And when we are here in this veil of tears, in this darkened-out place of mortality, we forget. And we think that all we can do is this small list of things that we limit ourselves to: "I can get married, I can go on a mission, I can have kids, I can make sure they go to the temple, and then I'm done. This is the definition of my life." And the truth is much greater than that. The truth is that we can part the heavens, we can invite angels into our room, we can move mountains, we can work every mighty thing. We literally have no limitation.

So the fulness of the gospel is this: that you take the lesser things that are commonly available to us. You take the greater things that we can lay hold upon if we will only believe that they're there, and pay the price to obtain them. And when you combine those things, you have what the scriptures call the fulness of the gospel. Do you want to know what the fulness of the gospel is? Read the first six verses in the Book of Mormon. Do you know what verse 5 is? It's about Lehi seeing God upon His throne. And from there on through the entire Book of Mormon is testifying that man can and should and does qualify for this great gift of entering into the presence of the Lord. And this is the fulness of the gospel.

This is D&C 6:7: "Seek not for riches, but for wisdom, and behold, the mysteries of God shall be unfolded unto you, and then shall you be made rich. Behold, he that hath eternal life is rich."

Then D&C 6:11 says, "And if thou wilt inquire, thou shalt know mysteries which are great and marvelous; therefore, thou shalt exercise thy gift, that thou mayest find out mysteries, that thou mayest bring many to the knowledge of the truth, yea, convince them of the error of their ways."

This is D&C 42:61: "If thou shalt ask, thou shalt receive revelation upon revelation, knowledge upon knowledge, that thou mayest know the mysteries and peaceable things—that which bringeth joy, that which bringeth life eternal."

So there is the key. I want to read this last statement. This is Bruce R. McConkie from *A New Witness for the Articles of Faith*, page 492:

> There is a true doctrine on these points, a doctrine unknown by many and unbelieved by more, a doctrine that is spelled out as specifically and extensively in the revealed word as are any of the other revealed truths. There is no need for uncertainty or misunderstanding. And surely if the Lord reveals a doctrine, we should seek to learn its principles and strive to apply them in our lives. This doctrine is that mortal man, while in the flesh, has it in his power to see the Lord, to stand in His presence, to feel the nail marks in His hands and feet, and to receive from Him such blessings as are reserved for only those who keep all His commandments and who are qualified for that eternal life, which includes being in His presence forever.

Let us at least sample the holy word and see what the Lord promised as to seeing His face and being in His presence while we are yet pilgrims far removed from our heavenly home. "Verily I say unto you, thus saith the Lord it shall come to pass that every soul who forsaketh his sins and cometh unto me and calleth upon my name, and obeyeth my voice and keep my commandments, shall see my face and know that I am." (D&C 93:1)

In the name of Jesus Christ, amen.

Triumph of Zion

Fireside given by John M. Pontius on August 16, 2009, at Heritage School in Provo, Utah. Approximately 300 people were in attendance.

I'm so grateful to be here. It is indeed a miracle that I am here. I was so incredibly close to death in March, and I knew over a year ago that I would be giving this fireside. I guess it shouldn't surprise me to see so many people here. But it does! And I ask for an interest in your prayers, because if anything good comes of this, it's going to be as big a miracle as the dividing of the Red Sea.

I want to tell you how this book, *The Triumph of Zion*, came about. I had been praying for many years for a particular blessing, and I thought that I was asking for the greatest thing that a mortal could ask for. After quite a bit of time asking for this, the Spirit overwhelmed me one day and said, "That is a righteous request, and I will surely grant it. But there is something more wonderful that you should be seeking after." And I thought, "What could be more wonderful?"

And so I thought, and I prayed, and I really studied and tried to figure out what would be more wonderful than that. I finally arrived at something I thought would be, and I did the same thing: I fasted, and I prayed, and the Spirit said the same thing. It said, "There is something more important that you should ask for." And this basically went on for fifteen years.

Then some time ago, about two years ago, I had arrived at what I thought was again the greatest blessing that a mortal could ask for. I am kind of audacious and I figured that if there's a brass ring, I'm going to go for it. I don't see any reason not to! I don't see any place in the scriptures that would discourage me from seeking the greatest things that have been offered. And so I knelt down and I said, "Father, this is the thing that I really want, for which I will dedicate my life and do anything you ask me to do." And the Spirit said back to me, "That is the greatest thing that you can ask for." And what I was asking for was to be able to enter into His presence in this life, and to ask for the privilege of being a part of the latter-day Zion. I wanted to be there when He came again. I wanted to be a part of the 144,000 who went out and gleaned the earth, to have the power of the priesthood in its fullest aspect; I wanted to see those atomic bombs trying to blow up Zion, and raise my hand to the square and turn them back, and say, "Yea, Lord,"—you know? I just figured it could be done.

And so after the Lord said, "Yes, that is a righteous request," then immediately I thought, "Well, I'm not exactly sure what Zion is going to be like." I just asked for it, but I wasn't exactly sure what I had asked for. And so I started studying everything I could find. And in the process of that, I concluded that the Zion that we are going to build in Jackson County, Missouri, was going to be a translated city, like Enoch's was. But I couldn't find anything that just authoritatively said that.

In the meantime, I had made a friend of Joshua Mariano. He had become an acquaintance of mine, and a matter of fact I met him for the first time tonight. I asked him in an email if he would do some research for me. He's a fantastic researcher and has an amazing library, and those of you who are familiar with his work, it's stunning! I asked him if he would look in his library and see if he could find any authoritative statements that could link our latter-day Zion and the principle of translation. He responded, "I've never heard that; I doubt if there is anything, but I'll look."

He wrote me back about a month later and said, "I'm finding a few things, and I'll let you know." I think it was probably three or four months after that that he sent me a 254-page document—two hundred and fifty-four pages of authoritative quotes and scriptures and statements by Brigham Young, and John Taylor, and Joseph Smith the prophet, Orson Pratt, and it literally stunned me. I read through that, and it was such an overwhelming amount of information, and it all corroborated the original premise: that our Zion was to be a translated society. And it stunned me.

The reason is that I am a student of the gospel. I am not a scholar of the gospel, but I am a student of it. And I had never read that; I had never latched onto that concept in an authoritative statement. And so the fact that there could be 254 pages of information to establish that principle was electrifying to me. Matter of fact, I sent the thing back to Joshua and said, "Joshua, would you please organize this by subject?" There was so much information that I had trouble categorizing it. And he was very kind, and he organized it into the categories of Translation; Translation of Zion; the Holy Priesthood of Zion; and laid out this amazing document.

And as I prayed and thought about it, the Spirit just worked on me and said, "You've got to write this into a book." And so, I took an entire month off from work, and I started the work on this, and then basically worked on it for two years, to put this information that Joshua had found into a book that could be read and understood, and something that could build your faith—my faith, I don't mean to say it that way—that would make it so that I could understand what he had found; so that it would be a joy to read, and it would be a joy to grab hold of; and it wouldn't be overwhelming, and it wouldn't say to you, "Oh yeah, somebody will be translated but probably not you." Because as I read it and as I studied, the joy of it changed my world view.

And it was so empowering to my soul, and so celestially enlightening to my view of the future, that I yearned and prayed and fasted, and was blessed to pen *The Triumph of Zion*. It was originally called *The Call of Zion*. And the reason that I called it that was because of my sister-in-law. I was minding my own business one evening, and my wife Terri handed me the phone and said, "This is Faith. Tell her what you told me about Zion." And so I said, "Hi, Faith!" and spent about ten minutes telling her what I just told you." And she basically said, "Oh, that's interesting. Let me talk to my sister again." And so I handed her the phone back and went back to what I was doing.

The next morning the phone rang and it was Faith. She said, "John, I didn't believe a word that you said last night. But I thought it was only fair, since it was a gospel subject, to pray about it. So I sat down and said, 'Heavenly Father, I know that John is barking up the wrong tree—but just in case it's true, I need to know.'" And she said, "The Lord sent the Spirit to me and said, 'Yes, it's true, and you and your husband must make this pursuit!'" And she said, "I guess

I have heard the call of Zion!" And I thought, "Oh, there's a good name for that book!"

Then my publisher, who I'm sure is all-knowing—I wasn't meaning that sarcastically—my publisher, who has done a great service to me for many years, thought that *The Call of Zion* could be misinterpreted to meaning me calling somebody to do something, and he wanted to avoid that concept. And so I changed it to *The Triumph of Zion*, which actually better illustrates the message of the book. Because the triumph of Zion is much different than what I thought it would be.

I went through Joshua's research, and as it springboarded me into other lines of thinking, I was impressed with the fact that not only is Zion to be a triumph in our day, but it is a possible triumph that is something that is well within our grasp. It is something that is already here, already available, already lying before us. We've had the capability of doing this for 170–something years, and that was what was in Joshua's research—this huge body of information about not only what Zion is but how to do it. And it was electrifying to me to realize what that message was inside there.

Now, one of the things that is kind of interesting about the true gospel of Jesus Christ is that it's possible to have a tremendous body of truth and have big chunks of it sitting about, that we know and believe and love, and yet not have the chunks arranged properly. Does that make sense to you? I wish this were a more intimate group and I could be down there, and you could say, "Yeah, yeah!" So, if you agree, nod, okay? Thank you! And if you don't have Zion, if you don't have the lens of Zion to look through, it isn't possible to entirely see the connection between those principles.

For example, if you want to turn with me to the 88th section of the Doctrine and Covenants, verse 68—pardon me, let's start at section 50, verse 26. "He that is ordained of God and sent forth, the same is appointed to be the greatest, notwithstanding he is the least and the servant of all. Wherefore, he is possessor of all things, for all things are subject unto him, both in heaven and the earth. The life and the light, the spirit and the power sent forth by the will of the Father through Jesus Christ, His Son. But no man is possessor of all things except he is purified and cleansed from all sin. And if you are purified and cleansed from all sin, ye shall ask whatsoever you will in the name of Jesus, and it shall be done."

Okay, if I were to ask for a show of hands, I would guess that every single person in this room would raise their hand and say, "Yes, I believe that that is true." If I ask for a show of hands and ask how many of you know how to pull that off, myself included, would leave my hand down—until a few months ago. This is because the promises there are so astronomical and so beautiful and fantastic that it almost requires faith beyond human ability to understand how I could be the possessor of all things, and have all things subject to my priesthood power; to be able to go forth and be the servant of all. How could that happen? And yet it's true—I know it's true. But if you have the lens of Zion to look through, and you understand that this society of people has that power and that priesthood inherent within them, if you are able to see that Enoch and his people had the ability to move mountains and to work miracles, and to defend their city by the power of God, and cause rivers to flow in the opposite direction, and all of the miracles that they performed, then they were a fulfillment of this scripture. And they had the same priesthood that we have! And so with the lens of Zion, we can look at these true principles and place them into their correct order.

And so, the concept of Zion is what I call the unified gospel theory. Remember Einstein was trying to find the unified field theory? What that was, was a search for a single idea or single principle that, if you could understand and define it, would explain everything. It would explain time, it would explain gravity, it would explain electricity, it would explain the creation of the earth, it would explain how everything interacts; and not only explain how it interacts, but give us the ability to control it. And so, he was looking for this one principle that would give him a unified understanding. In other words, would take all the scattered understandings of science and unify them into a single concept. He never accomplished it. It still, even today, is an illusive thought. But, the concept of Zion, is, in fact, the unifying principle of the gospel. It's the thing, if you could hold it up and use it as a microscope and view these vast and glorious promises that the gospel is laying before us, that it makes those principles drop into their proper place in the mosaic of the gospel.

This is a little quote from the book:

> When these glorious promises are viewed through the lens of Zion and translation, they fit with perfect alignment into the context of their own claims; which is to say that with Zion view, the language used in these scriptures can be interpreted literally, without pushing the promises into some post-mortal fulfillment. The language clearly promises these blessings to living mortals, and when we realize that these blessings have been repeatedly enjoyed by Zion-dwellers—a society of translated people—then these claims are literally true in the context of their own claims. Without an understanding of Zion, the promised glories are just too vast to fit into our commonly held paradigm of the gospel as we know it. If the idea of Zion and the blessings it promises are not immediately in our thinking, we might incorrectly push the fulfillment of these promises into the Celestial Kingdom, because their vastness seems to fit better there than here.

President Howard W. Hunter made this observation: "With God our Heavenly Father, all truth—whether profound or however apprehended—is circumscribed into one great whole." How many have heard that term, "circumscribed into one great whole"? If you have been to the temple you've heard it a lot. So what does it mean? See, this is the problem with me being up here and you being down there. There's too much of a disconnect. What does it mean? Somebody shout it out. "All truth can be circumscribed into one great whole." Okay, say it again! It means we can obtain that glory now—true. There's only one thing; it all fits into one great whole, and we, because we're mortal (I think what you're saying) breaking them out into a sequential event or into pieces of a puzzle like a mosaic, but they really belong into one great whole.

Another way to say this, another logical offshoot, is that God has done the same thing over and over again. When He created Zion in the past, He drew from this one great body of truth to create that Zion. He didn't invent new things for Enoch's Zion. He just simply drew from the gospel of Jesus Christ, and Enoch took those principles and that priesthood, and he created his Zion, using the principles that have always existed. When Melchizedek built his great city he used the same set of principles; it wasn't something that was unique to Melchizedek. When the Nephite society built their Zion that lasted for 200 years, they used the same principles, the same gospel of Jesus Christ, the same priesthood that belonged to Melchizedek, and he drew from that great whole.

In other words, there's only one gospel of Jesus Christ. It doesn't get reinvented for each dispensation. And the value of that realization, for me at least, is that we can go back and look at Enoch's Zion, and we can say, "When we build our Zion, it's going to be like that." Does that make sense to you? Elder Orson Pratt said, "The latter-day Zion will resemble, in most particulars, the Zion of Enoch. It will be established upon the same Celestial laws, will be built upon the same gospel, and be guided by continuing revelation. Its inhabitants, like those of the antediluvian Zion will be the righteous gathered out from all nations. The glory of God will be seen upon it, and his power will be manifest there, even as in the Zion of old. All of the blessings and grand characteristics exhibited in ancient Zion will be shown forth in the latter-day Zion."

So there you have it. And that was the value of Joshua's work. Because these guys understood this. They just said it over and over and over—hundreds of pages of it. And I have to say, I only used 10 percent of the quotes he gave me. There was so much of it that that book would be 500 pages long if I would have used everything he put in there. So, another way to say it is that the Lord's course is one eternal round. Have you heard that? What does that mean—that the Lord operates as one eternal round? I know it's intimidating, but I have to promise you, I'm more intimidated than you are!

Yes, He's the same yesterday, today and forever. And what He did with Enoch He did with another planet somewhere else. And what he's doing with our latter-day Zion He did with Enoch. In other words, he's just doing the same thing over and over and over. Why? Because, if something is true, it can't get true-er. If it's celestial it can't get celestial-er. If it's Zion, it can't get Zion-er. This is the only way it can work. It's the best way it can work. It's inspired, it's genius, and it's the workmanship of God. So if it will work for Enoch, that's the way it will work for us.

So if you want to know what our Zion is going to be like, read Third Nephi and read what they did; and that's what our Zion will be. Read Genesis chapter 14 in the Joseph Smith translation, and that will tell you what Enoch's Zion was like. And the book of Moses, and all those places where a Zion is talked about, and the characteristics are laid forth: They are not only talking about what they did with Enoch, they are talking about what will happen for us.

So, why are we concerned about this? What difference does it make anyway? It's actually a good question. Yes? Yes, excellent, you get a gold star. Would the ushers bring this lady a gold star? Oh, I'm sorry, I must have left them home. She said that because this all must happen before Christ must come again. Yes, Shawn? Yes, if it doesn't happen, the earth will be utterly wasted at His coming. Remember that? Front row, please? I love that. How many of you feel the same way? He says the reason it's so important is because there's something missing in his heart. And there isn't anything wrong with you; this is the human condition. It is the condition of a righteous soul.

Because you know—this is the reason I was searching for this, because I knew—the Spirit had whispered to me, "If Moroni can do it, you can, too." And I know that is audacious, but it says, "Go boldly unto the throne of grace." Right? And if the brother of Jared had an experience—if I approached it in the same inspired way that the brother of Jared did, then I could have those same blessings.

Matter of fact, Ether chapter 4 says that, doesn't it? It says, If the latter-day gentiles will acquire the same righteousness that the brother of Jared had, that I will show unto them all the things that I showed unto the brother of Jared. And believe me, it's not just a matter of looking, because he stood face-to-face with the living Christ, and saw a vision of all things, which he penned into the sealed portion of the Book of Mormon. And if you stand there, you're going to have not only just the information that the brother of Jared had, but you will have the privileges and the priesthood and the power and the revelation and the glory that he had. It isn't possible to be any other way. And so if it was possible for him—and the scriptures attest that it was—it is possible for us. And we must do it, as this sister says, before the Lord can come again.

My thought is, why haven't we? Well, the reason, in my opinion, is because we don't actually believe it's possible. Nobody shakes their head at that? There's a lot of people that—what? Exactly that! Okay, this brother says it's new and different, and nobody has really thought of this. And that's exactly right. And so my statement just got backed up by that. How can you believe something you have no idea exists? You can't. But the fact is that—who was counting these people for me? How many are there? There's 300 people here tonight! I was expecting fifty. Well, his fifty and my ten—that's sixty. And Ranelle warned me there was going to be a lot of people here; I was just expecting fifty. And to be quite honest with you—to be bluntly honest with you—I have known these things for a number of years. And the Lord has not let me talk about them. And that is the hardest and the loneliest thing that I've ever experienced.

I talked to my wife, Terri, about it. And she believed with me. Okay, sorry, I obviously love my wife. She is my fellow dreamer and my fellow Zion seeker-for-er. My fellow pilgrim. And she and I have acquired a unity in this belief, that there is a pathway. And the thing that I hope to do tonight is to open enough of a light so that you can look and say, "I know where my pathway to Zion is. I—fill in your name now—know where my pathway to Zion is." That's my goal. And so what I'm doing now is I'm trying to open the paradigm of Zion so you can say, "Yeah, I can see that might work, but how do I do it?" That's what I'm hoping to do.

She says it seems to her that there has to be a time for Zion, that it isn't a principle that is always available to all people. And this is true. But which dispensation are we in? We are in the dispensation of the fulness of times. We are in the "latter days." We are the people who will be there when Christ comes again. Whose job is it to build Zion? Is it "time"? It is—for you personally—if the Spirit tells you that. It may not be. Your pathway may lead you somewhere else, and God bless you, and I'll see you in the celestial kingdom. My purpose isn't to say that every one of you must do this. That's between you and your Savior. What I'm saying is that there is a pathway to Zion, that Zion must be built, that we are the people who will build it, and blessed are you if your inspired path leads you to Zion. And blessed are you if it doesn't! Matter of fact,

I think more blessed maybe, because you just go and watch from the sidelines. Maybe not! Maybe you will be out there wielding the mighty sword as a translated person. I don't know. But at any rate, not everyone will walk this path, but the path must be walked.

Okay, we got somewhere stuck on Zion must be built before . . . sorry! This is Moses chapter 7, verse 62: "And righteousness will I send out of heaven, and truth will I send forth out of the earth" —does this sound familiar?—"to bear testimony of my only begotten, His resurrection from the dead, yea, and also the resurrection of all mankind. And righteousness and truth will I cause to sweep the earth as with a flood, to gather out mine elect from the four corners of the earth unto a place where I shall prepare a holy city, that mine people may gird up their loins and be looking forth for the time of my coming, for there shall be my tabernacle, and it shall be called Zion, a new Jerusalem."

So, here's the order: Righteousness and truth will sweep the earth as with a flood. Can you see that happening? Can you see how many people are in this room? Matter of fact you resemble a flood, the way you go up like that. "The elect will be gathered from the four corners of the earth." Front row: (comment from audience). It's two pendulums: The pendulum of righteousness is swinging this way, and the law of opposition says that the further it goes out, the pendulum of wickedness must go out the same distance. And so when Zion finally is established, wickedness will be at its all-time high. So what is he saying? He's saying we're over here. He just referred to it by talking about the other side of the equation. If A equals B, and he's talking about A, then we understand that B is over here. Don't confuse me, Shawn!

So then after the elect are gathered out of the four corners of the earth, and I guess I don't have time to talk about all this stuff— I know that I don't. Read the book when it comes out. I apologize that it won't come out until March. And I'm not here to promote this book. I'm here to glory in my Christ, and to tell you what He has done for you, and shout His name in praise. And so the elect will be gathered out of the four corners of the earth, and a holy city—a new Jerusalem—will be built by the elect. The elect may "gird up their loins," which means what? There's a metaphor in "girding up your loins." There's two possible things. In the old times they wore a kind of wrap-around skirt, and if you're going to work in the fields or walk in the water to gather your nets, you take the back side of your skirt and pull it up in front, and tuck it in front: Gird up your loins so your clothes weren't dragging in the water. So the other thing is that it refers to taking courage; gird up your loins, take courage in Zion. And so we're going to work ourselves out in the service of God, with courage and dedication to do the works of the latter days. And then finally, according to Moses 7, the Second Coming will occur. So that's the order. And we can see it taking place.

Joseph Smith said this: "Zion and Jerusalem must be built up before the coming of Christ." Okay, that was the Prophet Joseph. Orson Pratt says, "The Christians of all denominations expect that he will appear in the clouds of heaven with power and great glory. The Latter-day Saints expect this in common with all other Christians, but before he appears in his glory, he is going to build up Zion, and that is, Zion must be built up on the earth. And if there is not a Zion built up upon the earth before he comes, or in other words, if there never is to be another Zion built up on the earth, then he never will come."

Did you hear that? If there never is a Zion built up, then He will never come. Why? There's no point! There's no point for two reasons. One is because the whole earth will be utterly wasted. And the other point is, He must come to Zion when He comes. That's what the prophecies say. Well, of course! Exactly right! Until we are prepared. . . . Yes, he can't come and institute a law that we aren't prepared to live. I'm not paraphrasing you exactly, but that's right.

Elder McConkie said this: "Though the day of the Second Coming is fixed, the day for the redemption of Zion depends upon us. After we as a people live the law of the Celestial Kingdom; after we gain the needed experience and learn our duties; after we become—by faith and obedience, as were our fellow saints in the days of Enoch—after we are worthy to be translated, if the purposes of the Lord should call for such a course in this day, then Zion will be redeemed, and not before." Does that electrify you? He says, "After we are worthy to be translated, then Zion will be redeemed."

This gentleman is saying there's a perception that we're afraid to covet "calling and election made sure," that we're not supposed to do any of that, that we accept authority and never look beyond that. Well, I'm not one that can judge what other people do. But I did that. And the fact of the matter is that the promises of the scripture are all personal. There isn't any problem relative to the Church that I know of—the Church is doing exactly what it supposed to do, exactly how it's supposed to do it, exactly on time. There isn't anything that you can find fault with in what the Latter-day Church is doing. Because it is Christ's true church, it is run by a living prophet, and it's doing exactly what it's supposed to do.

So then why aren't we building Zion? Well, then, that's because we as a people have not perceived that we're supposed to be. It's like the brother said in the back, how can you do something that you don't see? This sister says, it doesn't stop us from individually seeking—that's correct. When you as an individual perceive a pathway to a greater blessing, then it would be your obligation to seek that. And what I am hoping to do is to put a bright light upon that path. And when you see that—if you see it, if you choose to see it, if it is your inspired destination for your life—then it will become a thrill to you. It will change your world view. It will change everything you thought you knew about yourself, you relationship to Jesus Christ, and to The Church of Jesus Christ of Latter-day Saints. It will change it! It will modify it to something that is so profound and so beautiful that it will stun you. It will change you from this moment until the day that you enter the presence of Christ. That's how empowering this concept of Zion is.

As I sat and wept and read what Joshua had produced, and did my own research, and marveled at what the gospel was offering me, and connected the dots of what the temple was saying—the promises of the priesthood, the promises of the endowment, the promises of the marriage sealing ceremony—and you take all of those words, and you tie them all together, it creates a mosaic tapestry of exquisite beauty, that you can't see unless you're shining the light of Zion on the piece.

The Prophet Joseph Smith said this: "Every saint has an equal interest in building up of Zion of our God, for it is after the Lord has built up Zion that he will appear in his glory. We all look for the appearing of our great God, and our Savior Jesus Christ, but we shall look in vain until Zion is built, for Zion is to be the dwelling place of our God when he comes. How then is the Lord to dwell in Zion if Zion is not built up? This question we leave to the Saints to answer. The salvation of the Saints, one and all, depends on the building up of Zion, for without this there is no salvation. For deliverance in the last days is in Zion, and in Jerusalem."

Did you know that statement was ever made? I didn't, but there it is. I'm going to—who said that? Back row . . . red dress. You know, I'm not going to be able to get into this discussion of Alma 13 tonight, which is about the greater and the lesser portion of the gospel. There is a lesser portion of the gospel, but it is the gospel, and it is true. And it is glorious, and it is saving, and it is everything that you hope it is, and it will get you to the celestial kingdom. But there is also a "greater portion of the word." And that greater portion, you have to look at it with inspired vision. You have to specifically open your eyes to it. But it isn't meant to be invisible; it isn't meant to be a mystery that remains mysterious. It is simply meant for those people who have eyes to see and ears to hear.

Here's a statement by the Prophet Joseph: "Now the doctrine of translation is a power which belongs to this priesthood." I read that and I wept. There isn't anything else you can say about it. Is it possible, in this day, with the priesthood that we have? Do we have to wait for the prophet to say something else? Yes—if we are going to go back to Jackson County, Missouri, and as the Church, or as a people build the city. The prophet is the only one who can declare that time. But can you pursue it? Yes. Because the triumph of Zion is a personal triumph—and that's what the burden of this book is. It isn't something that you have to wait for the prophet to tell you to do. Why? Because it's 254 pages of having already been told! It's because the doctrine of the priesthood must distill upon our souls; and when it distills upon your soul it's going to take you to the same place that it took Enoch. Why? Because there's only one gospel! Because there's only one God, and His course is unchanging, and it is one eternal round. Because He's going to do the same thing for you as He's done for any other person who's ever approached Him.

Is that thrilling to you? This is the part where you go like this—thank you. Sorry, I need a little feedback. Otherwise all I can see is you frowning down there.

{Audience question} What about not being commanded in all things? Good point! He says we're not commanded, we shouldn't be commanded in all things; and we are following the prophet in everything he tells us to do. However, when the Holy Ghost opens to our view an inspired pathway—which means that if you can see it by the light of revelation—it is appropriate for you. Do you understand that? Because, according to 1 Nephi 3:7, the Lord will not put you upon a path that he hasn't opened the way for you to obtain. "I know that the Lord will make no commandment unto the children of men, except he shall prepare a way for them, that they may accomplish the thing that he commandeth them." So, if you can see Zion, if the Holy Ghost, who is a member of the Godhead, opens your eyes to that, by divine law there must be a way for you to obtain it. Does that scare you? It should! Because if you can see it tonight, then I'll see you in Zion. You don't have a choice now—I'm sorry! I should have told you that before you walked in and sat down.

Brother in white shirt here . . . Okay, let me restate this, because I doubt if this microphone picked you up. Boyd K. Packer came to a twelve-stake priesthood meeting and said that the whole church basically was in trouble because we weren't following the prophet, and he didn't know how we were going to escape the judgments of God, that we had to jettison Babylon and seek after the greater blessings in obedience to the gospel of Jesus Christ. Okay, so how do we do that? I mean, how many of you are not doing everything that you think you can do? How many are not working your assignments with all your might, mind, and strength? How many of you are not holding family prayers? I mean, I assume that since you are sitting here tells me that you are the wise virgins; you are the purest of the pure and the greatest of the great. You are the righteous of the righteous. You are the tithe of the tithe of the people of the Lord. So, what aren't you doing? You have yet, perhaps—I don't mean to be judgmental—but if you are like me, you have yet to see where all of this gospel of Jesus Christ is taking you. It's almost impossible—it is impossible, without specific revelation to you—to an individual—to understand that this gospel that you love and you live, is taking you to Zion.

Let me keep going. Elder McConkie made this statement. Now, think about this: "Raphael, whom we assume to have been Enoch, or someone from his dispensation, came and committed such keys as appertained to that day, meaning Enoch's day. No doubt those included the power to use the priesthood to translate men, as will be the state of all those who abide the day of the Second Coming." (Read again) Bruce R. McConkie, *The Millennial Messiah*, page 119. Is that thrilling to you? This is John Taylor: "And then when the time comes that these calamities shall overtake the earth, those that are prepared will have the power of translation as they had in former times, and a city will be translated."

Are you getting the picture? Did the Brethren—DO the Brethren understand about translation? Yes! Can they tell us that we have to go out and get it? No, they're too busy telling us to not beat our wives! You laugh, but you know it's true! Isn't it? What are they telling us—because that's the level we're at? "Don't do pornography, it will hurt you. Don't beat your wives, don't abuse your children. Read the scriptures, hold family home evening."

Who said that? Talk real loud . . . louder. Yeah, in six talks in the last conference, she says, they told us to go to the temple more often. And there's a very specific reason for that. It's not only to do work for the dead—very important labor—but it's in the temple that we learn our most precious and immediate truths, make the most pertinent covenants relating to Zion. I can't call on you all—I apologize; we'll be here all night, and I want to proceed, if you'll forgive me.

This is still President Taylor: "If there was anything associated with the Melchizedek Priesthood, in all its forms, powers, privileges and blessings, at any time or in any part of the earth, it would be restored in the last days. For this is the dispensation of the fulness of times, embracing all other times, all principles, all powers, all manifestations, all priesthoods and powers thereof that have existed in any age, in any part of the world." Okay, can I skip that now? Isn't that an amazing thing? I need to quit saying that, I guess.

A personal triumph: Now let's go onto the idea that Zion is a personal triumph. For the first part, let me just say this, that Zion will be the personal residence of Jesus Christ when He comes. He says, "I will come to Zion." That means He will be there. That means that people who live in Zion must be changed and be worthy to live in the presence of Christ. Which means that there's a fairly strict standard of conduct, right? What is it they do to you at BYU as a student? What do they call those standards? Honor code, okay? There's a pretty stiff honor code for Zion, right? Sorry, I'm going to run out of voice before this is over. I only have one kid left at home, so my shouting skills are way down. (She knows it's true.)

> The Lord once offered his people the chance to build that Zion from which the law shall go forth into all the world. They failed. Why? Because they were unprepared and unworthy, as it is the case with those of us who now comprise the kingdom of God. When we as a people are prepared and worthy the Lord will again command us, and the work will go forward, on schedule, before the Second Coming, and at the direction of the President of the Church. Until then, none of us need take any personal steps toward gathering to Missouri, to prepare for a landed inheritance there. Let us rather learn the great concepts involved and make ourselves worthy for any work the Lord may lay upon us in our day and time.

That's Bruce R. McConkie, *New Witness for the Articles of Faith*, page 586. Isn't that cool? Zion is a personal pursuit!

This is Elder Penrose: "The time will come when the saints of the living God will purify themselves before him, until they will be fit to receive these blessings." He was speaking of Enoch. "When the holy temple is built in Zion, God will take away the veil from the eyes of his servants, and the day is yet to be dawned when the sons of Moses and Aaron, having become sanctified to the renewing of their bodies, will administer in that holy house."

I don't have time to go through the logical sequence of why that term "renewed in their bodies" refers to translation, but can you see that it has to be? This whole process is bringing us towards a great promise that has to do with a change in our physical bodies. Isn't that what translation is?

Now, those of you who have been to the temple . . . I can't say any more about this, but what's it about? And now, let's go back.

There's only one gospel, right? Let's go back to the Three Nephites. At what point in time did they request to be translated? Where were they? Who were they speaking to? They were talking to Jesus Christ. Okay, if there's only one gospel, if there's only one way, if God never changes, if His course is one eternal round, and the Three Nephites made that request of Jesus Christ, then that is the way that it works. And it never works any other way. John the Beloved, who we know is translated, made the same request—of whom? Jesus Christ. That's the way that it works. And of all those people that we can go through scripture and find out that they were translated, they made the request personally of Christ. So why does the temple teach us to walk up to the veil and have an interview with Jesus Christ? Because, that's the process that brings us to Zion. Because you must part the veil and talk to Him and personally ask Him for a place within the latter-day Zion. So what is the temple teaching us about? How to approach the veil and make a very specific request . . . of the Lord.

Now, if you can connect those two dots, you will suddenly understand what the temple is about—what the endowment is about. It's actually stunning when you think about it. And when you can connect those two dots, then you start working backwards, and you go, "Okay, since that's my doorway to Zion—talking to the Savior, and asking Him personally—then the temple is giving me very specific steps: From obedience—which we understand is the most basic law of the gospel, right—through a number of priesthoods, a number of endowments, a number of ordinations and covenants, and then finally a trip to the veil.

. . . Have you read First Nephi? I think it's the most-read book in the world, right? First Nephi, chapter 1? Okay, where we get stuck on is, "I Nephi, having been born of goodly parents," and that's like, Okay, good parents, love the parents. What is the message of 1 Nephi chapter 1? "My father saw God sitting upon His throne. He came back to his bed and was overwhelmed. He told me about it, and I saw it myself, and then I had this vision, and it was of the tree of life." Do you understand? This is what the Book of Mormon is about! And when Lehi was in the presence of Christ, what did he ask for? It wasn't translation. It was to have his family spared the destruction of Jerusalem. So what I'm saying is, the temple isn't specifically teaching that we must ask for translation; it's specifically teaching us that we must get to the veil and ask to be endowed by something that is the proper and appropriate request for you when you get there. And if it worked this way for every single prophet of every book of scripture that we have, then this is the pattern of the gospel. This is the one eternal round.

And if you follow the same inspired path that they followed, if you dedicate the same strength and dedication and willingness to sacrifice that they gave, and if we are willing to pay the price—and there is a price—you will go there. You will! And the law of God, the law of celestial everything says that if it worked for Enoch, it must work for you. It can't take you somewhere else. You can't obey the same laws that Enoch obeyed and the same gospel that Enoch loved, and the same Savior that Enoch worshipped, and have it take you into the presence of Buddha. It does not work that way. It will take you the same place that it took Enoch. You understand that? I'm sorry, the Spirit beat me up when I said that. But nevertheless, it's true. It can't take you somewhere else than where it took him.

Okay, so here's a little quote from my book: "If any person comes to recognize Zion as a true principle, then that truth has distilled upon their soul by the power of the Holy Ghost. All truth comes from God. The mere fact that it is true, and that the Holy Ghost has borne witness to you, is prima facie evidence that the time of Zion has come for you personally; because divine law stipulates that the Holy Ghost cannot set you on a path that is unobtainable."

Would it be right of God to open your eyes to the celestial kingdom if it were not possible for you to go there? No. Of course, it requires the entire gospel course. It requires repentance, baptism, laying on hands for the gift of the Holy Ghost, and it goes on and on and on down the very path that you have been on your entire life. But what may not have occurred to you until this moment is that there was never a statement that said you can only go to Point X—and that is eternal marriage or some imaginary stopping point. What it says, if you read the scriptures with an eye of faith, it says that you can go all the way to the same distance of every prophet of any dispensation has gone to! You can! The message of the temple is this; You can talk with angels. You can have visions, you can have miracles, you can have revelation, you can go to the veil, you can talk with Christ. You can part the veil and He'll say, "What do you want?" And you'll say, "I want that," and He'll say, "Come on in! I've been waiting for you!"

I have a statement in this book by Bruce R. McConkie that says, "The Lord delights in our importuning pleas to part the veil." He *delights* in our heartfelt desire to part the veil. He stands ready at the other side of the veil to part it, when we simply turn the keys that we already possess, and the door that's already before us, to claim the promises that we already possess. Is that thrilling to you? It stuns me. It stuns me. It's the Aladdan's lamp of mortality. It's a sandbox full of diamonds that we sit and push our toy trucks around in, and think it's just sparkly sand. It's the Aladdan's lamp that we just don't rub, because we don't value it enough to clean it up. And yet, when we rub it, the genie of Zion and translation, and speaking with the Lord through the veil, will open before you as surely as God exists. Because He can't lie. He can't set you upon a course that's different from anyone else in the entire body of His whole creation—not just this earth, but worlds without number.

What can be more fantastic than this? There is, in fact, one truth that transcends even the glorious possibilities of Zion. And briefly it is this: that it is within our capacity to establish Zion in our lifetime. Everything we need, every doctrine, every priesthood ordinance, every truth and power and principle that is required of a mortal to personally qualify for and enter Zion exists today within the latter-day Church. Nothing is missing. Nothing remains to be revealed. No statement or proclamation of a living prophet needs to be made. It is all present now, in its complexity and its completeness. All we must do is see what we already possess with an eye of faith, believe that it is ours to claim, and then be willing to pay the price to do so.

Then I go back into, "The living prophet is the only one to tell us to build a city, but we can build Zion in our own life." Do you believe that? This is the part where you go like this (nod). Yes, you need to do that. You need to acknowledge to your own soul that you believe it.

Let me ask you a question. I intended to talk for an hour-and-a-half. We're thirty minutes late getting started. Do you want to go on for thirty minutes, or do you want to stop now? Okay. If you have an obligation that's going to take you out, vaya con dios, and thank you. Let's look at the 76th section of the Doctrine and Covenants, verse 50. "And again, we bear record, for we saw and heard, and this is the testimony of the gospel of Christ concerning them who shall come forth in the resurrection of the just." Okay now, this "them"—what period of time are we talking about? "Who shall come forth in the resurrection of the just?" We're talking about premillennial individuals. Do you buy that? Good.

The timeline of our present consideration is thus before the resurrection of the just, because we are speaking of those who shall participate in that mighty event.

Going onto verse 51: "They are they who receive the testimony of Jesus, and believe on His name, and were baptized after the manner of his burial, being buried under the water in his name, and this according to the commandment."

Okay, who are we talking about? They'd been baptized. Who are we talking about? The Latter-day Saints! Got that? Okay, what are we talking about? We're talking about people who are in this church, who are premillennial Latter-day Saints. Okay?

Verse 52: "That my keeping the commandments, they might be washed and cleansed from all their sins, and receive the Holy Spirit by the laying on of hands, of him who is ordained and sealed unto this power." Okay, who are they? They've had all their sins washed away. What does that imply? We're back to the standard of conduct—what did you call that? The honor code! This is the honor code. It's a high degree of obedience and righteousness. Can we do it?

Do you understand that the requirements for Zion are less than the requirements for entering the celestial kingdom? That was thunder telling you . . . it is! The requirement for Zion is less! Why? Because exaltation is a greater blessing; therefore, the requirements for exaltation are greater than that of Zion. It follows they're sequential. So, is it possible for you to acquire the worthiness to be translated? Well, if you have any inclination to believe that you can enter the celestial kingdom, you have to say, "Yes, it is!" Because you will pass through that requirement set, that standard of worthiness, somewhere on your way to the celestial kingdom. You may do that after this life. But it is also possible, and required, that somebody—some lots of somebodies—do it prior to their dying. They have to be mortals. Can you do it? Yes! It is not possible for the Lord to put you on a path that you cannot walk!

Verse 53: "And who overcome by faith, and are sealed by the Holy Spirit of Promise." The brother in front here mentioned having your calling and election made sure. Read Bruce R. McConkie, who talked extensively about the fact that being sealed by the Holy Spirit of Promise is having your calling and election made sure, which is simply this: That when you acquire the degree of righteousness necessary for these blessings of which we are speaking, in a time previous to their possible fulfillment, the voice of God will come into your soul and say something as simple as, "You shall be exalted," to possibly visions, miracles, manifestations, and angels singing glories in your bedroom. Somewhere between there in that range of event, you will know that when you die, no matter what happens, you will be exalted. It's also called "the more sure word of prophecy." I can't go into it any more than that, but I'm sure you understand it.

So, we are talking about people who have been sealed by the Holy Spirit of Promise. Does it happen in this life? Yes! Absolutely. I bear testimony to you that hundreds of thousands of Latter-day Saints have their calling and election made sure. They just don't say anything about it. They can't. The Holy Spirit restrains them. And most likely, I would guess that every third person sitting in this building has had an event that gives them that assurance. Is it possible? Yes. Does it happen? Yes. Can you obtain it? Yes.

Okay, section 88—no I'm going to skip that . . . time constraints. Verse 54. We're still talking about these people: "They are they who are the Church of the Firstborn." A whole chapter in this book is talking about what is the Church of the Firstborn. And basically it is this: When a person has the privilege of speaking to Jesus Christ in this life, they become a member of the Church of the Firstborn. It's a society of people who speak with the Savior face-to-face. Is it possible? Yes. I bear testimony to you that it does happen in this life. I bear testimony to you that hundreds of thousands of people have had that event. And this is the group of people we're talking about. Can you do it? Yes. It is not possible for the Lord to put you on a pathway that is impossible for you to obtain. "They are they into whose hands the Father has given all things."

Now, we read section 50, verse 26—remember that? "He that is ordained and sent forth, the same is appointed to be the greatest, notwithstanding he is the least, and the servant of all. Wherefore he is possessor of all things, for all things are subject unto him." We are talking about people who have been in the presence of Christ, who have there requested the privilege of being a Zion-dweller, and as a result of that, were given Enoch-like powers: the translated gifts, the power to divide. Did you know that Moses was translated? How did he get translated? What did he do at the burning bush? Who did he talk to? And on Mount Sinai? He was speaking with the Lord. At some point in that interview—we aren't told, but he probably said, "Lord, I'm an old man. I probably won't live long enough to see the children of Israel to the promised land." And the Lord said, "Don't worry about it, Moses, my buddy. I'm going to change you so that you cannot die." And Moses was translated. So when he divided the Red Sea he wasn't doing it as a normal person; he was doing it as a translated person.

And there is a whole set of gifts that follow translated people, that don't follow the typical priesthood-holder. Verse 56 now: "They are they who are priests and kings, who have received of his fulness and of his glory." Okay, now the way to receive of the fulness of Christ—and once again I talk about this extensively in this book—is that is referring to the fact that we have been in the presence of God. And we've received of His fulness. In other words, there's no veil parting us, separating us. So we have received of His fulness, we have embraced Him, we have wept at His feet, He has shown us the vision of all, and we have made our request of Him—whether it is translation or something else, doesn't matter—but we at that point have received of His fulness and of His glory. "And are priests of the Most High, after the order of Melchizedek, which is after the order of Enoch." Does that ring a bell?.

So, who are we talking about? We are talking here about people who have walked the path to Zion. Does it sound astronomical to you? Is your belief light? You know the red warning light on your dash "Danger, add more belief! Danger, add more belief!" Is that light flashing before you? It did for me. And here's what will turn that light off. Here's the oil that will make that engine not seize, and that is the fact that God will not put you on a path that is impossible for you to achieve! Have you written that down yet? I'm sorry, say it louder. Then do it! Is that a problem? Good for you, sister. You're on your way. Good job.

One other comment. I saw a hand. Anyone? Thank you, brother. And go back and read Ether chapter 4. What does he say? He says, "When the gentiles cast off that veil of unbelief which has kept them in darkness, then will I show unto them all the things that I've shown unto the Brother of Jared." See, the problem is not that we don't have the faith to do it, because we do. Every one of you believes that Enoch did what he did, that the Three Nephites did what they did. What you don't believe, maybe, is that it will happen to you. It's the "veil of unbelief." It isn't a lack of faith. And what has been a struggle for me is to take my faith that these things are true, and overlay it with the belief that it applies to me. And when you do that, when you get your faith and your belief in perfect alignment, then you will march right up boldly to the throne of grace, and you will make this request of the Lord, and he will part the veil and say, "Well done! Enter into my rest." Do you feel the burn? Do you feel that?

... We're almost out of time. I want to talk about the mystery of godliness (D&C 76). Verse 58: "Wherefore, as it is written, they are gods [small g] even the sons of God." And I might add, this is a personal insertion, daughters of God. How do we know that? The temple teaches us that there isn't anything that happens to a man that does not also happen to a righteous woman. The whole process is the same. And where there is a difference, the women have the better deal. Do you understand that? Okay, so when you follow this pathway, which the temple teaches, which this scripture is teaching, which we've been talking about all night, and you have this experience with Christ and become a Zion-ite, then you are a god (with a small g).

Why is that? It's because we have been in the presence of God, we are worthy to stand in His presence, and we have received of His fulness. We have the fulness of the priesthood, which is mentioned several times in the temple. Right, remember that? You'll be called back to get the fulness? And therefore, we then become godly. We don't become gods, because that's somewhere down the line.

Now here is a statement by Orson Pratt: "Speaking of the 144,000 which will begin from Zion and go out from there"—so they're going to be us. We will be the 144,000. "They," the 144,000, had a particular inscription in their foreheads. What was it? It was the Father's name. What is the Father's name? It is God, with a capital G—the being we worship. If, then, the 144,000 are to have the name "God" inscribed in their foreheads, will it simply be a plaything or something that has no meaning, or will it mean that which the inscription specifies. They are indeed, gods. Why is it, then, that verse 27 says, "Wherefore he is possessor of all things, and all things are subject unto him?" Because they are g-o-d-s.

Yes, hand? Orson Pratt, *Journal of Discourses*, volume 18, page 243. Okay, John Taylor said this, quoting John the Beloved: "And I looked, and lo and a Lamb stood on Mount Zion with the 144 thousand, having the Father's name written in their foreheads. Their Father's name—bless me! That is God! Well done for Mormonism! 144,000 gods!" That's John Taylor.

Now going onto verse 56 in section 76: "Wherefore all things are theirs, whether life or death, or things present or things to come, all are theirs, and they are Christ's, and Christ is God's." Now here is an interesting question: Can a resurrected person die? This is the part where you go like this . . . No! A resurrected person cannot die. Therefore this cannot be talking about resurrected people. Because a resurrected person does not have the option to die. And these people, "All things are theirs, whether life or death." That means that a translated person can fulfill their assignment and go, "I am done, Lord, I'm ready to go on with my life. I'm done being translated. And they die. They're changed. Their body does whatever does for a translated person, and they go on. So these are not resurrected people. "All things are theirs, whether life or death, or things present or things to come."

Think back to the temple. What's the first thing that happens . . . Why does it show us the creation? . . . And why do we have to see it over and over again? It's because when we enter into the presence of Christ, according to the pattern, this is what has always happened! Read the accounts that we have in detail of God appearing to somebody, and He shows them a vision of all things from the beginning of time to the end of what He chooses to show them. This is the reason Moses wrote Genesis. This is the reason 1 Nephi includes all of the stuff it does in the eleventh, twelfth, and thirteenth chapters of 1 Nephi. This is the reason that Mahonrimoriancomer, the brother of Jared, wrote the greatest vision that has ever been recorded and put to paper—gold plates in his case—because he saw it. Moroni saw our time. The brother of Jared saw it. All these people saw this vision. And if it happened to them, it will happen to us, because God's process is one eternal round.

So, why does the endowment—the endowment, think about it—start with a movie of the creation? It's because when you walk into the presence of Christ, your endowment will begin with a vision of the creation of the earth and go on from there. Do you see the beauty of this thing? When you start to connect, when you look through the lens of Zion, all these drop into place. It's an amazing thing.

So, going on with verse 60: "And they shall overcome all things." Okay, we've got g-o-d-s who are yet going to overcome all things. Now, how is that possible? It's because they are translated, and a translated person has not overcome death. They are still mortal. So they haven't overcome all things. They shall overcome all things. So who are we talking about here? Translated people. But you can't see that without looking through the lens of Zion. Verse 61: "Wherefore, let no man glory in man, but rather let him glory in God." Now, why would he say that? Isn't that an interesting statement? Here we have gods who shall overcome all things, and he says, "Let no man glory in man", because these people are men. They're mortals. "Let no man glory in their translated state, but rather let him glory in God, who shall subdue all enemies under his feet." Because this is still premillennial.

Now we're going to go to the future here. "They shall dwell in the presence of God and His Christ forever and ever." So it's pre-celestial kingdom, it's pre-millennial, it's pre-resurrection, it's pre-Second Coming. And yet we have g-o-d-s who are going to do these amazing things. We have the 144 thousand. Are you getting the picture? Premillennial. "They shall dwell in the presence of God and His Christ forever and ever. They are they who He shall bring with Him when He shall come in the clouds of heaven to reign upon the earth"—so we're still pre-Second Coming— "...These are they who shall have part in the First Resurrection"—pre-First Resurrection—" ...and who shall come forth in the resurrection of the just."

Now we return to the "are's"—to the present time. "These are they who *are* come unto Mount Zion." Do you need any explanation about that? Does that thrill you? Who are we talking about? See, the 76th section is largely billed as a vision of the celestial kingdom, and it is! But it also is a vision of Zion. (Audience comment) The 144,000 will be 12,000 from every tribe, which means that some of the tribes will necessarily come from Enoch and his Zion. They will be joined together and form that combined body. 144,000 translated people will leave the City of New Jerusalem to go out and gather the people out from among the war-torn and battling nations of the earth. And the reason they must be translated ... will be because they will not be able to survive the horror and the destruction and the onslaught and the bombs and the guns and the open warfare against Zion that they will have to survive, in order to gather these people home.

They will go by the power of God, which means they will take one step in Zion, and the next one will be in Africa, and they will go to the people they are assigned to. They will teach them, prepare them for the ordinances, take them by the arm ... and they'll return without even taking off their shoes—without haste—to Zion. Because they'll take one step in Africa, and one step in the New Jerusalem. They'll take them to the Holy City and introduce them to Christ, and then they will be translated, they will become part of the 144,000; they will be sent out perhaps within a day or so to go and do that work. So these people will be gleaning the earth and gathering to Zion the final gathering!

What a day that will be! Can you imagine doing that? Jesus Christ will come up to you and say, "Brother John! I have some people in the darkest part of the Congo who love me. Go and bring them home." And me and my wife will lock arms, and we'll take one step from the presence of Christ and we'll be in the Congo. And we'll gather those people home, and we'll work miracles, and we'll command the waters to part and the fires to cease, and we'll raise the dead and heal them, and teach them with the open arm of God, and we'll bring them home to Zion rejoicing. That's the 144,000! Do you want to be there? I do. Do you understand why, after fifteen years of searching, this was the thing that I was taught was the most glorious thing that a person could request in mortality? Do you understand that? What a thrilling thing that is. How I rejoice in that! How I rejoice in my Savior, and this great plan, this gospel that is so vast that babes can understand it and geniuses can barely see it! That we can sit here and talk about and rejoice and rejoice and rejoice in, what the possibilities are endless for us! How glorious this is! And how grateful I am! Okay, that did it. Now I can't even see my paper.

[Audience question] Absolutely. I just said I'm going to lock my arm with my wife and we're going to go to the Congo. I was kinda hoping for Paris, but wherever He sends us. "These are they who are come unto Mount Zion and unto the City of the Living God, the Heavenly Place, the holiest of all." In the midst of this war-torn world of atom bombs and death and a third part of the planet being destroyed, and a third part of all the seas being destroyed, a third part of all the animals dead, a third part of all mankind dead, with stars falling from heaven, and all the things that the book of Revelation teaches us will happen, we will be in Mount Zion, the City of the Living God, the Heavenly Place, the Holiest of All! Ya comin'? [Audience] I like that! That was better than a nod! "These are they who have come unto an innumerable company of angels, to the general assembly and Church of Enoch, and of the Firstborn."

We're out of time. Brothers and sisters, thank you so much for allowing me this opportunity. Thank you, Father in Heaven, for allowing me to live long enough to give this message. It almost didn't happen. And He told me almost a year-and-a-half ago that I would have the privilege of this day. And it's so wonderful. I was expecting 50 to 100 people! And here we are almost 300 of you.

I love you. Thank you so much for your faith. Thank you for your belief. Thank you for allowing me to share this part of the gospel with you. And, you always had it. I haven't said anything you didn't already know. Did you realize that? I haven't told you anything you didn't already know. All I did was take what you already knew and rearrange it, connect it.

I want to bear you my testimony that Jesus lives. I love Him. I know that He is my—*my*—Savior. And He has delivered me, both from the grasp of the grave and from the pains of the things that I have done wrong in my life. He has saved my soul. He has redeemed me and brought me back into His presence. And I love Him, and I am so grateful for this gospel of Jesus Christ. I know that it is true. I know that this is the true Church. But much more importantly than anything that implies, I know that it is within my power to seek and obtain Zion.

And I hope that now, you have that same testimony.

In the sacred name of Jesus Christ, amen.

About the Author

It was never John's intention to write LDS books or a doctrinal blog or website, but from his youth he had decided to discern the will of the Lord and flawlessly obey His voice, no matter where that lead him. Hearkening to the Lord's voice was not always easy, but John's often difficult journey ended in a far better place than he ever dreamed possible.

After living in Alaska for thirty-three years, raising a family there and building several successful careers, the Lord sent John and his family to Utah in 2010. John and his wife, Terri, who is the love of his life, both grew up in Utah but spent the majority of their lives in "the mission field." Returning to Utah was like coming home for John and brought him nearer to additional family and friends. Together John and Terri have eight children and thirty incredible grandchildren.

As a well-known author of LDS books, John had many opportunities to speak at firesides, write additional books, and maintain his website, "UnBlogMySoul." While fighting cancer during his last years, he continued to accomplish unexpected and amazing things that he claimed only the hand of the Lord could have brought to pass. About this he wrote, "I could not have written this book or any other eternally weighty thing without the Lord's hand. His hand has led me places I did not want to go, but when I actually got there, I recognized it as my 'far better land of promise.'"

John passed away peacefully in his home in 2012 after a lifetime of service to the Lord Jesus Christ. Following John's death, Terri compiled the first book of his UnBlogs, entitled *Journey to the Veil*. This second book, *Journey to the Veil II: Path of Discipleship* will complete the publication of those blogs, which are considered by many to be some of John's finest works.

Scan to visit

www.followingthelight.org

Scan to visit

www.unblogmysoul.wordpress.com